WEALTH & WISDOM

A Biblical Perspective on Possessions

JAKE BARNETT

NAVPRESS ®

A MINISTRY OF THE NAVIGATORS
P.O. BOX 6000, COLORADO SPRINGS, COLORADO 80934

The Navigators is an international Christian organization. Jesus Christ gave His followers the Great Commission to go and make disciples (Matthew 28:19). The aim of The Navigators is to help fulfill that commission by multiplying laborers for Christ in every nation.

NavPress is the publishing ministry of The Navigators. NavPress publications are tools to help Christians grow. Although publications alone cannot make disciples or change lives, they can help believers learn biblical discipleship, and apply what they learn to their lives and ministries.

Printed in the United States of America

Contents

To my father, John G. Barnett,
who consistently demonstrated
spontaneous generosity,
and my mother, Minnie Barnett,
who exemplified the financial disciplines
that make generosity possible.

Acknowledgments

This book developed in a living context—that of teaching what the Bible says about material possessions to a group of Christians in Brazil. The motivation to organize this biblical teaching, as well as much of the material itself, developed in this context. My Brazilian brothers contributed not only the opportunity for teaching, but innumerable insights of their own, plus much valuable feedback, demonstrating the universal nature of biblical teaching and application. Among these friends are Aldo Berndt, Mario Nitsche, Fernando Gonzales, Roberto Blauth, Oscar Almeida Filho, Dirceu Mattozo, Diomar Westphal, Fernando Korndorfer, and Dalby Karkle.

My friend Jim Petersen provided the opportunity in Brazil, a great deal of assistance in developing the concepts, and much encouragement. In addition, he served as one of three major editors, along with Herbert Schlossberg and Theofanis Stavrou. Ruth Myers, Meryl Glockner, and Ed Reis also gave valuable

7

editorial assistance. These ideas would not be in writing were it not for the patient instruction of Ronald Finelli and Robert Billars in guiding me through the intricacies of word processing. Gene Denler carried much of my workload during the writing, and developed the scripture index as well.

My wife, Marge, provided patient encouragement and assistance. In addition to her help, she suggested that I postpone a family project that was important to both of us.

My sincere thanks to each of you. I hope you will find the result worthy of your investment.

Author

Jake Barnett has been a builder and developer in Minneapolis, Minnesota since 1954. He served in the U.S. Navy in World War II. In 1952 he received a B.A. in Psychology from the University of Minnesota. While studying at Northwestern Bible College, Jake became involved with The Navigators and has served on the Board of Directors.

Jake has made major investments of his time and energy in God's Kingdom in many areas of service. These include involvement in the local church, teaching in adult education programs, counseling and training counselors for the Graham Association and World Wide Pictures, and conducting seminars on the Christian's financial matters and on evangelism. Most important to him have been the opportunities for involvement in the mission enterprise on several continents. He has had the privilege of meeting strategic needs and encouraging others to participate.

Jake and his wife, Marge, have two daughters, Melody and Sheryl.

Preface

This book stems from several sources, the first being my thirty-five years of experience in business as a builder and developer. These have been years of direct involvement with material possessions, not only my own but those of others. I have enjoyed years of close relationships with business associates: legal, accounting, real estate, and banking professionals; subcontractors; tradesmen; and government officials, as well as encounters with hundreds of young people who were making the major financial investment of their lives.

The insights I gained into human nature in relationship to money through those encounters were innumerable, and the truths I saw revealed were invaluable. Sometimes the lessons were deliberately taught, but usually they were communicated unconsciously. Some of the most valuable lessons came from people who did not share my faith as a Christian. Some lessons were positive and constructive, others were negative and served as warnings.

Perhaps an example would illustrate the latter. Shortly after graduating from the university and beginning my business career, I found myself discussing my future with a real estate advisor. I told him that my financial objectives were limited in scope because of the priority of the Kingdom of God. He laughed and replied, "Jake, you will be just like the rest of us. You may think you have limited financial objectives, but the goal will constantly recede. You may set $100,000 as a reasonable accumulation, but when you reach that objective you will move it up to $250,000, then to $1,000,000. It is impossible to be satisfied!"

What a warning! As a "successful" businessman, he had given me the most significant lesson of my lifetime on materialism. Dozens of times I have resisted the temptation for unnecessary expansion with his words echoing in my ears!

The second source of this book is my own experience in giving and investing in God's Kingdom and in encouraging others in these matters.

I grew up within the church and went through its formalities when very young, but did not become a Christian until age twenty-three. My commitment to Christ at that time involved the commitment of my life. Something in my religious background had left me with a presupposition that the only way one could serve God with all of his heart was as a pastor or missionary, which is commonly referred to as "full-time Christian service." I no longer find that phrase appropriate, because all Christians should be serving God all of the time. However, in my desire to truly serve God, I enrolled in seminary three weeks after my decision to follow Christ.

Three semesters of Greek, Hebrew, and systematic theology without any help in personal spiritual growth left me disillusioned. About that time Dawson Trotman, the founder of The Navigators, spoke in chapel. His theme was that *an ordinary Christian can be effective for God.* Afterward I contacted some Navigator men who taught me how to study the Scriptures for my own personal growth and develop my relationship with God. Trotman's theme—an ordinary Christian can be effective for God—was repeatedly confirmed by the Scriptures, relieving me of the misconception that I had to be a professional Christian. In fact, I have become convinced that there is no higher calling than to demonstrate the power of Christ in an ordinary life under His control: living a life based on the Word of God, instructed by the Holy Spirit, without the prestige of position, and with all the responsibilities of life as lived by our contemporaries. In this context we can function as salt and light, walking worthy of Christ's name and sharing the real meaning of life within our sphere(s) of influence. The Scriptures make it clear that the job of the professional Christian is to equip *us* for the work of ministry (Ephesians 4:11-13).

So with a clear sense of God's leading, I transferred to a secular university, graduated, and began my business career. My decision to be a "layman" (a term I use reluctantly because it is not biblical and generally carries a negative connotation) was the deliberate, conscious choice of God's best for me. My conscious effort to arrive at this conclusion focused my business career on the Kingdom of God. It is only natural that one of the facets of this focus is the financial—giving to and investing in the Kingdom.

At the beginning, I simply gave a portion of my income. I made certain that I carried my fair share of responsibility in my church and responded to the special needs of those within my circle of contacts. I found giving to be very satisfying and began looking for ways to increase my involvement.

I began to study the provisions of the tax code and found that there were tremendous incentives to give beyond the simple deduction. This was in the 1950s, and some provisions were very generous. Things have changed, but there are still tax advantages to giving. At the same time I found that there were strategic needs that I wanted to meet, but these opportunities required larger amounts of money than were generally available from income.

An incident from those early years illustrates my point. My sisters had married twin brothers who were missionaries in the Orient. Just two years after I began my business career they returned for a year of furlough. With two small children in each family, eight of them would be living and traveling together during that year. I recognized their need for adequate and reliable transportation, and arranged to purchase a new Chevrolet station wagon from a Christian dealer who made one available at cost. Because of our close relationship, I wanted to provide this for them personally, but did not have the funds readily available. Financing the car presented a problem because years earlier—as a young man who desperately wanted a car—I had promised myself that I would never borrow to purchase such a rapidly depreciating item. (I'll explain more about that philosophy later.) I finally compromised by purchasing the car with a short-term loan, and disciplined my finances to pay it off within a few months.

One of my brothers-in-law died during his next term on the mission field. Perhaps my fondest memory of him is the incredulity on his face when we gave him the title to the car. His surprise was rapidly transformed to "many expressions of thanks to God," and I had the privilege of experiencing 2 Corinthians 9:12-15:

> This service that you perform is not only supplying the needs of God's people but is also overflowing in many expressions of thanks to God. Because of the service by which you have proved yourselves, men will praise God for the obedience that accompanies your confession of the gospel of Christ, and for your generosity in sharing with them and with everyone else. And in their prayers for you their hearts will go out to you, because of the surpassing grace God has given you. Thanks be to God for his indescribable gift!

Another benefit of this experience for me was to recognize a basic truth: Capital has a legitimate function in a Christian's life, and when utilized within the Kingdom of God provides continuing benefits. The car did not depreciate! Because we purchased it at the dealer's cost and prices were higher in California where it was resold, the entire cost was recovered. The funds were then used to purchase a vehicle upon their arrival in the Philippines. With the help of many associates in giving, I have seen this pattern repeated over and over. I will tell you of other experiences that involved not only the multiple use of money, but the multiplication of capital within God's Kingdom.

Experiences such as these gave me insight into what can be accomplished through strategic giving of modestly larger sums of money. I also gained a little knowledge of the incentives provided in the tax laws. I recognized that it would be necessary to set up a tax-exempt foundation to realize the full benefits available so I approached an attorney who had experience in meeting the legal requirements. I had no reason to believe that he shared my interest in God's Kingdom, but as I explained my objectives, he became very excited. He felt that for too long only exceedingly wealthy people had utilized these opportunities. He was pleased to see an ordinary person make the effort to take advantage of these legal provisions to benefit others.

So far I have mentioned two sources for this book—my experiences in the business world and the privilege of giving to and investing in the Kingdom. The third is far more important. Since one of the focuses of my career was on giving to and investing in the Kingdom, it was only natural that I would study the Scriptures in this area. The first real opportunity to articulate the results of my study of Scripture came in 1970. A friend and his colleagues had been working among college students and young professionals in the major cities of southern Brazil. I was introduced to these new Christians as one of those who had made it financially possible for my friend to be in Brazil. They had been somewhat puzzled about his means of support (at first they thought he was a CIA agent!), and the idea of giving in this way was foreign to their thinking. It was a privilege to open the Scriptures to them. They were committed to the Kingdom of God and their response was very positive.

My friend was determined not to impose American forms and standards on them, and it was exciting to see them search the Scriptures to work out an expression of Christianity indigenous to their culture. They concluded that they needed a scripturally based philosophy of finances, and one of their first steps was to ask me if I would lead a weekend seminar for selected leaders from ten cities. Preparation for that seminar forced me to put together, in somewhat coherent form, the principles I had learned.

Since then I have presented this material in various forums here in the United States. On some occasions the presentations were complete seminars. Sometimes they were limited to one- or two-hour sessions, and often were simply brief conversational descriptions. Regardless of the format, the result has always been the same—encouragement to commit these ideas to writing. After a couple of years of encouragement, I set aside the time to undertake the task. I hope you consider it worthwhile.

Introduction

Christians do not have an adequate or biblically based philosophy of material possessions as evidenced by the variety and conflicting nature of the financial concepts we present to the world. We have taken a comprehensive look at the Scriptures in many areas, but not in this one. Perhaps the reason lies in our feeling that material things are somehow worldly and are inferior to the spiritual, and we desire—above all—to be spiritual. However there is no way to avoid dealing with material things, so everyone does have a financial philosophy whether he or she recognizes and admits it or not.

The absence of a comprehensive understanding of what the Scriptures say about material things leaves each individual or group vulnerable to oversimplification. Each selects a few fragmented ideas from Scripture and develops them into an oversimplified philosophy that often amounts to little more than a slogan. These ideas are then developed, extended, and defended to the exclusion of other biblical truth.

Many scriptural truths, when carried to seemingly logical conclusions in disregard of other truths, become gross distortions of truth. The topic of material possessions graphically illustrates this. We will examine some of these one-sided philosophies in chapter two of this book:

1. One prominent, current teaching about the Christian and money is that God wants every Christian to be wealthy. Material success is regarded as our heritage, and wealth as a sign of God's blessing. Helping others and sharing in community are not emphasized because all should claim the success to which they are entitled. Wealth is equated with spirituality.

2. Opposite to this first view is the idea that all wealth is positively evil. Since the poor are poor *because* others are rich, Christians have no right to participate in an affluent society. All wealth is the result of exploitation. Accepting a salary above a minimum level is stealing. God desires that we live on a subsistence level. Poverty is exalted because God is against the rich and on the side of the poor.

3. Somewhat related to the second view is the concept that the ideal material condition is to be completely dependent on God, day by day, for everything we need. Receiving is the ultimate act of faith. Since any provision for the future indicates a lack of faith; savings, insurance, and other financial reserves are undesirable. In this context, giving is leverage for further receiving. Since possessions are evil, or at least dangerous, the wealthy or successful are automatically suspect.

4. Some Christians do not recognize any connection between material possessions and faith. The material constitutes one aspect of existence and the spiritual another. This dichotomy results in a philosophy of material possessions identical to that of the world.

5. Those who avoid any of these extremes tend to treat material possessions rather lightly and concentrate on giving. Giving is presented as an obligation, almost always consisting of a

mandatory tithe that should be given to the church. While tithing is obligatory, it will be rewarded in two ways: the 90 percent remaining will produce more benefit than 100 percent did before, and great additional material blessings will be forthcoming. "Sacrificial giving"—giving everything without reserve—is encouraged and is described as the only true giving.

Since these views are based on a single emphasis, they are incomplete as philosophies. The fact that they contradict each other causes confusion to many. As Christians we need to move toward a more comprehensive, biblical philosophy of finances. All that I have read and heard leaves many areas unexplored and many questions unanswered. Here are some of the questions that prompted my investigation that I will attempt to answer through this book:

Are material things God's provision or a temptation?

Is money good, neutral, or evil?

Does God want all Christians to be wealthy, or does He want us to live on a subsistence level?

Does God want us to be immediately dependent on Him for everything, or does He want us to assume responsibility for our material welfare?

Do we understand biblical principles of economics, or even the elementary principles of contemporary economics?

Are we aware of the ways in which dominant economic systems either agree with or violate scriptural principles?

What should our attitude be toward the economic system in which we live?

Are we aware of the freedoms we enjoy, even though there may be much to criticize within any system?

Should our major concern be equality in the distribution of wealth?

What do the Scriptures say about the acquisition, production, and ownership of wealth?

Do the Scriptures teach anything about capital and its function in the creation of wealth?

Is there a relationship between our finances and our maturity in Christ?

Is giving an obligation or a privilege?

To whom should we direct our giving?

What is implied in the gift of giving?

These are only a few of the questions we must deal with in studying about the Christian and material possessions. I will not approach this subject from a purely academic stance, and certainly will not deal with these matters exhaustively or conclusively. My desire is to stimulate our thinking, and encourage further investigation of these ideas and how the Scriptures deal with them. The truths discovered need to be combined into a coherent philosophy of material possessions. I do not presume to accomplish that task, but hope to stimulate its beginning.

PART ONE
God's Economic Order

The objective of part one of this book is to determine whether the Scriptures present a unified view of material possessions. We will be looking for underlying principles that can be the foundation for a biblically based philosophy of material possessions.

In this section we will not attempt a detailed analysis or complete application or illustration of the principles we discover. Our purpose will be to understand basic principles and to determine if these principles are applied uniformly throughout the Scriptures.

Is God's revelation progressive and yet consistent, or did He make significant changes in His instruction to us concerning our relationship to the material universe? Some Christians believe that the teachings of Jesus in this regard contradict those of the Old Testament—that Jesus instituted a new era in our relationship to material things. Other Christians believe that every detailed instruction given to Israel must be followed today.

We will discover a perfect consistency in the basic principles, along with a progressive growth in the application. This is consistent with our growing understanding of God's revelation in other areas of theology.

To begin, we will evaluate how important a proper understanding of material things is to our spiritual maturity. The second step will be to look at man's convictions about material possessions and how he feels about the place and importance of possessions in his life. Then we will turn to the Scriptures to discover God's revelation on the subject, beginning with study of the book of Genesis.

ONE

Material Possessions and Maturity

We are physical-spiritual beings who live in a material universe. God created us with both physical and spiritual attributes. Our bodies are material and are sustained by the material. The material is a basic aspect of life that is impossible to ignore. The present material universe may be temporary, but Scripture does not indicate that it is inferior. So, the material is an important, central, and constant part of our lives.

If our philosophy of the material universe is out of harmony with our nature as God created us and the universe as God created it, serious problems will result. The Scriptures give us adequate instruction for developing a balanced philosophy of material possessions.

Money represents material things. As a medium of exchange and a store of value, it facilitates our handling of material possessions. So money is a basic, common concern of mankind. It is commonly said that we spend fifty percent of our lives occupied with money. This would mean fifty percent of our time, our attention, our mental energy, our emotional energy, our conversation, our successes, our failures, our problems—fifty percent of our *lives*. That is why there is so much in Scripture concerning money: who provides it for us, how we should and should not acquire it, what we should do with it, the problems and opportunities connected with it, and finally—and most important—what our attitude toward it should be.

Dr. A.H. Maslow, the psychologist, talks about a hierarchy of needs that begins with basic physiological requirements followed by safety and security, love and belongingness, and finally, self-actualization and esteem.[1] For Christians, each of these levels is affected and transformed by our relationship to God and His Kingdom. Self-actualization will be quite different within the Kingdom of God than outside it, but the levels still apply.

Maslow demonstrates that the lower levels of need must be satisfied before one is free to proceed to the higher levels. This doesn't conflict with the fact that Jesus placed our spiritual welfare at the foundational level: "But seek first his kingdom and his righteousness" (Matthew 6:33). Jesus is talking about our ultimate master—whether it be God or money—the basis of our trust and the attitudes and motivations of our lives. He goes on to promise that as we establish the proper order of priority, all levels of need in our lives will be fulfilled. If we assume that a solid spiritual foundation undergirds all of life, we still must deal with the reality of Maslow's analysis. We must still function on all levels of life, including the material. Placing God's Kingdom in first priority is the initial step, but Matthew 6:33 does not abrogate the many scriptural instructions concerning material things.

The economic aspects of life primarily relate to Maslow's basic levels—the physiological and security needs—but not entirely. The fulfillment of advanced levels may either be enhanced or distorted by one's economic philosophy. One may try to buy love and affection with money, another may feel unworthy of either because of economic failure. Accumulation of money can be equated with self-actualization and self-esteem. In contrast, generosity can demonstrate love and lead to self-actualization in serving others. But my point here is that if the lower levels of need are not met, it will be impossible to fully realize our potential on the higher levels. If the financial aspects of our lives are a constant struggle, we will not be free to concentrate on more advanced aspects of life and service.

Mike Vance, a former associate of Walt Disney, conducts excellent seminars entitled "Adventures in Creative Thinking." He lists five equities that must be present if an individual is to be successfully fulfilled: the physical, the intellectual, the spiritual, the psychological, and the financial. He contends that the psychological (equivalent to Maslow's self-actualization and esteem) is the most difficult, and that the financial is the easiest. I agree that the financial is the easiest because "equity" in this area is not measured by accumulation, but by attitude, discipline, and control.

God intends that we be in victorious and dynamic control of the financial aspect of our lives—that we be free. "So if the Son sets you free, you will be free indeed!" (John 8:36). A Christian can have genuine financial freedom, but not necessarily in the sense that the expression is usually used—to indicate an abundance of money. In fact, financial freedom has little to do with the amount we have, but much to do with our attitude toward money, the proper and disciplined use of what we have, and our understanding of and obedience to scriptural teachings about money and material possessions. Freedom involves several things:

Freedom from worry and continuing concern with possessions.
Freedom from servitude to material things.
Freedom to utilize material possessions for eternal purposes.
Freedom to enjoy God's material provisions without the bondage of materialism.

Many Christians are so concerned with avoiding materialism that they are unable to enjoy the positive freedoms. What emotions do you immediately associate with money? I have found that worry, concern, guilt, and desire are the most common. Joy, praise, and thanksgiving should replace them! Often if we have these positive feelings in regard to money, we tend to repress them. Somehow they seem "materialistic" to us. We forget that "God . . . richly provides us with everything for our enjoyment" (1 Timothy 6:17). Paul made this statement in the direct context of dealing with wealth. Money is part of the "everything" that God has provided for us.

Money is an essential aspect of life, and all of life is spiritual. The sacred-secular distinctions are artificial. We can bring glory to God with our finances. We can enjoy money with thanksgiving. Our relationship to God's material provision should be one of constant *celebration.*

One of the barometers of our spiritual life is maturity in relationship to money. Jesus said, "Whoever can be trusted with very little can also be trusted with much . . . so if you have not been trustworthy in handling worldly wealth, who will trust you with true riches?" (Luke 16:10-11). The "little things" are material wealth, the "true riches" are eternal values. Although the material is God's provision for us and is to be enjoyed and utilized with thanksgiving, it does not have permanent value and will pass away. The physical universe in its present form is a temporary arena for God's revelation. So money has neither eternal nor intrinsic value, but is only a means.

Satan uses money and possessions to produce greed, covetousness, selfishness, envy, pride, and idolatry. God, in contrast, uses material things to demonstrate His love and gracious provision for us. He desires to use money to bring us to maturity—to perfect us in love, generosity, selflessness, diligence, self-control, discipline, dependence, thankfulness, and many other spiritual qualities.

God is always interested in our maturity, growth, and progress in "attaining to the whole measure of the fullness of Christ" (Ephesians 4:13). As in any area of life, God's primary interest is in what takes place within us. He is more concerned with who we are than with what we do: "Man looks at the outward appearance, but the Lord looks at the heart" (1 Samuel 16:7). Thus what we do with money is secondary to what the process does to us.

In direct relationship to money, Paul desired that the Corinthians "also excel in this grace of giving" (2 Corinthians 8:7). Our focus tends to be on how much money we give. We easily forget that God is not in the business of raising money, but of bringing His children to maturity. He is interested in what we are *becoming*.

A Christian's financial life and philosophy should demonstrate God's grace and continuing work in our lives. Money is not only an important, basic, and constant part of life, it is also conspicuous. If this highly visible aspect of our life is in harmony with Scripture and thus in order, it will stand in sharp contrast to the world's standards. If it is in disorder, it will cast a shadow on other aspects of our witness. In the financial area we need to be "salt" and "light" to those around us (Matthew 5:13-16). To be salt and light, we must first be involved with the nonChristians around us rather than be isolated. Second, our philosophy of material things must be consistent, based on Scripture, and credibly demonstrated.

Dr. Joseph Aldrich, president of Multnomah School of the Bible, wrote the book *Life-Style Evangelism*.[2] In it he describes four different responses by Christians to the culture in which we live. Our response to our culture determines the effectiveness of our witness. He encourages us to maintain the "radical difference" that is necessary to our integrity and to our witness: "Do not conform any longer to the pattern of this world, but be transformed by the renewing of your mind" (Romans 12:2). At the same time, we must maintain the "radical identification" that is necessary to our presence. The four categories of response that he discusses apply with special significance to the economic realm, and I would like to use them here.

The first possible response to culture is rejection. This leads to withdrawal and results in isolation. Involvement in the economic life of our culture is held to the bare minimum. This is exemplified by the monastic movement and some Christian communal groups. Its most important manifestation, however, is in the "other-worldliness" of many Christians. This has its philosophical basis in the Platonic and neo-Platonic idea of the existence of a sharp distinction between the material and the spiritual, with the conviction that the material is inferior. This culminated in the Manichaeans of the third century, who believed that matter was inherently evil. There is a great deal of Manichaeanism in twentieth-century piety.

This response has serious consequences in the economic realm and produces negative results in many areas of life. Young Christians afflicted by this mentality are often poor students. They do not seriously develop their abilities in anticipation of a productive career. I have known many students with great potential who deliberately selected the easiest courses, were satisfied with barely passing grades, and were encouraged by their leaders to take this course of action in order to have more time for "ministry." These students join many others who are mediocre or poor employees, unwilling to give themselves to conscientious service because their interests lie in the "spiritual." They overlook scriptural examples of diligence as well as admonitions such as Paul's instruction to "obey your earthly masters with respect and fear, and with sincerity of heart, just as you would obey Christ . . . serve wholeheartedly as if you were serving the Lord, not men" (Ephesians 6:5-7). Even those who become employers and entrepreneurs often look for the easy path with minimal involvement.

In contrast, we see Hezekiah, who "in everything he undertook . . . sought his God and worked wholeheartedly. And so he prospered" (2 Chronicles 31:21). Paul continued this theme in

1 Corinthians 10:31, "Whatever you do, do it all for the glory of God," and in Colossians 3:22-24, "With sincerity of heart and reverence for the Lord." He continued, "Whatever you do, work at it with all your heart, as working for the Lord, not for men . . . it is the Lord Christ you are serving."

If we do not contribute to our economy and refuse to be involved in its capital structure, we forfeit the right and opportunity to influence the direction of society. We become beneficiaries of the system without contributing, enjoying its privileges without accepting its responsibilities. Our system is strong enough to permit this as evidenced by the counter-culture movement of the sixties and seventies. But Christians should not take this unfair advantage. In addition, we hinder the gospel by demonstrating a nonscriptural pattern of other-worldliness.

The second response to culture is immersion, which involves complete identification with the world around us. This is obviously in conflict with Jesus' prayer that we remain in the world but not be identified with it (John 17). Paul tells us specifically that we "must no longer live as the Gentiles do, in the futility of their thinking . . . darkened in their understanding and separated from the life of God" (Ephesians 4:17-18). Instead, we are to "live a life worthy of the calling [we] have received" and should "have nothing to do with the fruitless deeds of darkness" (Ephesians 4:1, 5:11).

When Christians adopt the identification response to culture, there is no radical difference in lifestyle between us and the world. This response overcomes the isolation that results from rejection, but the resulting presence in the world accomplishes little. Conformity to the world makes it impossible to be salt and light.

The third response is split adaptation, which is following biblical teaching within the religious sphere but adapting to cultural standards in the economic realm. This approach produces good Christians on Sunday, but no critical difference is seen in their lives during the week. The businessman who feels that he must compromise his standards to succeed in the marketplace is an example of this.

Split adaptation is the most inconsistent response because it involves knowledge without application to life. Joseph Aldrich refers to it as spiritual schizophrenia, a good description because it describes the tension involved in this ambiguity. Christians who deliberately compromise their convictions are the most uncomfortable.

Immersion and split adaptation have the effect of destroying our credibility as Christians and nullifying our witness. In the economic realm, they also render us ineffective in influencing our society for good. The isolation that results from the rejection response has the same effect, because even though we have truth to communicate, we are not in contact with those who need to hear. These three approaches to culture are not desirable.

The fourth and correct response is critical participation. This consists of involvment in our society and economy, including its capital structure, with a critical difference in evidence through our demonstration of Christian principles within that framework. This response consists of identification and involvement rather than isolation. Our participation in what is good gives us the right to criticize and seek to correct that which is bad. Participation gives us credibility, acceptability, and proximity.

Our economic affairs present a unique opportunity for us to demonstrate and affirm the Christian message. Jim Petersen, author of *Evangelism as a Lifestyle,* understands this truth and speaks of being "redemptive in our relationships."[3] Our relationship to money can be a demonstration of God's grace and our economic lives can be a vehicle for ministry to others as well as service to the Kingdom.

If we are going to participate in our society and its economy in a constructive manner, which is a demonstration of God's grace, we must understand what the Bible teaches about material possessions and the money that represents them and facilitates their use.

NOTES:
1. Abraham H. Maslow, *Motivation and Personality* (New York: Harper & Row, 1970), page 35ff.
2. Joseph C. Aldrich, *Life-Style Evangelism* (Portland, Oregon: Multnomah Press, 1981), pages 60-64.
3. Jim Petersen, *Evangelism as a Lifestyle* (Colorado Springs, Colorado: NavPress, 1980), page 71.

TWO

Looking at Our Assumptions

In his book *Idols for Destruction,* Herbert Schlossberg defines assumptions as "beliefs so taken for granted that it is not deemed necessary to prove them."[1] This succinct definition both states a fact and introduces a difficulty, for much of what we do and believe is based on unexamined and untested assumptions. This fact has been recognized by scientists, theologians, biblical writers, and practical analysts of human behavior.

Edward Hall, the contemporary anthropologist, explains it this way:

> The most important paradigms or rules governing behavior, the ones that control our lives, function below the level of conscious awareness and are not generally available for analysis. This is an important point, one that is often overlooked or denied. The cultural unconscious, like Freud's unconscious, not only controls man's actions but

can be understood only by painstaking processes of
detailed analysis.[2]

Christians are not immune to this tendency to be controlled
by untested assumptions, however much we may wish to think
otherwise. To the extent that we consider our assumptions to be
revealed truth, we are in ever greater danger of accepting them
without questioning. If we have failed to examine our assumptions, it follows that we do not really know their source. The result
is that we can follow the prevailing opinions of society without
recognizing our conformity.

The consequences are increasingly alarming, because the
conflict between the standards of society and the Christian faith is
rapidly increasing. Since we usually accept assumptions unconsciously, the tendency is not so much a temptation to which we
succumb as it is a trap that we slip into carelessly.

If assumptions were merely mental exercises they would be
relatively harmless, but they are more than that. They control our
actions. "We do not see the environment," as Os Guinness says,
"because we see *with* it. That means we are influenced by ideas we
do not notice and therefore are not aware of their effect on us."[3]
Francis Schaeffer states the problem simply: "People have presuppositions, and they will live more consistently on the basis of
these presuppositions than even they themselves may realize."[4]

Anthropologists contend that we are almost totally unaware
of our culture. Edward Hall says that culture is man's medium and
is a major determinant of our actions. Hall talks about "the
cultural unconscious" that controls man's actions and the difficulty man has in transcending his own culture because "one is
completely unaware of the fact that there is a system of controls as
long as the program is followed."[5]

I have found cross-cultural experiences to be invaluable in
producing and focusing an awareness of my own culture. The
prospect of presenting a financial seminar in Brazil caused me to

begin to look objectively at some of my cultural presuppositions. As an American faced with the prospect of presenting ideas concerning the philosophy of finances to a group of Latins—many of whom were Marxist in their orientation before becoming Christians—I realized that it was clearly desirable for me to communicate solid, biblical truth rather than my own cultural assumptions!

Since our assumptions have such a determinative effect on our beliefs and actions, it is necessary to deal with them. The first step is to become aware of them, the second is to submit them to analysis, and the third is to be willing to correct them on the basis of scriptural truth. Romans 12:2 describes the process: "Do not conform any longer to the pattern of this world, but be transformed by the renewing of your mind. Then you will be able to test and approve what God's will is."

Recognizing Our Assumptions

The first step in securing freedom is to isolate the wrong assumptions that lead to wrong conclusions. I have asked Christian audiences to help me compile a list of assumptions accepted by our society that relate to material possessions. At the beginning, I was surprised to find that the majority of the assumptions listed were of questionable validity. But a careful look at Schlossberg's definition reveals the reason for this; assumptions are beliefs, not proven facts, or they would not be assumptions. If we begin with false assumptions as premises, we cannot arrive at correct conclusions.

A look at the following list of assumptions that are accepted as truth by large segments of our society reveals why we have no adequate philosophy of wealth. It is little wonder that our economic policies are confused and fragmented by attempts to reconcile special interests. While each of these assumptions is prevalent in our society, each is not universally accepted. Some are contradictory to others. I simply list these assumptions here, commenting on them only to the extent necessary for clarity. All of these assumptions will be addressed in this book.

Assumptions Prevalent in Our Society

Material possessions can bring real satisfaction through power, status, happiness, and security.

Unlimited acquisition of wealth is a worthy goal in life.

Wealth is a measure of a person's real value.

Wealth is the measure of success. (Even professional success is measured by earning capacity.)

Ownership is absolute; what I possess is *mine* by right. (Individuals with this attitude fail to recognize that God is the ultimate owner of everything.)

Ownership is absolute; what I possess is *mine* individually. (Those with this attitude fail to accept the responsibilities of community.)

I have a *right* to an equal share. (This is often extended to legitimatize covetousness and envy, and encourages rising expectations that soon become regarded as entitlements.)

Getting is better than giving.

In regard to money, the end justifies the means. ("Anything goes" in getting money; it is a game of every man for himself.)

Consumption is a virtue. (On the individual level, spending is preferred to saving. On the level of society, consumption is stimulated in preference to investment.)

Capital and profit are wrong.

The earth is running out of resources to the extent that civilization itself is in danger.

Resources are unlimited, so there is no need for conservation.

Society is responsible for the problems of individuals.

Society is responsible to meet everyone's needs.
Redistribution of wealth is a legitimate function of the state.
Economic growth is the supreme test of a society's quality.
Capitalism is of questionable morality.
Socialism has the higher moral ground.
Economic morality is relative.
Moral conduct is detrimental to financial success.

This list is not exhaustive, but it is sufficient to explain why Schaeffer says, "The majority of people [have] adopted two impoverished values: *personal peace* and *affluence*."[6]

As Christians, we are told that we "must no longer live as the Gentiles do, in the futility of their thinking" (Ephesians 4:17). Yet we have allowed many of society's assumptions to affect us and go unchallenged.

In addition, we have a list of assumptions that are peculiar to the Christian subculture. Even when these assumptions are contrary to those prevalent in society, they may not conform to biblical teaching. Many of our assumptions are based on a superficial or false interpretation of Scripture. Some of the assumptions listed below contradict others, but all are accepted by substantial numbers of Christians.

Assumptions Common Among Christians

Money is evil, or at least the root of all evil. Wealth is inherently dangerous.

Material things are worldly. It is not spiritual to enjoy material things.

Rich people are materialistic. The poor are free from materialism.

Honesty is detrimental to gaining wealth, therefore the morality of those who possess wealth is questionable.

Because of these factors, wealth and those who possess it are condemned.

Spirituality is directly associated with wealth:
>   Wealth is the sign of God's blessing.
>   A truly spiritual person will be financially successful.
>   God wants all Christians to be wealthy.
>   Poverty is a sign of moral and spiritual weakness.

Spirituality is directly associated with poverty:
>   Poverty is a sign of God's blessing.
>   A truly spiritual person will renounce financial
>   success.
>   Wealth is a sign of moral and spiritual weakness.
>   Poverty is a virtue to be desired.
>   Christians should have a "bare necessity" lifestyle.

God wants us to be continually and immediately dependent
   on Him:
>   God provides only for those with immediate needs.
>   Provision for the future is not consistent with faith.
>   Savings and insurance are wrong.
>   Those in control of their financial situation are missing
>   God's blessing.

Living by faith means depending on God to supply every
   immediate need.

Living by faith is more spiritual than assuming responsibility for one's financial affairs.

God is orchestrating every detail of my life:
>   When anything good happens He is rewarding me.
>   When things go wrong He is correcting me.

Planning and providing for the future are not consistent
   with faith.

Therefore asking and receiving are more spiritual than
   assuming responsibility to be able to give. Receiving is
   better than giving.

God is against the wealthy and on the side of the poor.

I am responsible only for my own financial welfare; others
   can take care of themselves.

Financial affairs are a private matter. I need not discuss
these things with other Christians, and they should not
bother me with them. Financial matters are not a part
of fellowship.

Receiving is difficult. It is a great weakness to need help
from other Christians.

Giving is an obligation.

The tithe is the obligatory biblical standard for giving.

Giving should be primarily (or exclusively) to my church.

If I give, God is obligated to give back more.

Giving must be sacrificial to count with God:

I must give more than I can afford.

Giving from abundance is not really giving.

God needs the money I can produce for Him.

Analyzing Our Assumptions

These assumptions usually appear in syndromes that in effect
constitute a philosophy of material possessions for certain groups
of Christians. Three of these syndromes are popular today.

Perhaps the most widespread is the *guilt syndrome.* Money is
considered evil, or at least a very dangerous root of evil. Material
things are worldly. Possessions are positively dangerous. It is
immoral to participate in an affluent society. The poor are poor
because others are rich. Poverty is a virtue because God is on the
side of the poor and against the wealthy. All wealth is viewed with
suspicion, and capital and profit are evil. Christians have an
obligation to reduce their standard of living to the subsistence
level.

The result of this combination of false assumptions is guilt,
and false guilt makes us vulnerable to manipulation. The obsession against money is just as dangerous as the obsession with
money. The obsession against money can be just as enslaving, just
as detrimental to a balanced understanding of what the Bible
teaches, as the obsession of materialism.

Equally prominent in Christian circles is the *success syndrome*. While the guilt syndrome is based largely on false premises, the success syndrome begins with the essential goodness of God's creation. But this premise is distorted and developed with faulty logic, so the conclusions are wrong. In this syndrome not only poverty, but even modest success, is regarded as a sign of spiritual weakness. It is God's desire that every Christian be wealthy and successful. Wealth is a sign of God's blessing. The only thing standing between the Christian and wealth is a lack of confidence that God has created him or her to be successful. Self-aggrandizement becomes equated with spirituality, thus materialism is coupled with conceit.

This syndrome is not unique to contemporary Christianity. Paul referred to those who "think that godliness is a means to financial gain" (1 Timothy 6:5). I expected this syndrome to be most prominent in the affluent societies of Western cultures, but I have discovered it has great appeal to Christians in poor countries as well.

The third pattern is the *dependency syndrome*. Its proponents would like to call it the faith syndrome, but it represents the dead faith without action described in James 2:17. This syndrome consists of "opting out" of all responsibility and living in complete and immediate dependency on God. It is deemed impossible to live by faith if you have resources to meet your present needs, and providing for the future is viewed as even more "carnal." The only acceptable evidence of a life of faith is to be directly dependent on God to provide your immediate needs. In addition, God's provision is limited to the immediate time frame; He is not permitted to provide for even the near future. Receiving is considered more spiritual than giving and is emphasized accordingly. Personal benefit is presented as the primary motivation for giving. Giving is regarded as leverage for future receiving.

It is interesting to note that God often does supply one's immediate needs. But proponents of the dependency syndrome usually fail to note that God supplies through the generosity of productive and responsible members of the Christian community.

Opening Our Eyes to God's Truth

Somewhere between these extremes lies a more balanced, biblical perspective that we will attempt to discover. If we are to successfully understand biblical teaching on material things, we must impose several disciplines on ourselves: 1) set aside our assumptions, 2) accept truth as God has revealed it, and 3) determine the underlying principles of God's truth.

Jesus accused the Pharisees of nullifying God's Word by their traditions. Our assumptions can have the same effect, acting as blinders that focus our attention so narrowly that we see only segments of the truth, or obscure it entirely. For example, several years ago I was searching for the implications of the parable of the shrewd but dishonest manager mentioned in Luke 16. I read verse nine to a seminary professor: "I tell you, use worldly wealth to gain friends for yourselves, so that when it is gone, you will be welcomed into eternal dwellings." I expected him to affirm the obvious meaning, that we should utilize material wealth for eternal purposes. With a note of disdain the professor replied, "I'm not sure what it means, but it can't mean to use worldly wealth for eternal purposes!" The clear meaning of Scripture did not coincide with his assumptions!

When our assumptions are expressed in the forms and traditions of our culture or subculture, it becomes difficult to recognize them as assumptions, let alone to set them aside. If we have also come to look on our assumptions as revealed truth, it becomes nearly impossible to subject them to analysis. However, we must be willing to subject our assumptions to the test of Scripture and set them aside when they do not conform to it.

Truth will set us free. We often resist truth because it does not fit our assumptions and conflicts with our traditions, but these are not the only reasons. Truth in Scripture is often contrasted with sin, and the proper response to truth is obedience. We also resist truth because we do not desire to obey.

Another reason we resist truth is that we do not trust it. We have more confidence in our own formulas. There are many areas in which we distort the Scriptures to accommodate our assumptions. The topic of material possessions is one of these areas. For example, it is hard for us to believe individually that giving is better than receiving, and collectively that encouraging voluntary generosity will meet our needs better than imposing a mandatory obligation.

Yet we must begin with truth, with reality as God has revealed it through Scripture. In his seminar on creativity, Mike Vance gives some basic requirements for constructive and creative thinking. One of these is the Aristotelian concept of reality: "The thing *is* what it *is*." If A is A and different from B, we cannot succeed by starting from the premise that A is B. He also emphasizes the importance of recognizing cause-and-effect relationships. If we are to reach correct conclusions that lead to correct actions, we must begin with reality and focus on the causes. To quote Mr. Vance, "We must find out how the system works and make it work." The system of the material universe works in relationship to man the way the Creator intended it to work, so we need to discover and accept God's truth concerning it.

Many of us are much more comfortable with rules and regulations than with principles. With a carefully prescribed set of rules to follow, we do not have to study, discern, or make decisions. Yet spiritual maturity requires these exercises. Hebrews 5:14 describes mature people as those "who by constant use have trained themselves to distinguish good from evil."

Elisabeth Elliot, missionary to the Auca Indians after her husband was martyred by that tribe, wrote a short but outstanding book entitled *The Liberty of Obedience*. She reminds us that "it does not take practice to read a rule book. . . . God the Father intends to make of His children spiritual adults. He has called us *sons.* The son is not trained for a job, but for a life. If we as Christians regard the Bible as a list of unequivocal rules, we obscure or even annul this training." She concludes that God could have "summarized all of the rules in one book. . . and think of the crop of dwarfs He would have reared!"[7]

It is important to recognize that God's instruction to man is on several levels, but all instruction is based on the nature of God and His creation. Jesus makes this clear in Matthew 22:34-37. He gives the two principles underlying everything—love for God and love for our neighbor—concluding that "all the Law and the Prophets hang on these two commandments."

Out of these principles comes the second level of law, including the rest of the commandments. These laws are universal but are not absolute. There is a time when love for God and love for neighbor supersedes the law against killing, as in defensive warfare. Or when love for our neighbor supersedes the law against falsehood, illustrated by Rahab of Jericho, who was commended for saving the life of her neighbor through falsehood.

The third level of instruction is that of the rules and regulations governing a specific society. We will profit little from these by insisting on their universal application, but we can profit much by determining the purposes behind them. This does not make our task easy, but it does make our task rewarding.

We will look to the Scriptures for their underlying and universal principles. We will try to avoid the mistake of generalizing specific instructions or confusing principles with their immediate application, which is usually cultural and circumstantial. We will attempt to focus on function rather than form and on substance rather than detail. We must also avoid abstracting the principles and filling them with our own content. Sometimes these principles are clearly stated; sometimes we must use discernment to determine the purpose behind a scriptural statement. We will discover direct teaching on economic matters, and we will also find that many general principles apply to this area as well.

NOTES:
1. Herbert Schlossberg, *Idols for Destruction* (Nashville, Tennessee: Thomas Nelson, Inc., 1983), page 8.
2. Edward T. Hall, *Beyond Culture* (Garden City, New York: Anchor Press/ Doubleday, 1976), page 38.
3. Os Guinness, as quoted by Schlossberg, *Idols for Destruction*, page 7.
4. Francis A. Schaeffer, *How Should We Then Live?* (Old Tappan, New Jersey: Fleming H. Revell Company, 1976), page 19.
5. Hall, *Beyond Culture*, pages 38-39.
6. Schaeffer, *How Should We Then Live?*, page 205.
7. Elisabeth Elliot, *The Liberty of Obedience* (Waco, Texas: Word Books, 1968), pages 54-57.

THREE

The Principles of God's Economic Order

The Bible's teaching about material possessions can be divided into four phases that correspond to God's historical dealings with man. God's revelation in these phases is consistent yet progressive.

> The basic principles governing and affecting man's relationship to material things are established in the book of Genesis.
>
> A model of these principles is seen in the economic instructions given to the nation Israel.
>
> Jesus gave new spiritual meaning and depth to these principles after centuries of tradition had erased all of their ethical and spiritual implications. God's Law had been reduced to a series of self-serving rules and regulations that provided escape from obligations rather than fulfillment of brotherhood.
>
> The writers of the New Testament taught Christians how to

apply the basic principles within whatever society they found themselves.

The Random House dictionary defines economics as, "The science treating of the production, distribution, and consumption of goods and services, or the material welfare of mankind." For our purposes we will narrow this definition since the book of Genesis does not develop the details of the science of economics, but gives principles governing man's material welfare. We will also broaden the definition to include the teleological aspects of material things. Since God is the source of the material universe and has a design and purpose for it in relationship to man, it is not enough to consider economics only in its material or psychological aspects. We must also consider the theological aspects. With this in mind, let's look at Genesis to discover basic principles that reveal the nature of God's economic order.

The Origin and Nature of Material Things

We find in the book of Genesis the foundation for all the economic instruction that follows. Genesis reveals something of the nature of God, the nature of man, and God's purpose in creating man. It records man's earliest experiences with material things under God's tutelage. It records man's rebellion and its consequences, which affected man's spiritual being, physical being, and the material universe in which he lives.

God created the material universe, created man, and has defined the proper relationship between these two aspects of His creation. The universe works the way the Creator intended it to work. So we need to determine how God intended man and the material universe to function together.

In Genesis 1:1 we read, "In the beginning God created the heavens and the earth," so God Himself is the source of the material universe. The universe He created is truly incredible. Even the writer of Genesis waxed eloquent in Genesis 2:1: "Thus the heavens and the earth were completed in all their vast array." Mankind has only begun to explore the greatness and understand the intricacies of God's creation. Whether man looks far out into the macrocosm of space, or deep into the microcosm of subatomic structure, man finds what appears to be infinity.

We are related to the material universe in many ways. Our bodies are material, our sustenance is material, and our senses relate to the material. God's creation has a purpose that is related to man. The material creation provides man's physical body into which God infuses His image, and provides for that body as God carries out His purpose. The fact that God is the source of the material universe offers important instruction concerning our study of man's relationship to material possessions.

It is also important to note that there is no hint in Scripture that the physical universe is evil or inferior. The God who created the material universe announced His satisfaction by describing it as "very good" (Genesis 1:31). The material universe is different from the spiritual in that its purpose is more specific and limited and it is temporary, not eternal. Those limitations, however, do not make it less important in serving the Creator's purpose. The alleged spirituality that makes material things evil is not biblical.

False Conclusions About the Origin of Material Things

Historically, the failure to understand the source and nature of the material universe has led to false teaching. The Persian dualists regarded matter as evil. It was either coeternal with God or the creation of an eternal, evil spirit that was antagonistic to good. These ideas were introduced into Western thought and became prominent in Gnosticism.

There are great differences in Gnostic thought, but its fundamental belief is that matter is evil. Since matter is evil it could not have been created by God, but by a demiurge who resulted from a series of emanations from God that made the creator remote enough to justify evil. Some Gnostics practiced rigid asceticism, while others regarded the indulgence of the flesh as a matter of indifference. Still others held that the flesh should be destroyed through vice. These ideas culminated in the Manichaeanism of the third century.

Church historian A.H. Newman characterizes Manichaeanism as "absolute dualism"[1] in which matter is believed to be inherently evil. If the material creation is evil, it follows that our physical bodies are also evil. The Manichaeans dealt with this problem by advocating "the ascetical spirit, with degradation of marriage, the exaltation of virginity, the regarding of the sexual instinct as absolutely evil and to be overcome by all possible means."[2] If our bodies are evil, then the physical body of Jesus presents an even greater problem. The Docetics answered this problem by denying the reality of Christ's body, teaching that it was only an apparition.

While Christians today have resolved some of these basic issues, we have not completely overcome all uncertainty about material things. Somehow we have come to look on material things as "worldly." This word is so common in usage among Christians that I was surprised to discover that it is used only a few times in the Bible.

In Hebrews 9:1 "worldly" refers to God's temporary sanctuary here on earth, the Tabernacle. In this sense all material things are "worldly" in that they are temporal. This is simply a description of their term of existence. It has no negative connotations and does not imply that material things are unimportant, inferior, or evil. In fact, Paul cautions against making our relationship to material things the basis of our spirituality. We are not to submit to rules such as, "Do not handle! Do not taste! Do not touch!" These rules are deceitful, having "an appearance of wisdom, with their self-imposed worship, their false humility and their harsh treatment of the body, but they lack any value in restraining sensual indulgence" (Colossians 2:21,23).

Another use of "worldly" is in Titus 2:12, where the reference is made to "worldly passions." This use does have negative connotations, but it refers to the condition of man's heart. Paul is speaking of "sexual immorality, impurity, lust, evil desires and greed, which is idolatry. . . anger, rage, malice, slander, and filthy language" (Colossians 3:5,8). There are other similar lists in the Scriptures.

The only use of the term "worldly" in relationship to material things is found in Luke 16:9 and 11. Here Jesus uses the parable of the shrewd manager to make a distinction between worldly wealth and eternal values. He indicates that the trustworthy handling of material things demonstrates that we can be entrusted with true riches. Material things are described as temporal, but not as evil or undesirable.

So, from Scripture we see that material things are "worldly" only in the sense that they are not eternal. Elisabeth Elliot speaks directly to this:

> Jesus Christ gave us, with Himself, *all things* freely to enjoy. Paul reminds us that all things are ours. We are not asked to deny ourselves as many things as possible in order to set our hearts on the eternal. Things are not incompatible with Christ. They are all "worldly" in the simplest sense—they are for this world. They are not sinful for this reason. . . . It is our use of things that determines their effect on us.[3]

Since this wonderful universe is God's creation and provision, it should be a cause of continual celebration! As we see in 1 Timothy 6:17—"God. . . richly provides us with everything for our enjoyment." The material universe presents us with tremendous opportunity, yet we often treat it as a temptation. God did not create material things as a temptation to be avoided, but as a provision to be utilized. Satan can pervert man's mind so that he looks at material things with lust, covetousness, greed, and envy. But the error lies within man's heart, not in material things themselves.

God's creation is good! Not evil, or even morally neutral, but good. Very good.

Man's Dominion Over the Material Universe

"Then God said, 'Let us make man in our image, in our likeness, and let them rule over the fish of the sea and the birds of the air, over the livestock, over all the earth, and over all the creatures that move along the ground'" (Genesis 1:26).

Man was distinct from the rest of creation because he was made in God's image. As God's image bearer, man was given dominion over the rest of creation. God created man to rule over, fill, and subdue the earth. Man was to exercise dominion over every living thing and bring the earth itself under his control. The earth was created for man's benefit.

If the earth is running out of resources, then God's purpose for it is nearing completion. He knew what He was doing in creation, and the resources will last as long as His purpose for them lasts. This does not mean that there is no need for conservation or concern for ecology. Man was not given dominion so that he might destroy the earth. We need to avoid both extremes—living in fear of depleting resources or exploiting and wasting resources.

The command to subdue, fill, and rule over the earth implies the active application of man's intelligence. Man was not to be passive, but active—in creativity, problem-solving, and achieving. It is possible that we are just beginning to obey this command. Every new discovery opens up expanding horizons. The discovery and application of knowledge in science and technology are essential aspects of dominion.

Having dominion over the earth does not give man the right to act without restraint or guidance. God sets forth principles that govern man's dominion. Man was not created to act autonomously, but under God as God's image bearer. Since his rebellion, man has attempted to act autonomously. Because man was not created to be autonomous, this has been tantamount to turning his dominion over to Satan.

The text of Genesis 1:26-30 makes it clear that man's authority to have dominion over the earth relates exclusively to the physical creation. The extent of man's dominion is defined twice in this brief passage. If we make any extension to what God has included in this definition, we open the door to any doctrine that suits our fancy. Examples of such extension abound, both historically (the "divine right" of kings) and contemporarily. One major U.S. denomination, for example, is using the text to justify abortion! Reconstructionists extend man's dominion to the control of other men and all of society by enforcing the rule of God's Law through all the earth. I believe this extension is not justified, and this enforcement is in conflict with the free nature of man as God created him.

Man's Nature as a Physical/Spiritual Being

When I consider your heavens,
    the work of your fingers,
the moon and the stars,
    which you have set in place,
what is man that you are mindful of him?
    the son of man that you care for him?
You made him a little lower than the heavenly beings
    and crowned him with glory and honor.

You made him ruler over the works of your hands;
    you put everything under his feet:
all flocks and herds,
    and the beasts of the field,
the birds of the air,
    and the fish of the sea,
    all that swim the paths of the seas.   (Psalm 8:3-8)

This psalm confirms man's dominion over the earth, but also focuses our attention on man's most universal and persistent question: "What is man?" Philosophers, psychologists, anthropologists, and historians have joined the theologians in asking this question. All of us on a personal level have asked, "Who am I?" Those who have attempted to answer this question without the help of scriptural revelation have found the task difficult indeed. The historian Arnold Toynbee, in his book *Mankind and Mother Earth,* has a chapter titled "Riddles in the Phenomena." He approaches our question from this perspective: "It is now hardly possible any longer to believe that the phenomena of which a human being is conscious have been called into existence by the fiat of a human-like creator-god."[4]

Much discussion on the nature of man focuses on the difficulty of reconciling the physical with the spiritual. Toynbee points to this difficulty: "Every live human being that a human being knows or knows of, including himself, is a conscious, purposeful spirit that is physically alive in a material body. None of these components of a live human being have ever been encountered apart from the rest. They are always found in association with each other; yet their relation to each other is incomprehensible."[5]

Toynbee continues to wonder, "How . . . have life and consciousness come to be associated with matter? Why does life . . . strive to perpetuate itself or . . . reproduce itself true to type? Is this effort inherent in the nature of the species? And, if the effort is not inherent but is introduced, what is the agency that introduces it if we rule out the hypothesis of the operation of a creator-god?"[6]

The contemporary anthropologist Ernest Becker states the dichotomy succinctly: "Man is literally split in two; he has an awareness of his own splendid uniqueness in that he sticks out of nature with a towering majesty, and yet he goes back into the ground a few feet in order blindly and dumbly to rot and disappear forever."[7] Becker concludes that "the two dimensions of human existence—the body and the self—can never be reconciled seamlessly."[8] "Underneath throbs the ache of cosmic specialness"[9] for "man is the impossible creature!"[10]

The dilemma is not as impossible for Christians, since we accept the existence of a personal Creator-God and believe that we find a revelation of God and the purpose of His creation in Scripture. The two aspects of man's nature—the physical and the spiritual—are clearly articulated many places in the Bible, beginning with the account of the Creation as recorded in Genesis:

> Then God said, "Let us make man in our image, in our likeness. . . ." So God created man in his own image, in the image of God he created him; male and female he created them.
> (Genesis 1:26-27)

> And the Lord God formed man from the dust of the ground and breathed into his nostrils the breath of life, and man became a living being.
> (Genesis 2:7)

The reality of the dichotomy is evidenced by these two stages of creation. God breathed His spiritual likeness into man's natural body and man became a living being in God's spiritual image. We recognize ourselves as spiritual beings and physical bodies inexorably bound together. This binding is apparently for time and for eternity, even though our natural body will become a spiritual body (1 Corinthians 15:44) clothed with the imperishable and with immortality (1 Corinthians 15:53).

When God desired to become man, it was necessary that He take upon Himself a human body, again apparently permanently: "Christ Jesus: Who, being in very nature God . . . made himself nothing . . . being made in human likeness" (Philippians 2:5-7). The Scriptures record the Lord Jesus Christ's human body in its natural form before the Crucifixion and in its spiritual form after the Resurrection. His spiritual body retains many of the characteristics associated with our natural bodies: Jesus promised to drink wine with His disciples in the future Kingdom; He instructed the Sadducees that sexuality would not be an aspect of the resurrection body; the resurrected Jesus was recognizable; He walked and talked and touched; He showed them He had flesh and bones; He broke bread and ate fish with them. Yet He could disappear from their sight, appear through closed doors, and bodily ascend into Heaven.

Perhaps Paul was thinking of these characteristics of Jesus' resurrected body when he wrote, "We wait eagerly for . . . the redemption of our bodies" (Romans 8:23) and, "The creation itself will be liberated from its bondage to decay and brought into the glorious freedom of the children of God" (Romans 8:21). We have only a few interesting glimpses into eternity. Our present existence is much clearer.

Our physical body is composed of the chemicals of the material universe in living form. God infused a spirit in His image into this physical body. Thus our humanity consists of the physical and the spiritual. We are one person. Robert Banks, an Australian professor, says, "Man is not simply a soul imprisoned within a body but a physical being."[11] Our existence continues within an imperishable body after this perishable body ceases to function, and we should prepare for this future existence. But our present existence is within physical bodies in a material universe.

Our tendency to think in categories has caused us to separate the physical from the spiritual and to emphasize the dichotomy. We tend to make a sharp distinction between the secular and sacred, when in reality all of life is sacred. This distinction has led to all kinds of distortions in doctrine and practice—from asceticism and stoicism, to the withdrawal of monasticism, to the other-worldliness of many contemporary Christians. We are physical-spiritual beings because God created us that way, and we must not consider the physical inferior to the spiritual.

Aspects of Man's Nature that Relate to Material Things

Individuality. Man is created in God's image. Since it is impossible for us to comprehend God fully, it is impossible to determine exactly what this statement means. Even if we understood God perfectly, we would not have an accurate description of man since man was not created identical to God but in His likeness. By examining what the Bible reveals about God and observing the differences between man and the rest of creation, however, we can reach certain conclusions about what it means to be made in God's image.

Theologian Augustus Strong defines God's image as two-fold.[12] The first aspect is "natural likeness to God, or personality." Since God is a person, personality is the essence of His image reproduced in us. Personality involves self-consciousness and self-determination. Personality is realized through the exercise of intellect, emotion, and will. As originally created, man exercised his personhood toward the second aspect of the image of God, which is "moral likeness to God, or holiness." Man accepted God with his intellect, loved God with his heart, and followed God with his will.

Adam was created in God's image, so the essence of God's image was complete in Adam as an individual. This concept of individuality is essential to the proper understanding of man in his relationship to God and others. It instructs us in every aspect of man's relationship to material things. The instruction is not only to each individual, but to economic systems that correlate the interests of many individuals. Systems that violate the concept of individuality either do not work or result in enslavement. Attempts to obliterate individuality are attacks on the essential nature of man.

Freedom to choose. Choosing is universal to man because God created man with this capacity. Volition, the ability to will, is a significant aspect of God's image. Choosing is not an option, but an existential necessity. Freedom of choice is not a gift of government or society, but is a gift from God.

Adam was given the freedom to choose. "You are free to eat from any tree in the garden; but you must not eat from the tree of the knowledge of good and evil, for when you eat of it you will surely die" (Genesis 2:16-17). Strong defines this freedom as the will, "the soul's power to choose between motives . . . both an end and the means to attain it."[13]

Without getting into a theological discussion of free will, we can recognize that man makes choices, exercising his personality in self-determination. Eve made a choice between obeying God or defying His commandments. Adam made the same choice. Cain and Abel, the next two human beings, each made a choice: one to serve God and one to rebel.

The ability to choose makes man a moral being in contrast to the rest of creation. Because he was made in God's image, man can discern right from wrong and can choose between motives. As he chooses correctly, God provides the ability to conform to the rules of right conduct. Without freedom of choice there would be no morality in the fullest sense of the word (involving a moral agent and volition). There could be perfection and conformity if man had been created without the freedom of choice, but then man would not have been made in God's image.

The individual is the ultimate unit of moral choice. Each person exercises his personality in self-determination through the will. If this is not so, the individual does not have freedom. If each man has the freedom implied in being created in God's image, it follows that moral choices are made by the individual. This is borne out by the examples in Genesis we have referred to: Adam, Eve, Cain, and Abel. Each person made an independent choice and was held accountable or rewarded for that choice. God ignored their attempts to place the blame elsewhere.

All through Scripture, individuals are required to make choices. This does not mean that the individual cannot act in voluntary concert within a community. Individuals may agree in their choices and influence each other in choosing. They may also choose to follow a group decision that contradicts their own. We unconsciously recognize the ultimate unit of choice when we reserve our highest respect for those who have the courage to follow their own convictions.

Personal responsibility. Individual freedom of choice implies individual responsibility. From the very beginning, each individual was held accountable for his or her actions. Adam attempted to place the blame on Eve, and Eve on the serpent, but to no avail. God held each responsible and punished each accordingly. God spoke to Cain in terms of absolute, individual responsibility. "If *you* do what is right, will *you* not be accepted? Sin is crouching at your door . . . *you* must master it" (Genesis 4:7, italics added).

This does not prevent us from influencing one another for good or evil. Cain's descendants continued in rebellion, culminating seven generations later in Lamech's defiance of God. Seth replaced Abel and with his descendants followed God, culminating seven generations later with Enoch, who walked with God so intimately that he disappeared from the earth into God's presence. Eventually the godly descendants, "the sons of God" (Genesis 6:2), intermarried with the glamorous "daughters of men"—the rebellious line—and mankind became totally corrupt. The one exception to the corrupt world was Noah. Individually, and alone, he walked with God.

Just as Adam and Eve tried to pass the blame to others, today man prefers to blame parents, friends, society, circumstances, or even God. But responsibility is concurrent with freedom of choice. Just as the individual is the ultimate unit of moral choice, each individual is responsible for his or her choices.

Diversity. Moral choice is not the only aspect of our individuality. We were created as individual personalities with great diversity. One benefit of diversity is that we can complement each other in community. Another reason for diversity is that God did not choose to demonstrate all of His creative ability in any single person. It would have been impossible for Him to fully reproduce His image in one person without that person being God. Even in our final perfection, we will each be a *different* manifestation of

God's glory. Michael Novak refers to the writings of Thomas Aquinas in this regard: "Aquinas once wrote that humans are made in the image of God but that since God is infinite He may be mirrored only through a virtually infinite number of humans."[14]

The choices we make in self-determination not only reflect our diversity, but increase it. Each choice moves us in a given direction. Erich Fromm recognizes our diversity and the role of choices in the development of character. In an attempt to explain the horrors of human destructiveness, he refers to man's character structure.[15] He says that man's existential needs are expressed and met through syndromes constituting his orientation to life. Fromm talks of the "life-furthering syndrome" of love, solidarity, justice, and reason; or the "life-thwarting syndrome" of sadomasochism, destructiveness, greed, narcissism, incestuousness.[16] Together they constitute man's character, which is progressive. In the Bible we see that the choices of Abel, Seth, and Cain both stemmed from and contributed to their character and that of their descendants.

Every choice we make further develops our character in a given direction. This is true in the economic realm as well, which is the essential teaching of the book of Proverbs in regard to material things. Diligence leads to success, which provides the motivation as well as the basis for future success. Slothfulness leads to failure, which reduces future opportunity. Jesus makes the same point in Matthew 25:29: "For everyone who has will be given more, and he will have an abundance. Whoever does not have, even what he has will be taken from him."

Ownership. Ownership of material things is attributed to individuals throughout the book of Genesis and the entire Bible. Of course this ownership is not absolute, but is qualified in that God ultimately owns everything. Since God gives man dominion over His creation, our ownership is in reality stewardship as God's image-bearer. In relationship to God, we consider ourselves stewards. In relationship to man, individuals are the owners of property.

Individual ownership was implied in the commands, "You shall not steal," and "You shall not covet . . . anything that belongs to your neighbor" (Exodus 20:15,17). Long before this formal approval of individual ownership was given in Exodus, we see individual ownership by the patriarchs.

Abraham had significant possessions when God told him to leave Haran (Genesis 12:5). By the time he left Egypt, he was "very wealthy in livestock and in silver and gold" (Genesis 13:2).

Isaac inherited all of Abraham's wealth (Genesis 25:5), and greatly increased the wealth of Abraham, harvesting crops of a hundredfold in a single year. His wealth became so great that the envy of the Philistines prompted them to ask him to leave (Genesis 26:13-16). This wealth was accepted as a sign of God's blessing (Genesis 26:12).

Esau had the right to sell his birthright (Genesis 25:31-33).

Jacob fled to Haran with nothing and became wealthy there (Genesis 30:43), and God directly assisted him in the accumulation of wealth. Jacob took practical steps to preserve his wealth when faced with the anger of his brother Esau (Genesis 32:7-8,13-20).

Joseph became wealthy and powerful in Egypt, and "the Lord was with him and . . . the Lord gave him success in everything he did" (Genesis 39:2-3).

Job received material blessings at God's hand, and the book of Proverbs supports the same pattern.

In all of these references, an individual is described as the owner. Yet since man lives in family and in broader community, it is rare that wealth is accumulated and utilized solely for the interests of the individual. The family and community surrounding the patriarch benefited from his ownership. The sons eventually inherited his wealth while the daughters were given a dowry. The oldest son received a double portion, partially because he was responsible to provide for his mother. But as long as the patriarch lived, he was the owner. If he made distribution before his death, it was done voluntarily. In these examples we can see scriptural support for several ideas:

> Individual ownership of wealth.
> Legitimate acquisition of wealth, sometimes as a specific
> > blessing of God.
> Inheritance of wealth.
> Preservation of wealth.
> Increase of wealth by diligent enterprise.
> Individual freedom to be profligate or prudent.
> The proper utilization of wealth.

This pattern of individual ownership continues throughout the Bible.

The individual's right to ownership is more than an academic consideration. History shows that property rights are essential to freedom—both for individuals and for their voluntary communities. An individual's right to ownership extends to the communities that he or she forms. Private ownership—by individuals or communities—limits the power of the state, while its prohibition gives the state absolute power over the individual and leads to totalitarianism. While property rights do not guarantee freedom, they are absolutely essential to freedom. I know of no historical exception, no situation in which men were free without the right to own property.

The right to ownership can be abused, as can any of God's good gifts, if used for self-aggrandizement. Yet the right to ownership cannot be denied for this reason. As part of God's pattern for man's relationship to material things, individual ownership carries both privilege and responsibility. An individual cannot delegate these prerogatives of ownership, even to a Christian community. Individual ownership is a corollary of our creation as individuals.

Let me summarize the aspects of man's nature that bear heavily upon our study of man and his relationship with material possessions:

1. God created man as an individual person.
2. Freedom of choice is inherent in man's nature.
3. Man reaps the benefits or suffers the consequences of his choices.
4. Each individual is responsible to God.
5. Diversity is the rule in God's creation. This diversity is amplified by man's choices.
6. Individual ownership of property is essential to freedom and necessary for the application of these principles to economics.

Man as Community

Individuality is only one aspect of man's being. While it is essential that man be confirmed as an individual, individuals can find fulfillment only if they are dependent upon one another in community. Man was created as a social being, as evident in the book of Genesis.

God Himself is in some way community. "Let *us* make man in *our* image, in *our* likeness" (Genesis 1:26). This statement is more than rhetorical, yet it cannot contradict the fact that there is but one God. Ultimate truth is often incomprehensible to our finite minds. We can only grasp components of it that sometimes appear contradictory: The Father is God, the Son is God, the Holy Spirit is God, and yet there is but one God. Without fully understanding this, we can recognize that God's image involves both individuality and community.

Man as community is also evident in Genesis 2:18: "It is not good for the man to be alone. I will make a helper suitable for him." This statement is often too narrowly interpreted, because God's intention went beyond Adam and Eve's relationship to the extended community that originated with them. Eve was a helper to Adam in many ways, but most important was her role in the creation of life.

The first human community consisted of Adam and Eve,

who fellowshiped together with God. The community expanded with Cain and Abel, and they complemented each other by the division of labor and worshiped God together as they brought their offerings.

Marriage and family are the basic form of community. Early in man's history most communities were familial, and their identities extended through many generations. For example, Abraham's family community had grown to seventy individuals by the time they settled in Egypt. The nation of Israel was considered one community, but was divided into tribes and families.

Community continues all through the Scriptures. The most complete development and the most thorough instructions regarding community occur within the groups of New Testament Christians. This new community was not familial or national, but a voluntary association of local Christians.

A community is composed of individuals; one cannot exist without the other. The freedom of individuals extends to the choice of community. An individual's continuing participation in any community is voluntary, even though introduction into that community may have been involuntary. This is true even of the family community. Children can reject identification and fellowship with their families, and as adults can separate from that community completely. Christians may find themselves within a natural Christian community almost without conscious choice, but they choose whether to remain in that community. There are a few imaginable "lifeboat" situations where community is involuntary, but most communities are voluntary.

The need for community complements man's individuality and is rooted in man's nature as he was created—in God's image. It is not sufficient to say that individual man was created in God's image and needs to live in community. Community is just as much a part of God's image as is individuality. There is no conflict between these two aspects of God's image. They are complementary, not contradictory.

Community must be based on individuality and must respect the individual's nature and freedom. Michael Novak expresses the relationship between the two:

> In this scheme, the individual is not atomic. Although the individual is an originating source of insight and choice, the fulfillment of the individual lies in a beloved community. Yet any community worthy of such love values the singularity and inviolability of each person. Without true individualism, there is no true community.[17]

Historically, the most regrettable repressions and persecutions have resulted from a religious majority's determination to enforce its convictions upon everyone within the community. Believers tend to develop strong convictions and insist that others conform to them. The Galileo affair, the Inquisition, the atrocities in the "City of God" under Calvin, and the Salem witch trials are but a few examples. Methods are more subtle today, but many Christian communities have developed techniques for achieving conformity at the individual's expense. The tyranny of the majority is inevitable if individuals are not respected.

On the other hand, individualism without community is equally dangerous. Hannah Arendt, in one of her insightful studies on the human condition, has said that radical individualism, radical human autonomy (social atomism), paves the way for totalitarianism.[18] Multiple communities, each with a legitimate realm of authority, are buffers to a totalitarian state. Community, coupled with private ownership of property, provides an effective defense against totalitarianism.

In totalitarianism, the state becomes an involuntary community. Since voluntary communities are prohibited, the individual is atomized. Thus there exists neither the free individual nor true community. This is not in conformity with man's nature as a person or as community. Thus, under totalitarianism, man cannot function as man. The results are manifold. It is easy to confuse the genuine unity of community with enforced uniformity and solidarity. The feudal system had the latter components without individual liberty and freedom. The totalitarian states of today are modern examples. Collectivism is not community. Enforced community is not true community.

This is why Novak talks about "a community of free persons in voluntary association" and a "new type of human being, neither an individualist nor a collectivist."[19] Perhaps this is not such a new type after all, since it was envisioned by the Apostle Paul almost 2000 years ago:

> Make my joy complete by being like-minded, having the same love, being one in spirit and purpose. Do nothing out of selfish ambition or vain conceit, but in humility consider others better than yourselves. Each of you should look not only to your own interests, but also to the interests of others.
> (Philippians 2:2-4)

Man's Choice

Man was created as a moral being with the ability to discern right from wrong, with the freedom to choose between motives, and with a will to carry out his choices. Man chose to satisfy himself rather than to obey God. Eating of the tree satisfied his physical appetite (good for food), his emotional or aesthetic appetite (pleasing to the eye), and his intellectual appetite (desirable for gaining wisdom, Genesis 3:6).

It is important to note that the first recorded exercise of man's ability to choose introduced sin. Whether we believe that all of Adam's posterity was sinful because of Adam's sin, or that each of us has ratified Adam's choice by our own sin, or a combination of both, we recognize that sin is universal to the human condition. Sin cannot be eliminated since it is already present, and man remains free to choose good or evil. The reality of sin affects every aspect of economics. The results of sin extend beyond the nature of man to the universe in which we live.

The Curse and Economics

"Cursed is the ground because of you;
    through painful toil you will eat of it
    all the days of your life.
It will produce thorns and thistles for you,
    and you will eat the plants of the field.
By the sweat of your brow
    you will eat your food
until you return to the ground,
    since from it you were taken;
for dust you are
    and to dust you will return."   (Genesis 3:17-19)

Before the Fall, Adam was permitted simply to take and eat of the abundance of the garden. He was to take care of the garden, but without thorns and thistles his task was not strenuous. Then the land was cursed. In resistance to Adam's effort, it brought forth thorns and thistles. Earning a living became hard work. No longer could man simply pluck the fruit from the trees. Man had to struggle to subsist on the plants of the field.

The severity of the curse is emphasized in Genesis 5:29 when Noah was born: "He named him Noah and said, 'He will comfort us in the labor and painful toil of our hands caused by the ground the Lord has cursed.'" This was perhaps more prophetic than Noah's father realized, for Noah "found favor in the eyes of the Lord" (Genesis 6:8), and God modified the curse for Noah's descendants (Genesis 9).

The curse applied directly to the land, but extended to all of man's efforts. Ever since the curse, man's efforts have been characterized by futility. The book of Ecclesiastes is a graphic picture of the futility of man's efforts—even when he is the most successful! Whatever man does comes up as thorns and thistles!

The curse introduced a new element into man's life that forms the basis of all economic practice: scarcity. It would have been difficult to buy or sell in the Garden of Eden, for everything man needed was there for the taking. As a result of scarcity—and apparently it was very severe—man began to develop economic functions.

As we've seen, man has been created in God's image. One facet of this image is intelligence. It is predictable that man would use this intelligence to mitigate the effects of the curse. As the community of man increased, the application of intelligence became necessary for survival. Efficiency was desirable.

To achieve this efficiency, the first step in the development of economics was the division of labor. Man learned that he could be more efficient if he concentrated on one thing. This factor appeared as early as Genesis 4:2, in the case of Cain and Abel. One was a herdsman, the other a tiller of the soil. Other occupations were recorded in succeeding generations. Nomads who raised livestock, musicians who played the harp and flute, metal workers who worked in bronze and iron, farmers who worked the soil or vineyards, professional warriors, and hunters are among them.

This specialization required cooperation and enhanced community. It introduced the necessity for trade and exchange, beginning with the concept of barter. The man who limited himself to one specialty needed to enjoy the production of others. Eventually this led to the introduction of money—something that could function as a medium of exchange and a store of value. Money greatly facilitated the division of labor because it became easy to store and transport the results of enterprise.

Capital was always present in some form, both human capital and the physical capital of the land, animals, seed stock, etc. Man learned that efficiency could be increased by the application of monetary capital as well. Thus economics came into being.

Summary
Economics relates to the ownership, production, distribution, and consumption of material goods. As such, it affects the relationship

of man to God's material creation.

The book of Genesis records God's creation of man and the material universe and His direction of man's early history. So in Genesis we could logically expect to find the underlying principles of how God intended man and the physical universe to work together. These principles are important because the universe works the way God intended it to work. In review they are:

> God's creation is very good—not neutral or evil, but good!
> Man was given dominion over the earth, to subdue it and cause it to produce.
> Man's nature as created in God's image includes:
>> Individuality—Each individual is created in God's image, with equal standing before God.
>> Freedom of choice—The individual is the ultimate unit of choice.
>> Individual responsibility—Each is accountable for his choices.
>> Diversity—From one individual to another there is a variety of talents, abilities, energy, motivation, etc. Diversity implies inequality of results. Diversity is increased by choices.
>> Ownership—A person's ownership of property is essential to freedom and individuality.
> Community is part of God's image. Individual man can find fulfillment only in voluntary communities.
> Man's choice produced two results:
>> Sin became part of the human condition.
>> The curse made man's dominion difficult. The curse introduced the factor of scarcity, which is the basis of economic development.

Man's economic history in its successful manifestations demonstrates the validity of these principles. Man exercises his dominion over the earth and causes it to produce. Man is ingenious in applying his intelligence and enterprise to the fact of scarcity. Individual men act in ways that demonstrate their individuality through their freedom of choice and their diversity. Man is zealous to protect his right to own property, and if given the opportunity, he assumes responsibility for his material welfare.

Man in general recognizes the necessity of community and finds fulfillment in voluntary communities. This is especially true in the economic realm, because most economic activity requires the cooperation of many individuals. Man accepts the fact that sin is an aspect of the human condition, and structures his societies and economic activities accordingly. Freedom to choose is restricted only when the rights of other individuals or of society as a whole are threatened. Man is willing to submit to the disciplines that are necessary to overcome the effects of the curse.

Societies that structure their economic systems to accommodate these truths succeed. Those that violate them not only run into difficulties, but prevent their citizens from fully demonstrating God's image. If God's intention for man is to be realized, man's economic systems must be based on God's principles.

NOTES:
1. Albert Henry Newman, *A Manual of Church History* (Chicago, Illinois: The Judson Press, 1933), Vol. 1, page 195.
2. Newman, page 197.
3. Elisabeth Elliot, *The Liberty of Obedience* (Waco, Texas: Word Books, 1968), pages 35-36.
4. Arnold Toynbee, *Mankind and Mother Earth* (New York: Oxford University Press, 1976), page 2.
5. Toynbee, page 2.
6. Toynbee, pages 2-3.
7. Ernest Becker, *The Denial of Death* (New York: The Free Press, 1973), page 26.
8. Becker, page 29.
9. Becker, page 4.
10. Becker, page 50.
11. Robert J. Banks, *Paul's Idea of Community* (Grand Rapids, Michigan: Wm. B. Eerdman's Publishing Co., 1980), page 82.

12. Augustus Hopkins Strong, *Systematic Theology* (Chicago, Illinois: The Judson Press, 1949), page 514.
13. Strong, page 504.
14. Michael Novak, *The Spirit of Democratic Capitalism* (New York: Simon & Schuster, 1982), page 53.
15. Erich Fromm, *The Anatomy of Human Destructiveness* (New York: Holt, Rinehart and Winston, 1973), page 251.
16. Fromm, page 254.
17. Novak, page 356.
18. Hannah Arendt, *The Origins of Totalitarianism* (New York: Harcourt, Brace, & World, 1966), page 232ff.
19. Novak, pages 129,134.

FOUR

Israel:
A Model in Harmony with God's Economic Order

If the book of Genesis provides us with the basic principles of economics, then the next four books of the Bible give us an application of those principles. The time period recorded in Exodus, Leviticus, Deuteronomy, and Numbers is the one time in history that God set up an economic system under His direct control. So we would expect to see confirmation of basic economic principles and how these principles would be best expressed within the Hebrew culture at that time.

We must remember that this expression was within the framework of an agrarian society and within the limitations of economic development at that time in history. For this reason, we must avoid universalizing the details and discern the basic principles that have broad application. In general, these will be the same principles that were prominent in Genesis.

In most cases, there are three distinct aspects to the rules and regulations. First, and most important to us, is the purpose God

71

had in mind: what He wanted to accomplish. Second, there is often a symbolic aspect that pertains to God's special relationship to the nation Israel. The Israelites were a peculiar people, chosen by God for a specific purpose and placed in a land that God reserved exclusively for them. Thus many of the regulations contain symbolic elements peculiar to this special relationship. The symbolic elements may not apply beyond Israel, and the sacrificial elements are obsolete. Third is the detail of the regulations, which would no longer accomplish God's purpose if applied today. With these thoughts in mind, it is not difficult to sort out the essential truths from Scripture. These truths will be found as we discern God's purpose in His regulations.

The Concept of Ownership

The right to individual ownership of property established in Genesis is confirmed in the Ten Commandments. It is implied in the Eighth Commandment, "You shall not steal," and extended in the Tenth Commandment, "You shall not covet . . . anything that belongs to your neighbor" (Deuteronomy 5:19,21). The importance of individual ownership is emphasized by the fact that the Tenth Commandment is the only law of the second tablet that deals with an attitude rather than an action. The place to exercise control over inordinate desires is within the mind, which we will discuss further in the section on materialism.

The prohibition against desiring and stealing our neighbor's possessions firmly establishes the right to ownership. This right is further supported by the many regulations concerning judgments, redemptions, inheritance, and giving. It is not possible to give something you do not own! Thus the concept of ownership and all of the privileges and responsibilities it entails underlies the instructions given in these books of the Bible. This same pattern is followed throughout Scripture.

No example of institutional ownership or endowment is given in these regulations. In fact, God seems to avoid it on purpose. The priests and Levites were not given a direct inheritance in the land, but were made dependent on the production of land owned by others. Materials to build the Tabernacle came from property the people owned. Cities for the Levites were provided from each tribe's land inheritance. The only land in Israel that was communally owned was the pasture land around the Levites' cities. Individuals owned the houses in the cities. God could have heavily endowed the religious and governmental functions, but He deliberately made them dependent on His people.

We should note that the idea of state ownership did exist in the ancient world. In fact, Joseph arranged the affairs of Egypt in such a way that the ownership of all the land, and even the ownership of the people themselves as slaves, was transferred to Pharaoh (Genesis 47). So God's choice of private ownership was not because the concept of socialism was foreign to the people of that time. Rather, it was because private ownership better suited God's purposes for man.

The Concept of Money

During this time period money was not the prominent factor in economic affairs that it is today, but its usage was increasing. Early references to money refer not to coinage, but to weighed amounts of silver or gold.

Money was mentioned several times in Genesis in relationship to the patriarchs. Silver and gold were listed as part of their wealth. In Genesis 23:16, Abraham purchased land for a burial site from Ephron the Hittite. He weighed out the shekels of silver "according to the weight current among the merchants." Apparently at this time money was used primarily for trade with foreigners, while local transactions were usually bartered. Of course the money itself was a commodity—gold or silver—and not coinage or currency as we know it today. Yet money was much more transportable than merchandise and was convenient for the traveling merchants.

These early references verify the definition of money as a *medium of exchange*. Money serves as a *store of value* and *standard of value* that expedites commerce by freeing us from the barter system. Money becomes a substitute for the material goods for which it is accepted in exchange. Of course early forms of money—weighed silver and gold and subsequent coinage of the same metals—originally had value as a commodity. Since all value is imputed, any medium of exchange is valuable to the extent men accept it as valuable. So the paper money of today functions in much the same way that gold and silver functioned, as long as men accept it as having value. When today's paper money represents gold or silver held in storage, its stability is enhanced.

The basic function of money as a medium of exchange and a store of value is illustrated in Deuteronomy 14:24-27, where instructions are given to use the tithe for a joyful celebration at a place God would designate.

> But if that place is too distant and you have been blessed by the LORD your God and cannot carry your tithe (because the place where the LORD will choose to put his Name is so far away), then exchange your tithe for silver, and take the silver with you and go to the place the LORD your God will choose. Use the silver to buy whatever you like: cattle, sheep, wine or other fermented drink, or anything you wish. Then you and your household shall eat there in the presence of the LORD your God and rejoice. And do not neglect the Levites living in your towns, for they have no allotment or inheritance of their own.

Money is also a substitute for material things. The firstborn belonged to God, but could be redeemed by the payment of the specified weight of silver. One tenth of the increase from the land, whether crops or livestock, belonged to God, but anything except clean animals suitable for sacrifice could be redeemed by paying 120 percent of its value. Special vows for the dedication of people, animals, houses, lands, etc., could be redeemed at certain values. Slaves and land could be redeemed by owners or family members.

Many symbolic significances in these regulations, and the detailed instructions, have no relationship to society today. But they demonstrate that money had a legitimate function as a medium of exchange and a store of value. As such, money is a substitute for the material things it represents. So the scriptural teachings concerning material possessions apply to money as well as to other forms of wealth.

As a substitute for material things, money is good. God created the physical universe for man's benefit and pronounced it good. Material possessions are God's provision for us. They are good. Therefore, money as a legitimate substitute for material possessions is also good.

This is not to deny that the widespread use of money presents new opportunities for evil. In every area of life Satan distorts what God has provided as good, making it a temptation. It would be an exception to the rule if this were not true of money. Money has a legitimate role as a substitute, a store of value, and a medium of exchange. But when given status as an independent good, money becomes an object of idolatry.

The distortion of the good provision of money into evil is manifested in innumerable ways. Money facilitates greed by making it possible to hoard wealth on a virtually unlimited scale. Land and cattle are somewhat limiting, but the number of dollars one can accumulate is virtually limitless. Also, the monetary goals that one considers sufficient seem to constantly recede.

Perhaps the most significant temptation in regard to money in the world today is that of inflation. I use the word "temptation" because inflation is basically a fraud perpetrated by government. Money today no longer represents gold or silver and has no intrinsic value. It is fiat money, created by decree through printing press or computer entries, and is good only as long as people have confidence in it.

The fact that money today has no intrinsic value becomes detrimental when governments inflate, that is, create more money than can be said to represent real things. Governments do this for a variety of reasons. The basic reason the United States government persists in creating inflation is that so many special interest groups demand government funds. Politicians find it hard to resist these demands or to increase taxes to pay for them. The easy solution is to borrow money and eventually reduce the resulting debt by inflating the money supply.

Herbert Schlossberg writes, "When we understand that there is no *economic* difference between flooding the nation with money from counterfeiters' presses and doing the same thing with money from the official press, then we begin to comprehend the nature of modern inflations."[1] So inflation is a form of theft. When a man contributes value and takes money in return, reducing the value of his money by inflating has the same effect as robbing him at gunpoint. In Schlossberg's words, "Outright stealing is widely recognized for what it is, but the economic crime that accomplishes the same thing through debasing the money is not. Yet the motive and the effect are the same."[2]

The meaning of inflation has been distorted to signify an increase in prices, which is really only one result of inflation. An increase in the price of oil is not inflation. In itself a higher oil price would simply force consumers to spend less on other goods and services. Inflation is the government's response of increasing the money supply to prevent consumers from reducing spending. The increased money supply is quickly recycled into the economy and causes the general increase in prices that results from inflation.

The source of inflation is envy and greed. Inflation is accepted and encouraged by large segments of society because it serves their purposes. Debtors, of which governments are the largest, are the direct beneficiaries of inflation. Economists talk of "monetizing the debt" by greatly increasing the money supply, thereby making the payment of all debts easier. In this process the government's debt is reduced, but the wealth of others is destroyed. Politicians like the inflation process because it gives them virtually unlimited money to spend to meet the demands of their constituencies (that's us!). Reformers like the redistribution of wealth that occurs when capital is wiped out by inflation and printed money is available to distribute to favorite consumer recipients. Some of these reformers have honest concepts of justice; others are playing the political game. The end results, however, are the same. Finally, the recipients and beneficiaries like inflation and these range from very poor individuals to the world's largest corporations. The losers are those with fixed incomes (such as retired persons), those with no access to the new money injected into the system, and those with capital. The latter carries the most drastic implications.

Money in its proper form, as an aspect of God's material provision for us, is good—not neutral, but good. It is not money that corrupts, but man who corrupts God's good through avarice, covetousness, envy, and greed. Rich and poor are equally vulnerable to the temptation of materialism.

The Concept of Capital

Capital is any asset that produces continuing benefits. With this definition, it is obvious that capital falls into two categories: human capital and material capital. Human capital consists of our physical and mental abilities. These can be enhanced by training, education, and experience. Material capital consists of land, livestock, seed stock, buildings, houses, factories, equipment, businesses, etc.

Money is the third form of capital. It is unique in that it is not productive in itself, but only when converted into one of the other forms of capital. Buying a farm or building a factory converts money into material capital. This function is true to the nature of money as a store of value and a medium of exchange. As a form of capital, money has a legitimate time value expressed as a rate of interest. One person makes a contribution of value to the economy and stores this value in money. Another borrows the money and converts it into material capital to produce income. Interest is the share of this income allocated to the monetary capital.

In nearly every successful application, human capital and material capital are combined to produce continuing benefits. Institutions such as our legal and educational systems are good examples of this, as are corporations. Each kind or combination of capital produces unique benefits. The institutions mentioned above produce justice and education, while other institutions produce different non-material benefits. Human capital produces salary income and other desirable things. Material capital produces merchandise, produce, and monetary rewards; bonds yield interest; stocks pay dividends; real estate brings rent; and farmland produces crops.

Capital should be preserved and should not be converted to consumption. "Precious treasure remains in a wise man's dwelling, but a foolish man devours it" (Proverbs 21:20, RSV). Capital in the form of land was given to every family in the tribes of Israel. God arranged the economy in such a way that this capital could not be permanently squandered. If a family lost possession of its land, the land was to be returned to them in the year of Jubilee, which was to occur at fifty-year intervals. This was not a redistribution of wealth as some claim, but restoration of wealth to the rightful owner. It had to do with preserving capital in the hands of the owners to whom God had entrusted it. Jubilee was designed to make it impossible for the Israelites to convert their capital into consumption. Under this system, the sale of land was in reality a lease for the number of years remaining until the next Jubilee, and the price was determined accordingly. The land was to be the capital base for all future generations of the family. "A good man leaves an inheritance for his children's children" (Proverbs 13:22). Ecclesiastes 5:14 deplores the situation of a man who conducts his affairs so that "when he has a son, there is nothing left for him."

Human capital was protected in God's economic system as well. If an Israelite was forced into slavery, he was to be released after six years. He was not to be sent away empty-handed, but with liberal provisions (Deuteronomy 15:12-15). Debts between Israelites were to be forgiven on the Sabbatical Year. In this way no one was permitted to remain hopelessly in debt or perpetually in slavery. The underlying principle behind these regulations is the preservation of capital—the ownership of material capital and the freedom of human capital.

While capital should be accumulated and preserved, there must be a balance. The concept of capital can easily be used as an excuse for unlimited acquisition. The prophet Isaiah warns against this: "Woe to you who add house to house and join field to field till no space is left and you live alone in the land" (Isaiah 5:8). The writer of Ecclesiastes points out the futility of obsessively accumulating wealth to the exclusion of life's real values:

> There was a man all alone;
>> he had neither son nor brother.
> There was no end to his toil,
>> yet his eyes were not content with his wealth.
> "For whom am I toiling," he asked,
>> "and why am I depriving myself of enjoyment?"
> This too is meaningless—
>> a miserable business!   (Ecclesiastes 4:8)

We will be dealing with the dangers involved in money and capital in chapter 7. The scriptural warnings against the pitfalls of excessive accumulation are coupled with the admonition to be generous in meeting the needs of others in the community. Together, these warnings constitute a formidable preventive to selfish acquisition.

Stewardship comes into full function in relation to capital. Since capital produces a continuing flow of income, it is the most basic focus of stewardship. In the parables of Jesus, the steward's primary responsibility was to see that capital produced income. The Israelites were expected to give of the increase of the land, but to preserve their land capital. So our giving is primarily related to our income, while stewardship is a matter of preserving and utilizing capital. Putting money into the offering plate is not the basic part of stewardship. A generous giver is not necessarily a good steward if he dissipates his necessary capital.

The matter of stewardship is a subject that we will deal with more extensively later, but certain aspects of stewardship need to be emphasized here. The poor steward either dissipates capital or mismanages it so that the yield is poor. A good steward understands the nature and function of capital and therefore has a proper attitude toward it. He not only preserves capital, not converting it to consumption, but puts it to proper use and causes it to produce adequate income.

Stewardship responsibility regarding capital applies to society as well as to individuals. For decades our society has been destroying its capital base. This has been accomplished by taxing capital and distributing its proceeds to those who use it for consumption, and by destroying the value of capital through inflation. In a front-page article in a recent edition of my local paper, a national political leader—not known for his conservatism—deplored the fact that our country refuses to preserve its wealth for future generations.

In Israel, God provided the land capital for every family in the nation. Today, capital can be inherited; it can be accumulated through savings, thus converting income from human capital into material capital; and it can be created. Regardless of the method, capital is a provision from God. This is especially true of created capital. "For it is he [God] who gives you the ability to produce wealth" (Deuteronomy 8:18). An entrepreneur with the right creative ideas can put together a capital structure where nothing existed before. The production of existing systems, even natural systems such as agriculture, can be multiplied many times over with new ideas. This factor is often overlooked by critics of successful societies who believe that all wealth is gained at the expense of others, and that, therefore, the poor are poor *because* others are rich. Capital can be created. The origination of capital is always at the expense of the immediate gratification that the money could otherwise provide.

The economic system of every society is based on capital. This is true of communism and socialism as well as capitalism. Every society has and uses capital because, by definition, capital is everything that produces income. The differences in these economic systems lie in the ownership of the capital and the level at which decisions are made. In some systems there is private ownership and decision-making within the framework of a free market system. (Of course there is never absolute freedom without natural restraints and the regulatory restraints of the society.) Other systems involve state ownership with bureaucratic or autocratic decision-making. Many systems blend the two extremes, but all utilize capital.

The attitude of the world systems toward capital is in one way more realistic than that of many Christians. Capitalists, socialists, and communists alike recognize the function of capital and its necessity in any economic system. They differ regarding the ownership of capital. Many Christians, however, deny or fail to recognize the nature and function of capital and distance themselves from involvement with it, preferring to live in dependency on the capital of others. An important question in any society is whether capital can be controlled and utilized by the stewards of God. Capital is not a negative thing to be avoided, but a resource to be utilized.

Understanding capital benefits the poor as well as the rich. It can help the rich understand the responsibilities of stewardship and can enable the poor to move toward economic independence. Even very poor individuals can begin enhancing their human capital by gaining knowledge and developing skills. This can increase their income to the point where modest accumulation of material capital is possible.

Most of us possess sufficient physical and intellectual resources to make progress in the economic realm. We need to understand the nature of capital, recognize that its stewardship is not only our responsibility but presents great opportunity, and accept the scriptural instruction to be responsible in this area.

Individuality inevitably leads to diversity and inequality of results, which is acceptable in God's sight. Scriptures such as Romans 14 make it clear that diversity is to be accepted in the Kingdom of God. While Deuteronomy 15:4 states that "There should be no poor among you . . . for he [God] will richly bless you," verse 11 says, "There will always be poor people in the land. Therefore I command you to be openhanded toward your brothers and toward the poor and needy in your land."

Diversity exists especially in the economic realm, so the result of these lessons regarding capital will be different for each of us. Our involvement with capital will vary with our calling, ability, opportunity, inheritance, and other factors. It is clearly God's intention that each of us be responsible stewards of His material provision. Therefore we need to evaluate the elements of capital at our disposal, determine our responsibilities and what God desires of us, and preserve and enhance our capital to fulfill those responsibilities.

The Concept of Income

Income is the increase produced by human or material capital. Since God did not intend for the Israelites' land capital to be consumed, His instructions for disposition relate primarily to the increase or income from that capital.

Only ninety percent of the increase was income to the Israelites. God reserved ten percent for Himself. "A tithe of everything from the land . . . belongs to the LORD. . . . The entire tithe of the herd and flock . . . will be holy to the LORD" (Leviticus

27:30-32). God gave this ten percent to the Levites in place of the land capital that He gave to the others. *God* was the giver!

> "I give to the Levites all the tithes in Israel as their inheritance."
> (Numbers 18:21)

> "I give to the Levites as their inheritance the tithes that the Israelites present."
> (Numbers 18:24)

> "When you receive from the Israelites the tithe I give you as your inheritance, you must present a tenth of that tithe as the LORD's offering."
> (Numbers 18:26)

Clearly the tithe was never the property of the Israelites. So they were not the givers of the tithe but were to present the tithe that belonged to God. Under certain circumstances, they could redeem some of the tithe by paying 120 percent of its value (Leviticus 27). Since the tithe did not belong to them, they were stealing from God and the Levites if they kept the tithe. They were literally "robbing God" as explained in Malachi 3:8.

I believe that the tithe was symbolic of the special arrangement between God, the Israelites, and the land. It was not intended to instruct us concerning our giving today. Therefore, the tithe was not used by Jesus or the New Testament writers as a motivation or pattern for giving. The New Testament instruction on giving is on a much different spiritual plane.

There is, however, an underlying principle in God's instructions concerning the tithe. God did not choose to endow or independently subsidize Israel's spiritual leaders. He chose to relate their support to the welfare of His people at large, making people and leaders alike dependent on each other. The people were directly involved with the physical support of the priests and Levites, and the leaders were dependent on the welfare and obedience of the people.

In addition to ten percent of the increase (the income), God reserved the first fruits for Himself. The firstborn of clean animals were to be sacrificed if they were perfect. The imperfect firstborn of clean animals and all unclean animals were to be redeemed by cash payment. Firstborn sons were to be redeemed by cash payment. First fruits of the land were to be presented as offerings. This requirement was highly symbolic. God based His claim to the firstborn on the destruction of all the firstborn in Egypt, which culminated the struggle with Pharaoh in securing the Israelites' release (Exodus 13). Each firstborn sacrifice or redemption was a powerful reminder of Israel's dependence on God and His special relationship with them.

The underlying principle here is that God has the right to the first and best of all that we possess. If we are to regard the tithe as the mandatory requirement for Christians today, it is logical that we require the firstborn and the first fruits as well.

What remained after the tithe and the first fruits was income to the Israelites. While there were no comprehensive instructions as to how income should be used or in what proportions, there are many commands, instructions, and suggestions. Here are the most significant categories of income use:

> Freewill offerings and vows to God.
> Support of families.
> Personal enjoyment.
>> The land was to be flowing with milk and honey. They were to eat of the fat of the land. Every third year the tithe itself was to be utilized for a feast! "Then exchange your tithe for silver . . . use the silver to buy whatever you like: cattle, sheep, wine or other fermented drink, or anything you wish. Then you and your household shall eat there in the presence of the LORD your God and rejoice" (Deuteronomy 14:25-26).
> Giving to those in need.
>> Much of the instruction concerning giving involved giving and lending to the poor. The majority of the

loans were tantamount to gifts, especially as the Sabbatical Year approached. "If there is a poor man among your brothers in any of the towns of the land . . . do not be hardhearted or tightfisted toward your poor brother. . . . Give generously to him and do so without a grudging heart; . . . be openhanded toward your brothers and toward the poor and needy in your land" (Deuteronomy 15:7-11). Much of the instruction on giving in the New Testament also related to assisting the poor.

Providing for widows and orphans.

Providing for strangers and travelers.

Saving for the Sabbatical Year and the Year of Jubilee.

Increasing capital—breeding stock, seed, barns, money, etc.

Accepting Capital as a Means of God's Provision

Christians today often have guilt feelings concerning wealth. Earlier we talked about the guilt syndrome that is based on erroneous assumptions about the nature of material things and their distribution. This guilt becomes especially acute when we begin to consider capital. This is due in part to the fact that the function of capital is inadequately understood and because we have succumbed to the propaganda that profit and capital are evil. To counteract the guilt syndrome, we must learn to regard capital as a resource to be utilized within the Kingdom of God.

To some extent our concern about wealth is understandable, because the Scriptures are full of warnings against materialism. We have experienced the subtle trap of materialism and are aware of our weaknesses. The result is that we do not trust ourselves in matters of wealth in general and with capital in particular. I believe it is good that God has succeeded in putting us on guard.

However, the course of action that many Christians follow is not so good. We are aware that "the love of money is the root of all kinds of evil," that riches are deceitful, and that the trap of materialism is subtle. So we protect ourselves by running away. We refuse to be involved in the capital structure of our society. But by doing so, we lose the benefits of stewardship for ourselves and the Kingdom of God. In addition, we lose the opportunity to influence our society as responsible participants.

We need to remember that capital is not evil, that it is absolutely necessary to every society, and that capital is controlled by individuals in our system of democratic capitalism. Running away from the issue resembles the monastic attempt to be spiritual through isolation, the ascetic's denial of physical satisfaction, or the insistence that total abstinence is the only legitimate approach to the problem of alcohol. These responses illustrate a tendency to recognize a problem and solve it by avoidance. By responding in this way in the economic realm, we accept permanent immaturity in this area, which can affect our total maturity. The two markedly different phases in God's provision for Israel after they left Egypt illustrate the point.

Phase I. The Wilderness. In this emergency and temporary situation, God directly provided for the needs of His people. He provided manna as food and preserved it for the Sabbath. When they desired meat, He provided it through flocks of quail. He provided water as it was needed. God's people became immediately and continuously dependent on His provision.

Phase II. The Promised Land. It was not God's intention that the manna situation be permanent. In fact, it was to be of very short duration but was prolonged for forty years by their disobedience. God's promise from the beginning was to bring His people into a land flowing with milk and honey. Every family was to receive a permanent inheritance of land, which was their *capital.* This capital was to be preserved for future generations. God would provide for the needs of His people on a permanent basis through the animals and produce the land would bring forth. The manna was to be replaced by the fat of the land.

Thus the Promised Land was no less God's provision than

the manna! In fact, it was much better and much more advanta-geous. It provided the opportunity for work, for learning and growing, for utilizing and developing abilities and talents, and for enterprise. The people could enjoy the satisfaction that comes with responsibility, with providing for loved ones, and with the privi-lege of giving to God and others. They could assume their respon-sibility for dominion over the earth and for causing it to produce. They could be co-laborers with God in the creation of wealth.

This new economic arrangement involved risk on God's part. It was not as safe as the isolation in the wilderness where direct dependence on God was necessary for survival. There was the danger of exposure to the pagans in and around the Land and of being led into immorality and idolatry. There was the danger that the Israelites would become proudly self-sufficient and satis-fied, forgetting that God was still the source of their blessings. God was fully aware of these dangers:

> When you have eaten and are satisfied, praise the LORD your God for the good land he has given you. Be careful that you do not forget the LORD your God, failing to observe his commands, his laws and his decrees that I am giving you this day. Otherwise, when you eat and are satis-fied, when you build fine houses and settle down, and when your herds and flocks grow large and your silver and gold increase and all you have is multiplied, then your heart will become proud and you will forget the LORD your God, who brought you out of Egypt, out of the land of slavery.
> (Deuteronomy 8:10-14)

> You may say to yourself, "My power and the strength of my hands have produced this wealth for me." But remember the LORD your God, for it is he who gives you the ability to produce wealth, and so confirms his covenant, which he swore to your forefathers, as it is today.
> (Deuteronomy 8:17-18)

It would have been easy for God to protect the Israelites—and us—from all mistakes. Yet, as He did in the past, He consistently takes risks in order to bring us to maturity.

Abandoning the Manna Complex

Many Christians today have a manna complex. In some situation in life they have enjoyed the experience of "living by faith," completely depending on God, relying on His provision to meet immediate and critical needs. Or they have heard stories of how God provided for others in spectacular ways, which seems exciting in contrast to their less colorful experiences.

It is wonderful that God meets these needs, just as He provided manna in the wilderness. But this should not make us reluctant to accept God's permanent provision, whereby we can become productive members of society, and to utilize the human and material capital God has provided to meet our needs and help us meet the needs of others. "Living by faith" involves much more than finances, and it is unfortunate that the phrase is so commonly limited to that meaning. Even in the area of finances, the common usage of the phrase does not indicate maturity.

The productive life is no less a life of faith than depending on God for daily needs! Productivity does not in any way reduce our dependence on God. God is not pleased with perpetual financial immaturity any more than we would be if our children were permanently dependent on us. The comfortable position of immediate child-like dependency must give way to the responsibility of the mature son.

Christians with the manna complex focus on receiving as though it were better than giving. Most of the exciting stories about faith and finances emphasize receiving. Yet Jesus points out that the giving side of the equation is preferable: "It is more blessed to give than to receive" (Acts 20:35). Virtually all biblical teaching instructs the giver. The scriptural pattern is that those who have been blessed with material things should distribute generously to those in need. We become co-laborers with God by meeting the needs of others. For every receiver there is a giver. God always meets needs through others who are able and willing to distribute. So our objective should be to move wholeheartedly to the giving side of the transaction. We can only do this by being good stewards of our capital.

Perhaps one reason Christians are susceptible to the manna complex is that Christian workers today, especially in mission organizations, depend on the voluntary contributions of other Christians. This is not unscriptural, for Jesus lived that way during His three years of ministry and told His disciples, "The worker is worth his keep" (Matthew 10:10). Paul wrote, "The Lord has commanded that those who preach the gospel should receive their living from the gospel" (1 Corinthians 9:14).

Since these workers are leaders and challenge us often, we hear many stories of God's provision, which often sound more exciting than our own situation. Attitudes that may be appropriate for them as they receive may not be appropriate for those of us who have the responsibility and privilege of giving. In fact, I have often heard application made and advice given that was not suitable for the listeners.

Let us not limit God's provision to the manna method! The manna came every twenty-four hours, the land inheritance only once. Yet the land was no less God's provision.

I have a dear friend who had been a missionary for several years when her husband died. Earlier on a furlough I had encouraged her husband to buy a small insurance policy. It surprised me when my friend expressed her concern that this money was at her disposal: "My husband and I have been dependent on the Lord to provide each month through Christians who support us. I must continue to depend on Him to provide through others—and many of them are far from affluent—so I don't feel I can do this with money in the bank." She suggested that as the trustee I should donate the money to a Christian organization! I told her that perhaps she was placing unnecessary limitations on God and suggested the proceeds from the insurance policy were in reality God's provision. Together we worked out a compromise that satisfied her emotional needs and personal convictions. She had two children, so we divided the funds into three equal parts. We donated her share, and I invested the remainder on behalf of her children. In succeeding years we drew on the funds for several emergencies, provided major support for the children through their college education, and provided travel funds for a ministry trip to her former fields of service. When I turned over the account to her second husband, the fund approximately equaled the original amount. My friend is grateful for the financial provision and the broadened view this experience provided. We must not limit God's provision to the manna in the wilderness!

I am not proposing that we lessen our dependence upon God, but that we broaden our awareness of how God can provide for us. I am not suggesting an anxiety or preoccupation with material things, but faithful stewardship of what God provides. I am not advocating self-sufficiency, but I am encouraging appreciation and thanksgiving for the opportunities inherent in God's provision of material things. When we put Him first, the material things will be provided, just as He promised. This is true for all of us—not only those in need of manna.

Giving Capital to Others

The idea of capital is not only compatible with faith, but has a significant application to giving as well. We will discuss giving at length later, but now it seems appropriate to mention one thing in this context.

We can accept capital as a provision from God. This capital should then be preserved, not converted to consumption. At the same time, we should not permit the preservation of capital to serve as an excuse for unwarranted accumulation. We are responsible to give generously, placing the interest of others on an equal basis with our own (Philippians 2:4). Combined, this sequence of concepts introduces the idea of giving capital to others. In fact, a gift of capital is the most significant and permanent gift we can make to another, since capital produces continuing benefits over a long period of time.

I have found that gifts of capital are especially significant to those who have never had the opportunity to accumulate capital themselves. This includes missionaries who have been unable to build equity in a house or make other provision for returning to their home country for retirement. We can make gifts of capital to others, including our children, that will provide a lifetime of benefits.

These considerations have led me to a personal conclusion: I will give of my income to meet the immediate needs of others; and I will give of my capital to meet the capital needs of others.

I have found that when I give capital, three marvelous factors come into play. The first is that my personal satisfaction in giving is extended indefinitely as I observe the continuing results. The second is that in addition to the income, the capital often increases in value, providing additional benefits to the receiver. The third is that God often multiplies the benefits far beyond my expectations. He is still in the business of multiplying what we give—just as He did the loaves and fishes! I will give you some illustrations of this in chapter 11.

The Concept of Community and Brotherhood
We have emphasized the right of individuals to own property. This ownership involves capital and income, with money as the vehicle that facilitates the use of both. In the preservation of the land capital for future generations, and in the instructions for the utilization of income, we begin to understand the nature of brotherhood and community.

Debts were forgiven every Sabbatical Year, and Israelite slaves were freed after six years. While income was individually owned, it was to be utilized to support families and brothers in need, and to provide for widows, orphans, the poor, and even the strangers and aliens.

We see this pattern continued throughout Scripture. Individual ownership involves responsibility and must be exercised by generously meeting the needs of others. The privilege of giving is the most significant aspect of ownership.

This emphasis on community was reinforced by other Old Testament regulations. The edges of the field, the gleanings of the harvest, and the fallen or overlooked grapes or olives were to be left for the poor or the alien (Leviticus 19:9-10, Deuteronomy 24:19-20). Everyone was allowed to eat from the fields or vineyards, but not to harvest or carry home (Deuteronomy 23:24-25). The Levites, widows, orphans, and the poor were to be included in certain feasts (Deuteronomy 14:27-29). Israelites were to redeem property on behalf of their relatives, and were to redeem relatives that had become slaves (Leviticus 25:25,48). Business transactions were to be characterized by equity, fairness, and honesty. "You must have accurate and honest weights and measures" (Deuteronomy 25:15). "Do not take advantage of each other" (Leviticus 25:17). Security for loans was to be handled with consideration for the debtors' needs. Israelites who fell into temporary bondage to other Israelites were not to be treated as slaves, but as employees.

A very significant aspect of these regulations governing brotherhood was the prohibition against charging interest to a brother. "Do not charge your brother interest, whether on money or food or anything else that may earn interest. You may charge a foreigner interest, but not a brother Israelite" (Deuteronomy 23:19-20). "If one of your countrymen becomes poor . . . help him. . . . Do not take interest of any kind from him . . . or sell him food at a profit" (Leviticus 25:35-37).

All of the loans referred to here are loans to poor brethren in need. The Israelites were to be generous in giving or lending as the situation required. Loans were in some degree the equivalent of gifts, especially as the Sabbatical Year approached when all loans were to be cancelled. It is possible that the loan designation was somewhat of a face-saving mechanism since it was easier to ask for a loan than an outright gift. However, in some cases, security was pledged, which indicates that the lender actually expected repayment. It is possible that these loans were for seed or other goods that would produce a return. There were few direct investment loans as we know them today. In any event, no interest was to be charged to a brother.

The capital structure of that society was much different than it is today, and the time value of money was not as significant. Since inflation was not a problem, the value of money was constant so the lender did not lose any of the purchasing power of his money. The prohibition against interest was not universal, but applied only to Israelites when dealing with each other. For all these reasons we should not extend the regulations on interest into today's economy. There is an underlying principle, however, that we must be generous to brothers in need and never capitalize on their misfortune. For the Israelites, this meant giving generous assistance, not charging interest on loans, and not making a profit on a transaction with a poor brother.

Most of the giving described in both the Old and New Testaments was giving to the poor. Today the worldwide problem of poverty is so overwhelming and so structural that our token efforts seem futile. In our country, the government has assumed much of the responsibility for providing basic necessities for the poor, although many Christians and churches make valuable contributions. One area in which we have done very little is in assisting our brothers to work their way through financial difficulties. In our rugged individualism we expect each person or family to work out their own problems or pay the consequences. It does not occur to many Christians in difficulty to inform the Christian community of their need because they have not seen a pattern of willingness to help. So they go to financial advisors, counselors, debt consolidators, loan officers, and finally bankruptcy lawyers—but never to their Christian brothers. We will explore this problem further in the section on giving.

Assuming Our Responsibility for Conservation

The regulations on conservation had both symbolic and practical aspects. Human capital was to be conserved by the observation of the Sabbath, a day of rest. This was symbolic of God's rest after the six days of creation and a reminder of God's lordship over Israel. Jesus, however, gave us the practical reason behind the Sabbath: "The Sabbath was made for man, not man for the Sabbath" (Mark 2:27). The real purpose of the day of rest was to meet an intrinsic requirement of man himself.

Similar symbolism is found in regulations regarding the seventh year, when the land was to lie fallow, but the essential purpose of those regulations was conservation. Allowing land to lie fallow is still an efficient method of replenishing the soil, although modern farmers often enhance the process by planting and plowing under certain crops that will enrich the soil. An incidental benefit to this practice in Israel was that the poor and the alien had the right to the produce that sprung up naturally during the fallow year.

The underlying principle in these regulations was that of conservation. The productivity of the land, and indeed of all forms of capital, should be preserved. There may be other acceptable methods of preservation, but our dominion over the earth involves the responsibility of conservation.

Conclusion

In looking at Israel as a model of God's order, we have not attempted to look at every detail. We have discussed only the basic concepts that conform to the principles of God's economic order as expressed in Genesis. Certainly many additional things pertaining to our topic can be learned from the Old Testament. We will look at some of them in the topical studies of part two. But first, let's look at the basic New Testament teaching in regard to material things.

NOTES:
1. Herbert Schlossberg, *Idols for Destruction* (Nashville, Tennessee: Thomas Nelson, Inc., 1983), page 91.
2. Schlossberg, page 90.

FIVE

Jesus and the Epistles Harmonize on God's Order

God's revelation in Scripture is progressive, so we can rightfully expect to find the highest level of teaching on man's relationship to material possessions in the New Testament. Since the teaching on material possessions is so comprehensive, we will break it down into separate topics for study in part two of this book. At the moment, however, we need to determine whether Jesus and the New Testament writers confirm the principles of God's order found in Genesis and modeled in the nation of Israel.

Israel departed from the economic model God established and refused to heed the prophets who urged repentance and reform. In 1500 years since the revelation of God's economic model, much of what God taught had been forgotten, ignored, turned upside-down by rabbinic interpretation, distorted by a corrupt judicial system, or reduced to petty legalism. Jesus took every opportunity to correct these distortions and challenge debilitating traditions.

The Pharisees, together with most of the Jewish establishment, were comfortable in their self-serving traditions, although their traditions had been moving them in the wrong direction. It was necessary for Jesus to challenge these traditions before He could lead the people into new truth. The directness, clarity, and irrefutable authority of Jesus' teaching made the Pharisees and Jewish leaders uncomfortable. He made it clear that He would not be content to put new patches on old garments or pour new wine into old wineskins (Matthew 9:16-17). The spiritual plane of His teaching stood in sharp contrast to their legalism. He was challenging the system.

In these challenges, Jesus often silenced His antagonists with a few simple words or an illustration. In so doing He always spoke the truth, but often did not deal with the subjects comprehensively. He left their fuller development to His followers who would write the New Testament. With this background in mind, let us look at some of the major New Testament themes regarding material possessions.

The Priority of the Kingdom of God

Jesus came to proclaim the Kingdom of God. He announced its presence, revealed its secrets, and illustrated its nature. Then He called for commitment to it. Allegiance to God's Kingdom supersedes everything else.

Jesus called His disciples to instant commitment. At a word, Peter, Andrew, James, and John left their fishing nets and followed Jesus (Matthew 4:18-19). Levi simply stood up from his tax collector's booth and followed (Mark 2:14). Clearly the Kingdom takes priority over one's profession.

In return for His followers' commitment, Jesus promises no material reward—not even a place to sleep (Matthew 8:20). Following Him takes priority over traditional responsibilities and personal relationships (Luke 9:60-62). Love for Jesus must exceed family love (Matthew 10:37), and following Him involves bearing a cross and losing one's own life (Matthew 10:38-39). Using the word in a relative sense, Jesus calls for "hatred" of parents, children, brothers, and sisters—even one's own life—as the price of following Him (Luke 14:26-27). Jesus demands absolute priority: "Any of you who does not give up everything he has cannot be my disciple" (Luke 14:33).

The results of this order of priority are positive. On the one hand, Jesus' followers are free to lay up treasures in Heaven (Matthew 6:20). In addition His followers are free to enjoy God's provision for their physical, social, and spiritual needs: "Whoever loses his life for my sake will find it" (Matthew 10:39). "And everyone who has left houses or brothers or sisters or father or mother or children or fields for my sake will receive a hundred times as much and will inherit eternal life" (Matthew 19:29). "But seek first his kingdom and his righteousness, and all these things will be given to you as well" (Matthew 6:33).

We must remember that the things of Matthew 6—life, family, possessions, food, and clothing—are not wrong for they are God's provision. But if given priority as the objectives of life, they become idols. Therefore they must be kept in perspective as the result of our commitment to God's Kingdom.

Faith Should Replace Worry

We saw that in the temporary wilderness experience, God's people were immediately dependent upon His direct provision. He led them into a more advantageous situation in which their welfare was related to their stewardship of the land capital that He provided. This offered new opportunities and new dangers. God was fully aware of the risks involved in financial maturity. He cautioned His people to recognize their continuing dependency on Him, warning them not to say, "My power and the strength of my hands have produced this wealth for me." He reminds them that "it is God who gives you the ability to produce wealth" (Deuteronomy 8:17-18).

This emphasis of depending on God is amplified in the New Testament. In one of His major discourses on material things, Jesus warns against investing our lives in the service of money and building earthly treasure rather than heavenly treasure (Matthew 6:19-24). Then He continues:

> "Therefore I tell you, do not worry about your life, what you will eat or drink; or about your body, what you will wear. . . . Who of you by worrying can add a single hour to his life?
>
> And why do you worry about clothes? See how the lilies of the field grow. They do not labor or spin. . . . So do not worry, saying, 'What shall we wear?'
>
> But seek first his kingdom and his righteousness, and all these things will be given to you as well. Therefore do not worry about tomorrow, for tomorrow will worry about itself. Each day has enough trouble of its own."
>
> (Matthew 6:25-34)

The essence of Jesus' message about material things is simple, "Do not worry" because God provides adequately. Underlying this exhortation are more important issues: the allegiance of our hearts, the attitude of our minds, our reason for existence, and the source of our confidence. Jesus talks about our loyalties and priorities. Whom do we serve? What is our master? What is the source of our strength? Jesus cautions us to make money our servant, not our master; to avoid materialism, the love of money, and the preoccupation with material things; to avoid worry, undue concern, and the obsession with material things that stems from self-dependency. In short, Jesus challenges us to recognize our dependence on God.

In this same context, Jesus promises us that "all these things will be given to you as well" (verse 33). His desire is not to deprive us of these things, but to free us from worry about them. What Jesus says does not contradict the basic principles of economics that we've considered. It does not negate the biblical admonitions to be diligent rather than careless, frugal rather than wasteful, wise rather than foolish, hardworking rather than lazy, and able to give rather than to be dependent on receiving. It does not nullify the implication of Jesus' parables that good stewardship is a virtue. Freedom from worry about tomorrow does not prevent prudent provision for the future when such provision is possible.

What Jesus says must not be so narrowly interpreted that it conflicts with the rest of Scripture. It cannot conflict with our responsibility to provide for our families (1 Timothy 5:8), to work with our hands to gain the respect of outsiders (1 Thessalonians 4:11-12), or to follow Paul's example of working to provide for life's necessities (2 Thessalonians 3:7-12). Paul did not regard his practical instruction as in conflict with what Jesus taught, for he reaffirms Jesus' teaching that we be free of worry and be dependent on God:

> Do not be anxious about anything, but in everything, by prayer and petition, with thanksgiving, present your requests to God. . . .
> And my God will meet all your needs according to his glorious riches in Christ Jesus.   (Philippians 4:6,19)

Depending on God frees us from worry and anxiety. It does not free us from being responsible stewards. It does not change the principles governing our relationship to the material universe that God has provided.

God Is the Source of the Material Universe

The fact that God in the Person of Christ is the source of the material universe is confirmed in the New Testament. Jesus demonstrated His creative power at Cana of Galilee by turning water into wine and again, on two occasions, by multiplying a few loaves and fishes to feed the multitudes. He demonstrated His power over nature by controlling the wind and waves, by causing the fig tree to wither, and by providing the miraculous catch of fish after His resurrection. His power to heal the human body was often demonstrated. He showed His power over death on two occasions, and finally in His own resurrection.

John put these demonstrations into words at the beginning of his gospel. "Through him [the word] all things were made; without him nothing was made that has been made" (John 1:3). Paul also confirmed, "He [Christ] is the image of the invisible God, the firstborn over all creation. For by him all things were created: things in heaven and on earth, visible and invisible . . . all things were created by him and for him. He is before all things, and in him all things hold together" (Colossians 1:15-17).

What God has provided is good! God knows our need for material provision (Matthew 6:32), gives good gifts to those who ask Him (Matthew 7:11), and provides good and perfect things for us (James 1:17). Paul summarized God's provision in 1 Timothy 6:17, "God . . . richly provides us with everything for our enjoyment." The essential nature of God's creation was not destroyed by the Fall, so Paul stated clearly that "everything God created is good" (1 Timothy 4:4).

Dominion, Not Slavery, Should Be Our Goal

In the book of Genesis, man was given dominion over the earth. He was instructed by God to subdue the planet by bringing it under his control, to rule over all life on the earth, and to multiply and fill the earth. Israel was instructed to subdue the land of Canaan. By the time the New Testament was written, the process of bringing the earth under control was well under way and its success inevitable.

Thus there is no need in the New Testament to repeat the original command, but great need to deal with the perils that accompany man's success. Rather than exercising control over the material universe, man in the New Testament was in danger of being controlled by his possessions. Likewise, man today is susceptible to the slavery to material possessions that we call materialism.

Jesus deals with this enslavement directly: "No one can serve two masters. Either he will hate the one and love the other, or he will be devoted to the one and despise the other. You cannot serve both God and Money" (Matthew 6:24). Jesus gives the illustration of the prodigal son who greedily demanded his inheritance early (Luke 15:12), and gives us the sneering reaction of the Pharisees who loved money (Luke 16:14). He tells us of the covetous man who sought his brother's inheritance (Luke 12:13) and the rich farmer who was the victim of possessiveness (Luke 12:16ff). He describes the futility of anyone who "stores up things for himself but is not rich toward God" (Luke 12:21).

Paul also warns that the love of money is the root of all kinds of evil and that the desire to be rich is a trap leading to destruction (1 Timothy 6:9-10). The writer of Hebrews warns against the love of money and encourages contentment (Hebrews 13:5). Jesus talks about the "deceitfulness of wealth" (Mark 4:19), and warns about "all kinds of greed" (Luke 12:15).

Material things are God's provision for us, but wealth is dangerous when it becomes an idol. God intends that we exercise dominion over material things, not be enslaved by them.

Man's Individuality Is Confirmed

Jesus confirmed each aspect of man's nature, constantly demonstrating each individual's worth by His actions. Most of His miracles, such as those of healing and raising the dead, directly benefited one individual at a time. He usually spoke to the multitudes in parables because He did not expect them to understand Him. In fact, the mass response was almost always wrong. He reserved the full revelation of Himself for individuals, primarily for the Twelve He had chosen.

He called the Twelve individually to leave their professions and families and follow Him. He turned from the crowd to heal blind Bartimaeus, dine with Zacchaeus the tax collector, and cleanse a leper. He indicated that the result of individual choices would divide families (Luke 12:52-53), and that at His coming "one will be taken and the other left" (Luke 17:34).

In all of this, Jesus recognized and accepted individual diversity. He talked of different kinds of human heart soil into which the Word was planted, different responses to truth, and different results in judgment. Economic disparity is included in this diversity.

Yet Jesus also introduced a new facet to the matter of diversity. In Matthew 13:12 He introduces a principle that He applies to the understanding of truth: "Whoever has will be given more, and he will have an abundance. Whoever does not have, even what he has will be taken from him." So we can conclude that spiritual disparity tends to increase.

In Matthew 25:29, Jesus applies the same principle to economic matters: "For everyone who has will be given more, and he will have an abundance. Whoever does not have, even what he has will be taken from him." This principle was also implied in the Old Testament wherever the economic results of action were described. The prudent and the diligent increased, the foolish and the lazy decreased. Therefore, those who base their economic actions on truth will prosper, while those who violate truth will not. Our economic choices increase the disparity. This principle has tremendous implications for both individuals and nations.

How is individual economic disparity justified? First, it simply describes cause and effect. It is the way things work. Second, it relates to ownership and stewardship: "Whoever can be trusted with very little can also be trusted with much, and whoever is dishonest with very little will also be dishonest with much" (Luke 16:10). In the spiritual realm, Jesus did not entrust the truth to those who could not receive it. In the material realm, God does not give great stewardship opportunities to those unable to exercise stewardship. Third, it relates to generosity: "With the measure you use, it will be measured to you—and even more" (Mark 4:24). Generosity and distribution increase economic disparity, but in the opposite way to what we would expect. "Give, and it will be given to you" (Luke 6:38). Paul told the Corinthians that "whoever sows generously will also reap generously," and promised that if they gave generously they would "be made rich in every way so that [they] can be generous on every occasion (2 Corinthians 9:6,11). Proverbs 11:24-25 is an explicit statement of this principle:

> One man gives freely, yet gains even more;
> another withholds unduly, but comes to poverty.
> A generous man will prosper;
> he who refreshes others will himself be refreshed.

In 1 Corinthians Paul discussed diversity in relationship to gifts and abilities. "Each man has his own gift from God; one has this gift, another has that" (7:7). This was in the context of physical ability—in regard to self-control and the discipline of a bodily appetite. Paul also emphasized the diversity of spiritual gifts. "There are different kinds of gifts . . . there are different kinds of service . . . there are different kinds of working" (12:4-6). Paul pointed out that diversity comes from God and we have no right to consider ourselves superior to others because of the gifts He has given to us. "Then you will not take pride in one man over against another. For who makes you different from anyone else? What do you have that you did not receive? And if you did receive it, why do you boast as though you did not?" (4:6-7).

I believe it is obvious that Jesus and His apostles confirm man's individuality, diversity, freedom of choice, and personal responsibility in general as well as in economic applications.

The Concept of Individual Ownership

The private ownership of property, almost always attributed to individuals, is confirmed throughout the New Testament, just as it was in the Old Testament. Most of Jesus' parables were stories about individuals and their possessions, but carried no hint of a negative attitude toward the possessions themselves. He spoke of those who accumulated wealth, expanded their farms, built vineyards, hired managers, and entrusted their wealth to others to invest. He respected the rights of the owner of the colt on which he rode into Jerusalem and of the house where He observed the Passover. He encouraged generosity in giving, the use of resources to help others (as in the good Samaritan), and the utilization of wealth for eternal purposes.

New Testament writers continue the same universal approval of individual ownership. I will choose but one example out of many because it is so often misconstrued. This example is in Acts 4, where the believers "shared everything they had" (verse 32). Even here, private ownership was respected; the sale of property and distribution of the proceeds were voluntary. Joseph owned the field he sold (verses 36-37). In another instance, Peter reminds Ananias, "Didn't it [the property] belong to you before it was sold? And after it was sold, wasn't the money at your disposal?" (Acts 5:4).

The fact that giving is kept on a voluntary basis in the New Testament is a powerful attestation to individual ownership. It is impossible to give something you do not own.

The Privilege and Responsibility of Community

The New Testament affirms man's nature as an individual created in God's image with God-given freedom of choice, individual responsibility, diversity, and a right to own property. At the same time, New Testament teaching greatly enhances the concept of community. Jesus teaches His followers to love their enemies, do good to those who hate them, bless those who curse them, pray for those who mistreat them, give to everyone who asks, lend without expecting to receive it back, and treat others as they would like others to treat them (Luke 6:27-36). He concludes this instruction by saying, "Be merciful, just as your Father is merciful." Jesus explains that His ultimate intention for community is "that all of them may be one, Father, just as you are in me and I am in you" (John 17:21).

The Incarnation, in which God Himself in the Person of the Son entered into the community of man, is the foundation of enhanced community. This leads us to Philippians 2:1-8, where Paul uses the Incarnation as the motivation to community:

> If you have any encouragement from being united with
> Christ, if any comfort from his love, if any fellowship with
> the Spirit, if any tenderness and compassion, then make my
> joy complete by being like-minded, having the same love,
> being one in spirit and purpose. Do nothing out of selfish
> ambition or vain conceit, but in humility consider others
> better than yourselves. Each of you should look not only to
> your own interests, but also to the interests of others.
> Your attitude should be the same as that of Christ Jesus:

> Who, being in very nature God,
>> did not consider equality with God something
>>> to be grasped,
> but made himself nothing,
>> taking the very nature of a servant,
>> being made in human likeness.
> And being found in appearance as a man,
>> he humbled himself
>> and became obedient to death—
>>> even death on a cross!

One way to gain insight into community as described in the New Testament is to study the phrase "one another." This phrase describes both individuality and community.

Eighteen times we are told to love one another. We are described as members of one another in the same Body. We are to be in harmony. We should be humble and submissive to one another. In our attitudes we should honor others above ourselves, being patient, forbearing, kind, compassionate, sympathetic, and forgiving. We should use our gifts to minister and serve one another—to instruct, teach, admonish, encourage, build up, and to spur one another on to love and good deeds. We should pray for one another and confess our faults to each other. We should fellowship together and increase our love for each other. We should be hospitable. Our concern for one another should equal our concern for ourselves. We should not slander one another or take each other to court. We need to stop passing judgment on one another, making comparisons with one another, showing favoritism to one another, or taking pride over one another. We should not provoke our brothers. We should not be envious, hateful, or grumbling. We should not lie one to another.

All of these words describing brotherhood are directly from the New Testament. Although this is certainly not an exhaustive study of the concept of community, I believe it is sufficient to demonstrate the New Testament's elevated concept of community.

Paul describes the ultimate community in Romans 12:5, "So in Christ we who are many form one body, and each member belongs to all the others." The two aspects of God's image are obvious here: individuality and community. Other Scriptures represent us as belonging to God: "You are not your own, you were bought at a price" (1 Corinthians 6:19-20) and "redeemed . . . with the precious blood of Christ" (1 Peter 1:18-19). In addition, we belong to each other! The right kind of community respects and enhances our individuality and personhood, but does not allow individualism in the sense of a self-centered philosophy of life.

Author F.F. Bruce, in *The Spreading Flame,* places great importance on the nature of the early Christian community. In explaining why an obscure and persecuted sect in the Roman Empire called "Christians" could not only survive but prosper, he points to their loyalty to one another. They shared their possessions within and between churches, supported their own widows and orphans, cared for the sick when the pagans surrounding them put their own into the streets to die, respected the slaves, did not expose their children to death, and visited their own in prison at great personal risk.[1] This was community in action, where the individual assumed responsibility for his brother and human needs were not the responsibility of institutions.

A New Concept of Giving

God instructed the Israelites to be generous in giving. In the wilderness, God directly provided all of His people's needs with manna, quail, and water. One of the benefits of the Promised Land was the opportunity for God's people to utilize their land capital to meet the needs of others. They were to be faithful in setting aside the ten percent that God had given to the Levites, and the first fruits that He had reserved for Himself. Then they were to give offerings to God, give with an open hand to those in need, give to widows and orphans, and give to strangers and travelers who were in need. While these instructions involved the concept of brotherhood, they were also mandatory. Later in the Old Testament, most notably in the book of Proverbs, some of the spiritual benefits of giving were emphasized. But in the New Testament giving is elevated to a purely spiritual plane.

John the Baptist set the tone for giving by his statement, "The man with two tunics should share with him who has none, and the one who has food should do the same" (Luke 3:11). This instruction has a different emphasis than the instructions given in Leviticus and Deuteronomy, where one sees the image of the wealthy and successful giving to the needy and unfortunate. In the New Testament, the image presented is that of equals sharing everything they have.

Jesus repeats Moses' instruction to "give to the one who asks you, and do not turn away from the one who wants to borrow from you" (Matthew 5:42). We also are to "lend . . . without expecting to get anything back" (Luke 6:35). Jesus tells us that giving is meaningless without fellowship with our brothers (Matthew 5:23-24). He teaches that we are not to resist those who would take advantage of us (verse 40). He goes on to tell us that our generosity should extend to those who do not love us (verse 44), and that our giving should not be ostentatious unless we are satisfied with the publicity as our sole reward (Matthew 6:1-3). His story of the good Samaritan expands the definition of the neighbor whom we should love according to the Second Commandment, and to whom we should give.

Jesus also introduces a new standard for measuring generosity. He observes the rich who give out of their wealth and the poor widow who gives two small copper coins. He says, "This poor widow has put in more than all the others. All these people gave their gifts out of their wealth; but she out of her poverty put in all she had to live on" (Luke 21:3-4). In 2 Corinthians 8:11-12, Paul encouraged the Corinthians to give "according to your means. For if the willingness is there, the gift is acceptable according to what one has, not according to what he does not have."

Jesus also promises that God's generosity to us will be proportionate to our generosity to others. This is true in regard to judging, condemning, forgiving, and giving. "Give, and it will be given to you. A good measure, pressed down, shaken together and running over, will be poured into your lap. For with the measure you use, it will be measured to you" (Luke 6:38). Paul told the Philippians that because of their continuous generosity toward him, "My God will meet all your needs according to his glorious riches in Christ Jesus" (Philippians 4:19). In 2 Corinthians 9:6 we read, "Whoever sows sparingly will also reap sparingly, and whoever sows generously will also reap generously." So generosity multiplies itself! Since God has given generously toward us, an increase in our generosity is possible. "Now he who supplies seed to the sower and bread for food will also supply and increase your store of seed and will enlarge the harvest of your righteousness [the righteousness of generosity]. You will be made rich in every way so that you can be generous on every occasion" (2 Corinthians 9:10-11).

In the New Testament, giving is elevated to the status of privilege. Jesus plainly states that "it is more blessed to give than to receive" (Acts 20:35). The Macedonian Christians recognized this and "they urgently pleaded with us for the privilege of sharing" (2 Corinthians 8:4). In Philippians 4:17 we see that Paul was not as interested in the gift he received as in the benefits to the giver. He concluded his description of the benefits of giving with the words, "Thanks be to God for his indescribable gift" (2 Corinthians 9:15), which I believe refers to the privilege of giving.

Later in this book we will treat the New Testament teaching on giving more comprehensively. For now it is sufficient to recognize that the New Testament confirms the responsibility to give that was first established in Israel, elevates giving to a spiritual plane, and makes giving the essence of brotherhood. As community develops into a genuine brotherhood of unity in the Lord Jesus Christ, giving should become so natural that it nearly loses its identity as giving and could be more accurately described as sharing.

The Concept of Capital

Jesus does not specifically teach on the subject of capital: He simply takes it for granted. Examples of this are numerous. In the parables of the sower, the seeds, and the mustard seed, He refers to the owners of the fields and their servants. The seeker of the lost sheep owned many sheep. The unmerciful servant owed a legitimate debt to his master. The rich young ruler possessed legitimate wealth. The landowner hired workers for his vineyard and was generous to them as he pleased. In the parable of the tenants the landowner planted a vineyard and rented it out to farmers. Those who refused to attend the wedding banquet went instead to their fields or businesses. In the parable of the talents, the businessman entrusted capital to his managers and expected an adequate return on his capital. Even the foolish, rich farmer was not rebuked for his success in causing his land to produce, but for placing his confidence in the resulting riches.

These parables involve the concepts of ownership, capital, and legitimate return on capital in the form of income. If these concepts were evil or undesirable, there would have been at least a note of disapproval in Jesus' teaching.

In Acts 4, many of the believers owned land and houses. Some of them voluntarily liquidated these capital assets to meet the needs of the community of believers. Paul gave special instruction to those who possessed wealth, which usually implied its use as capital. So, as seen in Jesus' parables and Paul's instructions to the wealthy, stewardship comes into its primary function in relationship to capital.

Oppression, Injustice, and Poverty

God established justice in the economic relationships of His people in Israel. Then He went beyond justice and instructed them in generosity, compassion, and brotherhood—the foundations of community. However, His people not only ignored the latter instruction, but corrupted justice itself. So the gross oppression and injustice that prevailed in Israel was a consistent theme of the prophets as seen in Amos:

> This is what the LORD says:
> "For three sins of Israel,
>   even for four, I will not turn back my wrath.
> They sell the righteous for silver,
>   and the needy for a pair of sandals.
> They trample on the heads of the poor
>   as upon the dust of the ground
>   and deny justice to the oppressed." (Amos 2:6-7)

You trample on the poor
and force him to give you grain.
Therefore, though you have built stone mansions,
you will not live in them;
though you have planted lush vineyards,
you will not drink their wine.
For I know how many are your offenses
and how great your sins.
You oppress the righteous and take bribes
and you deprive the poor of justice in the courts.
(Amos 5:11-12)

Hear this, you who trample the needy
and do away with the poor of the land,
saying,
"When will the New Moon be over
that we may sell grain,
and the Sabbath be ended
that we may market wheat?"—
skimping the measure,
boosting the price
and cheating with dishonest scales,
buying the poor with silver
and the needy for a pair of sandals,
selling even the sweepings with the wheat.
(Amos 8:4-6)

When John the Baptist called the people to repentance, they asked, "What should we do then?" (Luke 3:10). They were undoubtedly surprised that his response was not some profound spiritual truth or religious exercise. He simply answered, "The man with two tunics should share with him who has none, and the one who has food should do the same" (verse 11). Tax collectors asked the same question and he said, "Don't collect any more than you are required to" (verse 13). His answer to the soldiers who came to him was, "Don't extort money and don't accuse people falsely—be content with your pay" (verse 14). Clearly John's message of repentance was one of brotherhood and justice: share your possessions, don't extort by accusations, and be content with your pay.

We need to remember that Jesus came into a situation in which the entire establishment—including the religious—was corrupt. Corruption at the top set the tone for the entire society, and greed, selfishness, and cheating were perceived as necessary for survival. In any corrupt society, the rule becomes every man for himself.

A just God is an ally of the oppressed and is against the oppressor. This fact, however, has been misconstrued to mean that God is on the side of the poor and against the rich. Jesus certainly had compassion on the poor, just as He had toward everyone in need. Yet He accepted the fact that because of freedom of choice and human diversity there would always be rich, poor, and average people: "The poor you will always have with you" (Mark 14:7).

At the same time, when poverty was the result of oppression, the New Testament writers were as direct as the Old Testament prophets. James wrote, "Look! The wages you failed to pay the workmen who mowed your fields are crying out against you. The cries of the harvesters have reached the ears of the Lord Almighty. You have lived on earth in luxury and self-indulgence. You have fattened yourselves in the day of slaughter. You have condemned and murdered innocent men, who were not opposing you" (James 5:4-6). James is talking to people who hoarded, failed to pay due wages, lived in self-indulgence, and even murdered innocent men to gain wealth.

To be poor is difficult in itself, but the situation of the poor in a corrupt and unjust society becomes hopeless. Perhaps this is why the poor responded so readily to Jesus. Jesus recognized that His disciples were poor, hungry, sorrowful, hated, excluded, and insulted.

> Blessed are you who are poor,
>> for yours is the kingdom of God.
> Blessed are you who hunger now,
>> for you will be satisfied.
> Blessed are you who weep now,
>> for you will laugh.
> Blessed are you when men hate you,
>> when they exclude you and insult you
>> and reject your name as evil,
>>> because of the Son of Man.   (Luke 6:20-22)

The *New English Bible* says, "How blessed are you who are in need; the kingdom of God is yours." Jesus does not advocate poverty, hunger, sorrow, or rejection, but points out that these conditions were disguised blessings that made His followers willing to respond to Him. He further indicates that persecution would likely continue and increase because of their identification with Him. The hatred of the world that rejected Christ would certainly continue, but the conditions were temporary and would eventually be reversed.

Jesus does not elevate poverty or declare His partisanship for the poor. Rather, He points out that their situation in life has turned to their advantage by making them willing to follow Him, while the more fortunate have rejected Him because of their self-sufficiency.

A Proper Concept of Wealth and Its Use
In Luke 6:20-22, Jesus addresses those who followed Him as poor, hungry, sorrowful, and rejected. In contrast, He speaks a warning to the establishment that rejected Him:

> But woe to you who are rich,
>> for you have already received your comfort.
> Woe to you who are well fed now,
>> for you will go hungry.

Woe to you who laugh now,
    for you will mourn and weep.
Woe to you when all men speak well of you,
    for that is how their fathers treated the false prophets.
                                                (Luke 6:24-26)

The contrast Jesus makes is between those who follow Him and have experienced poverty, hunger, sorrow, and rejection; and those who have rejected Him because they enjoy wealth, plenty, laughter, and popularity. These sayings are not a general condemnation of wealth any more than they are a condemnation of having sufficient food, enjoying happiness, or having a good reputation. To interpret these sayings as condemning the rich is to ignore everything else Jesus taught about wealth, His relationships with wealthy people, and the rest of Scripture.

Since victims of the "guilt syndrome" regard wealth with suspicion, we need to examine the Scriptures that commonly form the basis for this negative attitude. They are really very few.

James has been construed as denouncing the rich. In reality, James presents three themes that relate to the rich, the poor, or the average. The first is the ultimate equality of those in humble circumstances and those who are rich:

The brother in humble circumstances ought to take pride in his high position. But the one who is rich should take pride in his low position, because he will pass away like a wild flower. For the sun rises with scorching heat and withers the plant; its blossom falls and its beauty is destroyed. In the same way, the rich man will fade away even while he goes about his business.   (James 1:9-11)

The rich need to recognize their humanity and the fleeting nature of life. This is in no way a condemnation of the rich, but is a warning against pride.

James' second theme is a warning against favoritism: "If you show special attention to the man wearing fine clothes . . . have you not discriminated among yourselves and become judges with evil thoughts?" (James 2:3-4). Special attention and special favors for the rich amount to discrimination.

The final theme is a condemnation of oppressors:

> Is it not the rich who are exploiting you? Are they not the ones who are dragging you into court? Are they not the ones who are slandering the noble name of him to whom you belong?   (James 2:6-7)

> Now listen, you rich people, weep and wail because of the misery that is coming upon you. Your wealth has rotted, and moths have eaten your clothes. Your gold and silver are corroded. Their corrosion will testify against you and eat your flesh like fire. You have hoarded wealth in the last days. Look! The wages you failed to pay . . . are crying out against you. The cries of the harvesters have reached the ears of the Lord Almighty. You have lived on earth in luxury and self-indulgence. You have fattened yourselves in the day of slaughter. You have condemned and murdered innocent men, who were not opposing you.   (James 5:1-6)

James condemns the rich who had dragged the poor into court, slandered Christ's name, hoarded wealth, lived in indulgence, and murdered for gain. He condemns them as oppressors and gives a graphic picture of that oppression, but does not condemn them merely because of their wealth.

Jesus had a good number of involvements with wealthy people. Perhaps the most notable is His encounter with the rich young ruler, an incident recorded in three of the gospels.

Jesus had the ability to discern the thoughts and motivations of those He encountered. The rich young man was sincere and Jesus dealt with him forthrightly. Mark tells us that "Jesus looked at him and loved him" (Mark 10:21). In fact, Jesus invited the rich young ruler to be a disciple. Jesus' instructions to sell what he had were related to this invitation, "If you want to be perfect, go, sell your possessions and give to the poor, and you will have treasure in heaven. Then come, follow me" (Matthew 19:21). The perfection Jesus spoke of was not in the selling or giving, but in following Christ! In this case, the idolatrous possession of wealth prevented the young man from following Christ.

What Jesus demanded of the rich, young ruler was not a great departure from previous demands. He had asked the Twelve to leave their professions and follow Him. He had clearly stated that following Him must take priority over family, friends, and possessions. He had encouraged His followers to lay up their treasures in Heaven. In dealing with the rich young ruler, He challenged him to do all of these—because Jesus loved him. Jesus' discernment enabled Him to identify the area of life that needed to be surrendered.

The lessons Jesus drew from this encounter are significant. "How hard it is for the rich to enter the kingdom of God!" (Mark 10:23). The selfish possession of riches is an impediment to commitment. The disciples were amazed when Jesus repeated and strengthened His statement. Their response was, "Who then can be saved?" (verse 26). This response indicates they understood that the implication of what Jesus was saying went beyond the matter of wealth. *If everything must be surrendered,* they thought, *then who will qualify?* Jesus assured them that all things are possible with God.

The specific exhortation to the rich, young ruler should not be generalized. Jesus did not generalize it. He simply pointed out the broader extent of the difficulty. Although Jesus encountered many wealthy people, He did not repeat this instruction to others. Some, like Zacchaeus, voluntarily distributed a portion of their possessions. The general New Testament instruction to the wealthy regarding distribution is to be generous, but they are not required to reduce themselves to poverty.

Jesus accepted the wealthy Zacchaeus and went to visit him, even before Zacchaeus promised to give one-half of his possessions to the poor. Jesus accepted the expensive jar of perfume from a woman who was able to afford it, and commended her generosity just as He had commended the widow who gave the two small coins. Mary, Martha, and Lazarus were people of some means who opened their home to Jesus. Joseph of Arimathea was wealthy enough to have had a private tomb prepared for himself. Dorcas and Cornelius used their wealth for generous and continuous contributions. Lydia of Philippi was a successful businesswoman and opened her home for the ministry. She was undoubtedly the stimulus behind the Philippians' generosity. Jesus and the Twelve were financially supported in part by women who were able to give: "These women were helping to support them out of their own means" (Luke 8:3). Obviously these people had not been instructed to sell and give everything, or they would not have had the continuing ability to provide financial support.

Clearly the self-centered possession of wealth is wrong, not simply the possession. However, this does not mean that the problem is not extensive, because Jesus indicates that it is: "It is easier for a camel to go through the eye of a needle than for a rich man to enter the kingdom of God" (Mark 10:25). The wealthy young man found that his wealth was more important to him than the opportunity to follow Jesus. Just as Jesus discerned the condition of the young man's heart, the Holy Spirit can use the Scriptures to reveal the condition of our own hearts to us. If our hearts are free from the idolatrous elevation of material things, the proper response to wealth is stewardship rather than divestiture.

Jesus' parables set forth the example of good stewardship. Stewardship goes beyond the advantageous management of material possessions; it involves using these possessions to achieve eternal benefits. The manager in Luke 16 acted dishonestly, but shrewdly, in utilizing his master's property for his own future. In the application, Jesus says, "I tell you, use worldly wealth to gain friends for yourselves, so that when it is gone, you will be welcomed into eternal dwellings" (Luke 16:9). In other words, lay up your treasure in Heaven. Jesus specifically told the rich, young ruler that by following Jesus' instructions regarding his wealth, he would be laying up treasure in Heaven (Matthew 19:21).

Paul gave specific instruction to the rich. He warned against the dangers of coveting riches, then instructed Timothy concerning those who possessed riches:

> Command those who are rich in this present world not to be arrogant nor to put their hope in wealth, which is so uncertain, but to put their hope in God, who richly provides us with everything for our enjoyment. Command them to do good, to be rich in good deeds, and to be generous and willing to share. In this way they will lay up treasure for themselves as a firm foundation for the coming age, so that they may take hold of the life that is truly life.
>
> (1 Timothy 6:17-19)

Conclusion

This overview of the New Testament's economic teaching demonstrates the unity and consistency of biblical teaching on material things. The principles found in Genesis, the model of Israel, and the teachings of Jesus and the New Testament writers are in harmony. In part two, we will take a more detailed look at some of the subjects introduced in previous chapters.

NOTES:
1. F.F. Bruce, *The Spreading Flame,* (Exeter, England: The Paternoster Press, 1982), page 188ff.

SIX

A Model for Living in God's Order

We examined the book of Genesis to determine the principles underlying God's order in regard to the material universe. We looked at Israel as a model of the application of these principles within a specific culture, and finally looked at the New Testament to find confirmation of God's order. Now we must attempt to answer, in broad terms, how to live in accordance with God's order.

Our purpose is not to develop a blueprint for the perfect Christian economic system. Systems are the product of their time in history, circumstances, and the character of the people involved. So systems are a result rather than a cause. Since God has not established a universal economic system, it follows that systems are to be made by man. Different systems may have a greater or lesser degree of conformity to the principles of God's divine order, but all of man's systems are imperfect—even those established by righteous men.

In Israel, we find the one occasion in history when God established a system based on the principles of His order.

If God's purpose in establishing Israel's economic system was to realize a just and righteous society, the effort was a failure. His purpose, however, was to demonstrate the impossibility of man achieving righteousness through his own efforts, even though such efforts were within a system established by God Himself. Paul explains that "before this faith came, we were held prisoners by the law, locked up until faith should be revealed. So the law was put in charge to lead us to Christ that we might be justified by faith" (Galatians 3:23-24).

Israel's economic system was established on the principles of God's Law. But by the time Jesus came, the principles were forgotten or turned upside-down and replaced by an endless number of complex rules and regulations based on tradition. Jesus said, "You nullify the word of God by your tradition" (Mark 7:13).

Economic righteousness, like all righteousness acceptable to God, is based on a regenerate heart. It is clear that the purpose of the New Testament economic instruction is to guide Christians' behavior within the framework of any economic system. The tenor of the New Testament is that Christians are aliens within a hostile environment. Jesus compares our role to that of salt that seasons, or a lamp that penetrates darkness.

The New Testament speaks to us as individuals, individuals in community, and to the community itself. It gives instructions as to how we should live. As the first step in broadly describing our economic lifestyle, I want to reemphasize three ideas from the preceding chapters.

The Concepts of Creation, Capital, and Community

I recently visited six cities in Brazil to interview the young Christian leaders who had been present at my original seminar on man and material possessions three years earlier. They had translated my notes into Portuguese, studied the Scriptures carefully, held weekend seminars, and were well into the process of applying scriptural truth within their own culture. I was amazed at how the basic principles I had presented survived their critical analysis and made the transition into another culture. These men are discerning, independent thinkers and students of Scripture, not at all prone to accept any "Americanisms." It was interesting to me that these men, living in several different parts of Brazil, had focused on the same principles as the most applicable in their situations. This led me to believe that there are three generic ideas that, if understood in all of their significance and applied, would revolutionize the thinking of Christians on economic matters. I would like to review and reemphasize them here.

The first of these ideas is that of creation. God created the physical universe and pronounced it "very good." Our bodies are part of this material universe and our sustenance depends on it. God gave man dominion over the material universe, with instructions to subdue the earth and to subject it to his needs. This incredible universe is God's provision for man and as such is not evil or inferior. Thus it should be received with thanksgiving, and our attitude toward material things should be one of constant celebration!

Money is included in the goodness of creation because, as a medium of exchange and a store of value, it represents material things. God provided material things for our good, our benefit, and our enjoyment. We must remember that temptation stems from within our hearts, not from God's creation. Money (and the material goods it represents) is not evil, or even morally neutral; it is good.

Since we are physical-spiritual beings, it is undesirable to regard the physical as inferior. Our tendency to divide life into the secular and the sacred is counterproductive. All of life is sacred. Our relationship to material things must be based on the recognition of the essential goodness of God's creation.

The second significant idea is that of capital. Capital is any asset that produces benefits (income or increase) over a period of time. It includes both human capital—our talents, abilities, skills, education, experience, etc.—and material capital—land, factories, buildings, and money. This makes capital universal, since everyone has capital in some form and every economic system requires capital.

Stewardship functions in relationship to capital. Good stewards preserve their capital, increase it, and manage it in such a way that it produces continuing benefits. Good stewardship is a sign of economic maturity and leads to innumerable benefits. These benefits include the satisfaction of assuming responsibility, the privilege of providing for family, the experience of growth and enterprise, and—most significantly—the opportunity for giving. Good stewards become coworkers with God in producing material wealth and using it within His Kingdom. God has promised to meet His people's needs. He does this through the productivity of good stewards and their willingness to distribute their wealth.

My friends in Brazil found the concept of capital to be very helpful. One of them said, "This was a really important thing. My problem was division and conflict between my Christian life and my professional life. When I began to see my profession as a form of capital, I could see it as an expression of my Christian life and a means of fulfilling God's purposes for me. The immediate effect was the idea of special courses to improve my ability in my profession." Another said, "This was a new idea: to understand that capital is not bad but a resource that is good, that can be used to serve God."

In chapter 4 we studied a significant application of the idea of capital, when God provided capital in the form of land for every family in Israel. This was much more beneficial than God's direct provision during the wilderness experience. We, too, need to mature beyond the dependency experience of the manna in the wilderness and progress into the productive privileges of the

Promised Land.

The first two ideas find their fulfillment in the third, which is the concept of community. The benefits of God's creation are experienced in community, and the function of capital is to enhance community. The beauty of God's creation is best experienced when we share it with someone. The benefits of capital are not realized in isolation. Since community is an aspect of God's image in man, everything in life relates to it.

We have emphasized the individuality of man and the importance of property ownership, but ownership is virtually meaningless to the completely isolated individual. An example of this is a miser who hoards his gold and finds his only satisfaction in counting it. This kind of ownership is of no benefit to the individual or to those around him.

Stewardship, however, does not involve the accumulation of wealth as much as it does the utilization of wealth. Beneficial utilization of wealth is almost always a function of community. The completely selfish person, the traditional miser, is rare indeed. Man must live in community to express God's image, and the majority of people conduct their economic lives in relationship to some community, at least that of family.

We have looked at some of the New Testament descriptions of what God means by community: "Each of you should look not only to your own interests, but also to the interests of others" (Philippians 2:4). "All the believers were one in heart and mind. No one claimed that any of his possessions was his own, but they shared everything they had" (Acts 4:32). The ideal is a community in which each member's individuality is inviolable and diligently protected, and where each individual regards the welfare of every other member as equally important to his own. In economic matters, this means that individual ownership of property is coupled with community responsibility. Robert Banks, in his book *Paul's Idea of Community,* comments on the liberty in a community that "opens up a freer, non-idolatrous use of possessions,"[1] and says that "the physical expression of fellowship by the sharing of material possessions was to take place, but not compulsorily."[2]

Most of us do not experience this kind of community. We may salve our conscience a little by giving to some international agency that endeavors to help mankind. We may distribute food baskets to the needy at Christmas, contribute to the food shelves, or give used clothing. Our church may have a special fund for the poor. On rare occasions we may help someone directly. But all of this distribution is either on an impersonal basis through an agency, or is on the level of "giving"—not the sharing among equals that is the essence of community.

Is it possible that we have deliberately designed our institutions in a way that relieves us of the responsibilities of community? Most of the giving in the Scriptures was to individuals in need, while today the major emphasis is on giving to institutions or religious projects. The New Testament churches were small, intimate groups of Christians who met in someone's house. Today, size is equated with success and provides the funds for elaborate buildings, programs, and professional leaders. Such an elaborate organization renders dependence on each other in community impossible. Many Christians even prefer, and have deliberately chosen, the anonymity that is possible in a large fellowship. The need for more intimate community is recognized when large churches establish smaller fellowship groups within the large body.

Mosaic Law made children responsible for their elderly parents in certain situations, but the rabbis circumvented this requirement by allowing the substitution of gifts to the religious establishment (Mark 7:9-12). I wonder whether we also have replaced our responsibilities of living and sharing in community with allegiance and giving to institutions.

The nature of a community that makes sharing possible is a worthy subject to consider. The small churches of the New Testament were ideal. Perhaps no organization of the twentieth century can be expected to provide this opportunity. Yet I believe there is ample opportunity for each of us, in our own sphere of influence, to establish and practice true community.

These three ideas—creation, capital, and community—can form the basis of an economic lifestyle that conforms to the scriptural pattern. If we follow the biblical teaching, we will be characterized as "communitarian individuals."

The Concept of the Communitarian Individual

We will always be individuals because God created us that way. In our discussion regarding man's nature (chapter 3) we used words such as personality, self-consciousness, and self-determination (exercised through the intellect, emotions, and will). Our conclusion was that attempts to obliterate individuality are attacks on man's essential nature. Diversity, freedom of choice, personal responsibility and even true community, depend on individuality. Individuality does not imply selfishness, because this is the opposite of God's nature. So we're not talking about the narcissistic preoccupation with the self that could be implied by the term "individualism," or the arrogant self-sufficiency implied by "rugged individualism." Instead we are talking about personhood.

The other important aspect of man's creation in God's image is community. Man was not created to be autonomous, but to be under God's authority. He was not created to be isolated, but to function in community. We need to accommodate the individual personality and responsibility inherent in man's nature as created by God, as well as the full expression of community. Both are necessary because they are aspects of God's image in man.

True community must be voluntary, because enforced community does not leave room for the individual's freedom. While our introduction to certain communities may be involuntary, our continued participation in them is voluntary. This is true of the family, the church, even the nation. And even when it is impossible to separate physically from the community, we can separate ourselves by alienation. Positive participation in a community is voluntary.

It is easy to recognize that the "community of all" in a totalitarian state is enforced community. We need to go one step further and recognize that enforced *conformity,* even within a voluntary community, can nullify individuality in the same way as enforced *community.* We cannot escape the responsibility of our individuality by surrendering our will to that of the community, and a genuine, voluntary community of free individuals will not demand that we do so. Christian communes may exhibit many desirable features, but they often do not allow the expression of individuality or the fulfillment of individual responsibility.

Communitarian individuals, however, fully acknowledge both community and individuality. In economic affairs, communitarian individuals will follow the scriptural pattern of individual responsibility and ownership, but freely utilize all resources to meet the entire community's needs. The basic needs of every member of the community will be met. This will be done in ways that will enable the recipients to reassume their individual responsibility with dignity, never in ways that encourage permanent dependency. Beyond the basic needs, there will be a genuine interest and participation in the concerns of others. Resources will lie within the voluntary community. Giving will be better than receiving. Helping others will bring more satisfaction than pursuing self-interest. All of this sharing will be motivated by the giver's generosity. It will never originate in the receiver's "entitlements."

Communities will take many different forms, depending on the unique characteristics of the particular body of believers. Yet the essential ingredients will always be present because they develop from scriptural principles and conform to man's nature in relationship to the material universe. Diversity of individuals and communities is the rule in God's Kingdom. It would be futile to attempt to describe the ideal Christian community's form and structure. Instead, we will attempt to delineate scriptural principles that form the basis for individual attitudes and actions, and thus describe the communitarian individual. Based on the principles found in Genesis, the history of Israel, and the New Testament, the communitarian individual will:

- Accept with thanksgiving God's provision of the material universe as good, not evil: as an opportunity, not a temptation.
- Assume the responsibility of dominion over material things. This can be characterized as stewardship (since God is the ultimate owner), or as ownership (since God has given ownership to us).
- Never become enslaved to the material things over which he has been given dominion.
- Maintain dependence on God, living by faith without worry.
- Give absolute priority to the Kingdom of God.
- Practice and demand justice in economic matters. Oppose oppression and injustice on personal and societal levels.
- Recognize our creation in God's image, involving individuality, freedom of choice, personal responsibility, and diversity.
- Accept the responsibility of individual ownership of property, recognizing that money represents God's material provision.
- Limit money to its proper role as a medium of exchange and a store of value.
- Never regard money as an end in itself or a worthy objective of life.
- Recognize the nature of capital and its legitimacy in a Christian's life.
- Recognize that stewardship involves the creation, preservation, and proper utilization of capital.

Utilize income in accordance with scriptural priorities.

Use material things, both capital and income, for eternal purposes.

Recognize that the individual, even though created in God's image, was not created to be autonomous and independent.

Recognize that God's image also involves community.

Voluntarily participate in Christian community, using gifts, abilities, and material resources to benefit the Body of Christ, without pride because God is the source.

Demonstrate interest in the welfare of others in the community that will equal or exceed interest in our personal welfare—including economic welfare.

Be generous in utilizing economic resources for the benefit of others in the community. This will involve generous giving and lending, but will go beyond that. It will be done by sharing in the context of brotherhood, enjoying together what God has provided.

Mature independence will be balanced with natural interdependence.

Individual responsibility will be balanced with community accountability.

In all of these ways, the communitarian individual balances his or her individuality with community. This makes possible the fullest expression of the image of God in which man was created.

NOTES:

1. Robert J. Banks, *Paul's Idea of Community* (Grand Rapids, Michigan: Wm. B. Eerdman's Publishing Co., 1980), page 27.

2. Banks, page 90.

PART TWO

The Communitarian Individual and His Possessions

So far I have attempted to present an overall view of the biblical teaching pertaining to man and material possessions. I have suggested that Christians in contemporary society who apply the scriptural teaching on God's economic order could be described as communitarian individuals. Communitarian individuals recognize the essential goodness of God's material provision, understand the role of capital in the stewardship of material things, and accept the responsibilities of both individual ownership and community.

In this part of the book I present many of the same biblical teachings and concepts already covered, but approach them as separate topics in order to treat some of them more thoroughly. To have attempted this more detailed study in part one would have distracted from the development of the overall thesis. We will look at many of the same ideas and Scripture passages, some of which have already been applied in several contexts. So there will be some repetition, but only what is necessary to provide a fuller understanding of these ideas.

The topics we will discuss in this section fall into two major categories. We will deal first with matters of money and wealth in general, and then will turn our attention to the topic of giving and receiving. Together, they describe the correct relationship of the communitarian individual to his or her possessions.

SEVEN

Matters of Money
and Wealth

Almost immediately after receiving dominion over the earth, man attempted to act autonomously. Since man was created to bear God's image and exercise dominion under God's authority, man's efforts toward autonomy violated his nature. God gave man the freedom to choose, but not the power to be autonomous.

Man's attempt at autonomy led to his bondage to Satan. Man's choice is not between autonomy and submission, but between two masters—God or Satan. When man chooses God as his master, he is free to be what God created him to be. When man chooses Satan, the result is enslavement. As servants of Satan, rebellious men effectively turn their God-given dominion over to Satan.

Satan is not very good at originating, because God did not give him the power to create. But Satan is very skilled at perverting the good that God created. All sin finds its foundation in something God originated as good that Satan perverts and distorts.

Examples of this are numerous. Our God-consciousness and need to worship are expressed in false religions, cults, and degrading idolatry. The greatness of God's image in man gives rise to the self-worship of humanism. The incredible, natural universe provides the temptation for nature worship and scientism. The need for legitimate government leads to stifling bureaucracies or totalitarianism. Love is reduced to lust, natural appetites to gluttony and drunkenness. Appreciation of beauty becomes vanity and pride. Talents and abilities are misdirected toward the desire for fame, wealth, and power. Scriptural truth is twisted into false teachings. The brotherhood of believers is distorted into impersonal, domineering institutions. The desire for truth leads to persecutions and inquisitions. Concern for the poor produces welfare systems that degrade and produce permanent dependency.

The list of Satan's perversions of God's good creation is endless, since it includes every sin of society or individuals. The elevation of something to the status of an "independent good," which means to give something value apart from its proper place and purpose in God's order, is inherent in many of these perversions.

The Trap of Materialism

Materialism is the perversion of God's provision of the material universe. It is the reversal of dominion, whereby man becomes enslaved to material things rather than controlling them. Schlossberg describes materialism well as "the idolatrous elevation of money and material possessions it will buy as the goal of life."[1] If a man lives to accumulate material things, he becomes a slave to the material. The New Testament speaks to this problem: "Don't you know that when you offer yourselves to someone to obey him as slaves, you are slaves to the one whom you obey?" (Romans 6:16); and, "They . . . worshiped and served created things rather than the Creator" (Romans 1:25).

The word "materialism" is commonly used in two different

ways. The first is that of philosophical materialism, which is the belief that the physical universe represents all of reality. There is no spiritual dimension to man, no God, nothing that transcends the physical universe—only what can be perceived by man's five senses. The material is all there is! The result of philosophical materialism is practical materialism, which is making the acquisition and enjoyment of material things—including the physical body—the primary objective of life. The material is all that matters!

Practical materialism has been present throughout history, but it is especially virulent today because the dominant philosophical systems are materialistic. Our philosophical ideas have consequences in daily life. Schlossberg emphasizes the effect of intellectuals' ideas on society: "These philosophies may come down in transmogrified form, but come down they do."[2] The current practical materialism we see in our society is related to the philosophical materialism that dominates our education systems.

Christians, too, may become practical materialists. One way we do this is by deliberate, conscious choice: "This is my primary objective in life." This, however, would be difficult to do because it conflicts with our stated beliefs. We can also become materialistic by unconsciously elevating material things to top priority, even though other things rank higher in our stated value system. The fact is, whether we make a conscious or unconscious choice, we "are slaves to the one whom [we] obey" (Romans 6:16).

Western man is especially susceptible to materialism because we have a highly developed goal orientation. This orientation is in sharp contrast to many societies of the past and many contemporary non-western cultures. We are concerned with time, efficiency, the creation of wealth, change, growth, and progress. It is natural that Christianity and Judaism are future oriented because both view God as having a purpose in history. Michael Novak says that we "understand salvation as a vocation in history," and have a "sense of a future different from the past."[3] Rifkin and

Howard go so far as to suggest that "the Reformation provided both the liberating energy . . . and the vision necessary to establish the new capitalistic order."[4] Biblical principles may have contributed more than we realize to the progressive nature of Western culture. Many Western Christians consider this highly developed goal orientation to be an essential aspect of man's nature.

I do not believe our goal orientation and consciousness of the future is in itself wrong or unscriptural, for Jesus Himself focused on the future as well as the present. Paul also took his responsibilities seriously, was concerned with growth and change, and looked forward to future rewards. The danger in such a perspective is that we may choose the wrong goals.

Paul's goals were in relationship to his calling in God's Kingdom. Jesus tells us to "seek first his kingdom and his righteousness, and all these things will be given to you as well" (Matthew 6:33). The patriarchs became wealthy men, but Hebrews 11 tells us that faithful obedience to God was the primary motivator in their lives; the wealth was incidental. When our goals are primarily material, we become victims of materialism.

Without actually using the term, the Scriptures have much to say about materialism:

> People who want to get rich fall into temptation and a trap and into many foolish and harmful desires that plunge men into ruin and destruction. For the love of money is a root of all kinds of evil. Some people, eager for money, have wandered from the faith and pierced themselves with many griefs.   (1 Timothy 6:9-10)

> Keep your lives free from the love of money and be content with what you have.   (Hebrews 13:5)

> Watch out! Be on your guard against all kinds of greed; a man's life does not consist in the abundance of his possessions.   (Luke 12:15)

But the worries of this life, the deceitfulness of wealth and the desires for other things come in and choke the word, making it unfruitful. (Mark 4:19)

These and many other verses help define materialism as slavery to material things. Materialism involves the love of money, an inordinate desire for material things, and preoccupation with material things. The acquisition of material things becomes the objective of life, and the obsession with material things supercedes other values. We come to believe that material things provide security, so we rely on them rather than God. We must remember that materialism does not refer to the nature or possession of material things, but to our attitude and conduct in relationship to them.

The proper attitudes and actions regarding material things are in sharp contrast to materialism. With a proper attitude we can accept with thanksgiving the things God has provided. We can enjoy them without guilt, knowing that God has created them for our benefit. We can exercise intelligent stewardship of material things, utilizing the capital at our disposal to produce an increase. We can give generously and save for the future.

The possession of wealth is not a sign of materialism, nor does poverty indicate its absence. The poor are in danger of being materialistic, too. In fact, it is probably more difficult for them not to be materialistic.

The Manifestations of Materialism

Covetousness, possessiveness, greed, envy, avarice, selfishness, and pride are the natural manifestations of materialism. Jesus dealt with several of these topics in Luke 12:13-21.

Someone in the crowd said to him, "Teacher, tell my brother to divide the inheritance with me."

Jesus replied, "Man, who appointed me a judge or an arbiter between you?" Then he said to them, "Watch out!

Be on your guard against all kinds of greed; a man's life does not consist in the abundance of his possessions."

And he told them this parable: "The ground of a certain rich man produced a good crop. He thought to himself, 'What shall I do? I have no place to store my crops.'

"Then he said, 'This is what I'll do. I will tear down my barns and build bigger ones, and there I will store all my grain and my goods. And I'll say to myself, "You have plenty of good things laid up for many years. Take life easy; eat, drink and be merry."'

"But God said to him, 'You fool! This very night your life will be demanded from you. Then who will get what you have prepared for yourself?'

"This is how it will be with anyone who stores up things for himself but is not rich toward God."

Jesus' first example was the covetous man who wanted his brother's inheritance. His second example was the rich farmer who selfishly held onto his wealth and placed his confidence in riches. The first man provides an example of covetousness—desiring what belongs to another. The second man exemplified possessiveness—the selfish retention of everything we have. Between the illustrations Jesus warns, "Watch out! Be on your guard against all kinds of greed." Or as the *King James Version* says, "from all covetousness." A.T. Robertson, the Greek scholar, translates this passage as, "*Every kind of greedy desire for more.*"[5]

The Tenth Commandment, in Deuteronomy 5:21, is the only one of the last five commandments that deals with an attitude rather than an action: "You shall not covet . . . you shall not set your desire . . . on anything that belongs to your neighbor." In this instance covetousness means to desire what belongs to another. Jesus, however, uses the word in a broader sense to mean, as Robertson implies, "every kind of greedy desire for more."

Covetousness is usually part of a broader allegiance to material things as described in 1 John 2:15-16: "Do not love the world or anything in the world. If anyone loves the world, the love of the Father is not in him. For everything in the world—the cravings of sinful man, the lust of his eyes and the boasting of what he has and does—comes not from the Father but from the world." In Luke 16:13, Jesus makes the issue crystal clear: "No servant can serve two masters . . . you cannot serve both God and Money." Paul takes the final step of identifying greed (covetousness) with idolatry in Colossians 3:5 and Ephesians 5:5.

Covetousness is closely related to envy, which is listed among the things that are greatly displeasing to God. Covetousness is to possessions what envy is to persons, but with a slightly different objective. The objective of covetousness is to possess. The objective of envy is to destroy what cannot be possessed. The two attitudes are often simultaneous, but either can lead to the other. For instance, our desire for another's possessions is much more palatable if we regard the person as totally unworthy, so we initiate envy, which leads to hatred. Also, our envy of another's ability may take concrete form in our desire for that person's possessions.

If we fall into the trap of materialism, we elevate money and material possessions as our major goal in life. We have an inordinate desire for material things that is expressed in covetousness. One sure sign of covetousness is the desire to gain wealth quickly. Another sign is insatiability. Schlossberg points out that "the legitimacy of such desires may be judged in part by our ability to satisfy them. All true needs—such as food, drink, and companionship—are satiable. Illegitimate wants—pride, envy, greed—are insatiable. By their nature they cannot be satisfied."[6]

I'm sure the terms are outdated, but years ago psychologists talked of the relationships between needs, the drive to realize them, and the goal or fulfillment of those needs. The process of fulfillment begins with a need that produces a drive to develop an appropriate mechanism for fulfillment. It is possible for the mechanism to become its own drive, causing the process to continue long after the initial need and drive have disappeared. This concept aptly describes the final stages of covetousness, in which the greedy desire for more motivates men who already have more than enough.

If covetousness is the wrong attitude regarding what we desire, possessiveness is the wrong attitude toward what we already have.

We have talked about the legitimacy of wealth and have seen that God expects us to utilize wealth as communitarian individuals. Possessiveness makes this community utilization of wealth impossible. In Psalm 62:10, the writer first warns against gaining wealth through immoral means, then turns his attention to the problem of possessiveness of legitimate wealth: "Though your riches increase, do not set your heart on them." Solomon continues the theme, saying, "I have seen a grievous evil under the sun: wealth hoarded to the harm of its owner" (Ecclesiastes 5:13). Proverbs 11:24-25 depicts the results of both possessiveness and generosity:

> One man gives freely, yet gains even more;
>> another withholds unduly, but comes to poverty.
> A generous man will prosper;
>> he who refreshes others will himself be refreshed.

The clear message here is that we are to hold our possessions loosely!

Possessiveness is the opposite of generosity. The rich farmer in Luke 12 is an extreme example of selfishness; every other word is "I, my, myself." In contrast to this selfishness is Paul's exhortation in Philippians 2:3-4 that says, "Do nothing out of selfish ambition or vain conceit, but in humility consider others better than yourselves. Each of you should look not only to your own interests, but also to the interests of others." This includes financial interests! An extreme example of such generosity and unselfishness is found in Acts 4:32-37. Here are a few of the key phrases from this passage.

All the believers were one in heart and mind.
No one claimed that any of his possessions was his own,
    but they shared everything they had.
There were no needy persons among them.
From time to time those who owned lands or houses sold
    them and brought the money from the sales.
It was distributed to anyone as he had need.

This situation is sometimes construed as an example of communism in the early Church, but a careful evaluation does not support this meaning. Rather than implying communism, this situation was an example of brothers who lived as communitarian individuals—with individual ownership and responsibility coupled with the voluntary, generous use of resources to meet community needs. The right of individual ownership was never violated, but was specifically affirmed. Peter said to Ananias, "Didn't it [the land] belong to you before it was sold? And after it was sold, wasn't the money at your disposal?" (Acts 5:4).

While the spirit of generosity in this emergency situation was commendable, the wisdom of disposing of capital was questionable. The capital was converted to consumption, resulting in the loss of resources. Within a few years these Christians were in poverty to the extent that Paul raised money from the Macedonians—who were themselves suffering from poverty and great affliction—to help them (2 Corinthians 8:2). I'm not saying that these Christians should not have done what they did, only that the consequences were to be expected.

If possessiveness and generosity are antinomies, the opposite of covetousness is contentment. Contentment means that we are willing to accept ourselves as God created us, with our gifts, abilities, talents, and opportunities. Contentment in regard to material things is not a passive acceptance, but an active acceptance. Being content enables us to accept the responsibility that accompanies our calling and our situation. In application, this means different things for each of us. In Proverbs 30:8-9, Agur defines his own personal area of contentment:

> Give me neither poverty nor riches,
>   but give me only my daily bread.
> Otherwise, I may have too much and disown you
>   and say, "Who is the LORD?"
> Or I may become poor and steal,
>   and so dishonor the name of my God.

Paul accepted his situation in life even though it involved a variety of financial circumstances. In giving his life to ministry to the Gentiles, he set aside all financial pursuits except the tent-making that provided the basic necessities. Our calling may be different and our circumstances may be different, but Paul's attitude is still applicable: "I have learned to be content whatever the circumstances. I know what it is to be in need, and I know what it is to have plenty. I have learned the secret of being content in any and every situation" (Philippians 4:11-12). In the same vein he writes, "But godliness with contentment is great gain. For we brought nothing into the world, and we can take nothing out of it. But if we have food and clothing, we will be content with that" (1 Timothy 6:6-8).

The results of covetousness and possessiveness are found in the words and phrases used in the Scripture passages quoted above: greed, pride, lust, evil and harmful desires, all kinds of evil, grief, trouble, diminishing, hurt, poverty, ruin, and destruction. These words describe a selfish person who is deceived by wealth, loves money, loves the world, lives in iniquity, serves the wrong master, and is totally dissatisfied because his or her appetites are insatiable. Money is a wonderful servant, but a terrible master!

The antidote to such misery is to saturate our minds with the warnings and exhortations found in these same Scriptures. We

need to recognize the negative results of covetousness and possessiveness. We need to guard against the love of money and all kinds
of greed. We need to seek God's Kingdom, love God, and serve
the right Master. We need to realize that wealth is not a worthy
objective of life. And we need to deliberately and purposefully
"lay up for ourselves treasures in heaven."

In short, we must practice contentment to combat covetousness. We must practice generosity to combat possessiveness.
Covetousness and possessiveness lead to pride, but contentment
and generosity lead to gratitude and humility.

A Proper Basis for Our Confidence

> The name of the LORD is a strong tower;
>   the righteous run to it and are safe.
> The wealth of the rich is their fortified city;
>   they imagine it an unscalable wall.
>
> (Proverbs 18:10-11)

Material possessions are God's provision for us and are not
wrong in themselves. However, our attitudes toward material
possessions can be wrong. The rich farmer in Luke 12 is the perfect
example of a man with misplaced confidence. In his self-
centeredness, he based his confidence for the future on his grain
and goods rather than God. Both Paul and David cautioned
against such misplaced confidence:

> Command those who are rich in this present world not to
> be arrogant nor to put their hope in wealth, which is so
> uncertain, but to put their hope in God, who richly provides
> us with everything for our enjoyment.   (1 Timothy 6:17)

> Surely God will bring you down to everlasting ruin:
>   He will snatch you up and tear you from your tent;
>   he will uproot you from the land of the living. . . .
>   they will laugh at [you], saying,

"Here now is the man
who did not make God his stronghold
but trusted in his great wealth
and grew strong by destroying others!" (Psalm 52:5-7)

Riches are an unreliable basis for our confidence, and Scripture gives us several reasons why:

Dishonest money dwindles away,
but he who gathers money little by little makes it
grow.   (Proverbs 13:11)

Whoever trusts in his riches will fall,
but the righteous will thrive like a green leaf.
(Proverbs 11:28)

Do not wear yourself out to get rich;
have the wisdom to show restraint.
Cast but a glance at riches, and they are gone,
for they will surely sprout wings
and fly off to the sky like an eagle.   (Proverbs 23:4-5)

Whoever loves money never has money enough;
whoever loves wealth is never satisfied with his
income.
This too is meaningless.   (Ecclesiastes 5:10)

He that loveth silver shall not be satisfied with silver;
nor he that loveth abundance with increase.
(Ecclesiastes 5:10, KJV)

First, wealth gained dishonestly or quickly tends to disappear. Secondly, God's pronouncements assure the ultimate failure of those who trust in wealth. Third, even if it can be retained, wealth cannot bring satisfaction.

Clearly God Himself is the only proper basis for our confidence. When our confidence is in Him we can claim all of His promises that He will provide everything we need. One of these promises is found in Philippians 4:19: "And my God will meet all your needs according to his glorious riches in Christ Jesus." Although this verse is often generalized to apply to all Christians in all situations, the promise was given in the context of the generous gift that Paul received from the Philippians. This gift was only the most recent manifestation of their continuous support. So the promise is to those who have the proper attitude toward material things, have placed their confidence in God Himself, and are generous in sharing what they have with others.

Establishing Priorities of the Heart

I have mentioned previously that, in contrast to many of the other commandments, the commandment to avoid covetousness deals with an attitude rather than an action. This is because our attitudes establish our priorities and determine our actions. "Above all else, guard your heart, for it is the wellspring of life" (Proverbs 4:23).

Only God Himself has full knowledge of our hearts' condition. We may have insights into ourselves, but these can be easily distorted as stated in Jeremiah 17:9, "The heart is deceitful above all things and beyond cure. Who can understand it?" Perhaps the greatest benefit of an intimate relationship with God is that He reveals to us the condition of our hearts. The psalmist says, "Search me, O God, and know my heart; test me and know my anxious thoughts. See if there is any offensive way in me, and lead me in the way everlasting" (Psalm 139:23-24). In 1 Samuel 16:7 we see that God deals with us on the basis of inward reality, not external appearances: "Man looks at the outward appearance, but the LORD looks at the heart."

Much of Scripture's teaching on material things pertains to the attitudes of our hearts. Just as Jesus had warned about our attitude toward possessions, Paul tells us that "the love of money is a root of all kinds of evil" (1 Timothy 6:10). This is also emphasized in 1 John 2:15-16:

> Do not love the world or anything in the world. If anyone
> loves the world, the love of the Father is not in him. For
> everything in the world—the cravings of sinful man, the lust
> of his eyes and the boasting of what he has and does—
> comes not from the Father but from the world.

To the extent that this passage refers to material things, it teaches that it is not the things we possess that are wrong, but our attitude of pride—our love of material things—that makes us boast about them. The problem is not in what we possess, but in what possesses us.

It has never been easy to avoid the love of money. In this age of affluence, which is dominated by materialistic philosophies and consequently geared to materialistic values, it seems more difficult than ever to refrain from devoting our life's energy to acquiring wealth for personal enjoyment. Affluence amplifies the temptation of materialism because the more we have, the more we desire. In primitive societies, expectations were limited, but in twentieth-century America they seem endless. However, in order to develop the right solution, we must correctly diagnose the problem. The existence or possession of material things or money does not constitute the problem. The problem lies with our attitude.

The key word in the passages above is the word "love," meaning the love of material things. Love is a function of the heart. God's primary concern is not with the quantity of our possessions, but with our attitude toward them. We can have many possessions and not be guilty of loving them. We can have very few possessions and still love them.

Ultimately our attitude toward possessions boils down to the matter of priority. We either love our possessions or we love God. Many passages of Scripture address this issue of priority.

> No one can serve two masters . . . you cannot serve both
> God and Money.   (Matthew 6:24)

But seek first his kingdom and his righteousness, and all
these things will be given to you as well.   (Matthew 6:33)

Do not store up for yourselves treasures on earth . . . but
store up for yourselves treasures in heaven. . . . For where
your treasure is, there your heart will be also.
(Matthew 6:19-21)

Better a little with the fear of the LORD than great wealth
with turmoil.   (Proverbs 15:16)

Better a little with righteousness than much gain with
injustice.   (Proverbs 16:8)

A good name is more desirable than great riches; to be
esteemed is better than silver or gold.   (Proverbs 22:1)

The rich, young ruler of Mark 10 illustrates the result of
wrong priorities. He sought out Jesus and asked the secret of
eternal life. Jesus looked at him, loved him, and invited him to be
His disciple, but tested him to determine his priorities. The young
man had to decide which came first, his desire to follow Jesus or to
retain his wealth. How many of us would pass the test if it were
that specific?

Does God expect all of us to give up our possessions like
Jesus asked this young man to do? Not if our priorities are in
order. It has been said that God can be happy for us to be wealthy
if we can be happy not to be. If our priorities are in order and our
attitude toward material things is correct, we are in the perfect
position to be good stewards of what God has entrusted to us.

Stewardship

God is the ultimate owner. He created it all! However God gave
Adam dominion over the earth. So in a valid sense we are owners
as God's representatives, as God's image bearers.

The earth is the LORD's, and everything in it.   (Psalm 24:1)

> The land is mine and you are but aliens and my tenants . . .
> throughout the country that you hold as a possession.
>
> (Leviticus 25:23-24)

> "The silver is mine, and the gold is mine," declares the
> LORD Almighty.   (Haggai 2:8)

> For every animal of the forest is mine,
>   and the cattle on a thousand hills. . . .
>   For the world is mine, and all that is in it.
>
> (Psalm 50:10,12)

Perhaps we could best describe our relationship to material possessions by defining it from two perspectives. As far as God is concerned, we are stewards under His ultimate ownership. As far as man is concerned, we are the owners of whatever God has entrusted to us.

In addition to being the ultimate owner of all that is, God gives each of us the abilities we have, including the ability to gain and create wealth. In Deuteronomy 8:18, God reminds His people of this fact: "But remember the LORD your God, for it is he who gives you the ability to produce wealth." Paul reminds his readers of this fact, too, by asking, "What do you have that you did not receive?" (1 Corinthians 4:7). Since God ultimately owns all material things and gives us our abilities, we are really stewards and caretakers of property that belongs to God. Since money is a substitute for material things, our relationship to money is one of stewardship. God is the true owner of money.

Jesus gave us the basic, scriptural teaching about stewardship in two parables. The first is the parable of the talents in Matthew 25:14-30. This parable about stewardship is used in an illustration of the Kingdom of Heaven. The servants were expected to use their trust productively. Those who did so were rewarded proportionately. Jesus concludes the second parable about stewardship by saying, "Whoever can be trusted with very little can also be trusted with much, and whoever is dishonest with very little will also be dishonest with much" (Luke 16:10).

Paul tells us that faithfulness is the chief requirement of a steward. "Now it is required that those who have been given a trust must prove faithful" (1 Corinthians 4:2). In the parables above, Jesus portrays faithfulness as putting talents to productive use to produce an increase, which is commonly described as profit.

Of course stewardship in God's Kingdom involves more than money. In fact, money is the "very little" mentioned in Luke 16:10. But our stewardship of finances may well be a test of our trustworthiness in greater things. Jesus implies this in 16:11, "So if you have not been trustworthy in handling worldly wealth, who will trust you with true riches?"

Although stewardship involves more than money, stewardship comes into full play in relationship to capital. We described capital as anything that produces continuing benefits over a long period of time: gifts, talents, abilities, skills, and education, as well as land, buildings, factories, businesses, and money. Stewardship has to do with producing and properly using wealth. Thus stewardship is not passive; it involves the active application of our intelligence. There is a biblical basis for planning and action. Giving is one aspect of properly using wealth, but giving is not the primary definition of stewardship.

We need to correctly understand stewardship and ownership. The selfish and self-centered individual thinks of ownership in the absolute sense. A "rugged individualist" would say, "I am the owner of everything I possess. What is mine is mine. I have earned it and am entitled to it. If any other person has needs, let him earn and provide for himself as I have. If I choose to be generous and give something away, it is an act of supererogation, and I should be commended for it. In this way, even giving serves my self-interest."

A good steward would say, "God has entrusted me with certain of His possessions. As far as men are concerned I am the owner, but as far as God is concerned I am a steward. As such it is my responsibility to utilize these possessions in conformity to God's character and instructions. These possessions are not really mine, and my stewardship cannot be exercised exclusively in self-interest. If in my stewardship I demonstrate the Owner's character through acts of love, generosity, and unselfishness, He must receive the credit."

To summarize, our ownership is really stewardship under God's ownership. Faithfulness is the chief requirement of a steward. Stewardship comes into full play in relationship to capital. The faithful steward causes the capital entrusted to him to produce a return. Our stewardship of material things can demonstrate our trustworthiness for greater things.

Utilization of Income

The principle of individual ownership makes stewardship primarily a personal responsibility, although the family and other communities can be vehicles of stewardship, too. The utilization of wealth, however, takes place primarily in relationship to community.

The Old and New Testament patterns for the use of income are nearly identical. In the Old Testament, God gave each family in the twelve tribes of Israel capital in the form of land. This capital was to provide for future generations, and rules were established to preserve it. God reserved ten percent of the income from the land capital for Himself. He gave this ten percent to the Levites in lieu of a land inheritance. The remaining ninety percent was income to the Israelites, which they were to use according to the following priorities that God established:

First fruits and freewill offerings to God.
Support of families.
Care of widows and orphans.
Giving and lending to the poor.
Providing for strangers and travelers.

Essentially the same pattern is found in the New Testament. Individual ownership was accepted as the norm, capital continued to produce income, and the income was used to meet the needs of the entire community. By both instruction and example in the New Testament we see a pattern of priorities for the use of income:

Providing for family.
Providing for the needs of brothers in difficulty.
Providing for widows and orphans who had no families.
Providing for the poor.
Providing for spiritual leaders.
Showing hospitality to travelers and strangers.
Giving for the extension of the gospel.

Illustrations of sharing in community abound in the New Testament. They range from the willingness of certain women to systematically assist Jesus and His disciples, to the pleading of the Macedonians to be allowed to contribute to the poor Christians in Jerusalem, to the generosity of the Philippians in supporting the Apostle Paul. Perhaps the ultimate example of this sharing community is found in Acts 4:32-35.

All the believers were one in heart and mind. No one claimed that any of his possessions was his own, but they shared everything they had. . . . There were no needy persons among them. For from time to time those who owned lands or houses sold them, brought the money from the sales . . . and it was distributed to everyone as he had need.

Using Wealth for Eternal Purposes

The book of Proverbs points out many disadvantages of poverty. It is full of warnings regarding wealth that is gained dishonestly through actions motivated by greed and the desire for quick wealth. It portrays poverty as preferable to greed. It also emphasizes the benefits of wealth gained properly by the diligent application of our God-given talents and abilities.

One of these statements is rather surprising, until one realizes that it is more of a statement of reality than an instruction to action.

> Wealth brings many friends,
>> but a poor man's friend deserts him.
> A poor man is shunned by all his relatives—
>> how much more do his friends avoid him!
>
> (Proverbs 19:4,7)

This is not an instruction to buy friendship, but is simply a statement of fact. Poverty tends to isolate, while even modest resources make friendship possible. And friendships are the Christian's opportunity to relate to our world as salt and light.

In Paul's instructions to Timothy, which he intended for Timothy to pass on to wealthy Christians, Paul said, "Command them to do good, to be rich in good deeds, and to be generous and willing to share. In this way they will lay up treasure for themselves as a firm foundation for the coming age" (1 Timothy 6:18-19). Jesus also instructed His followers to build up treasure in Heaven (Matthew 6:20). What treasure did Jesus and Paul refer to? The reward from God that is promised for even a cup of cold water offered in Jesus' name! The joy of sharing in the lives and ministries of other Christians now and throughout eternity! Participation in bringing people into the Kingdom of Heaven and enjoying their fellowship forever!

Jesus addresses the issue of utilizing wealth in His application of the parable of the steward in Luke 16:9: "I tell you, use worldly wealth to gain friends for yourselves, so that when it is gone, you will be welcomed into eternal dwellings." We can easily miss the significance of this parable by focusing on the unjust steward's actions rather than on the application Jesus made. Jesus' message is obvious. We should utilize the "worldly" wealth at our disposal to gain friends for eternity: material possessions for eternal purposes!

Responsibility to Work

The Fourth Commandment, which gives God's instructions for using our time, has two aspects. When considering this commandment, we usually limit our focus to the seventh day, the day of rest. But the commandment also says, "Six days you shall labor and do all your work" (Exodus 20:9). We talk about the "Protestant work ethic," and perhaps this scriptural principle has been inappropriately applied. But we must remember that work is extolled in both the Old and New Testaments.

One of the blessings the Lord promises to those who fear Him is that "you will eat the fruit of your labor; blessings and prosperity will be yours" (Psalm 128:2). The writer of Proverbs promises that "wealth gotten by vanity shall be diminished: but he that gathereth by labour shall increase" (Proverbs 13:11, KJV), and repeatedly uses the word "diligent" to describe labor that leads to profit and plenty, and "slothful," "sluggard," and "lazy" to describe those headed for poverty. The teacher in Ecclesiastes found that it was good for man "to find satisfaction in his toilsome labor . . . and be happy in his work—this is a gift of God" (Ecclesiastes 5:18-19).

Paul is even more specific about our need to work.

> We gave you this rule: "If a man will not work, he shall not eat." We hear that some among you are idle. . . . Such people we command and urge in the Lord Jesus Christ, to settle down and earn the bread they eat.
>
> (2 Thessalonians 3:10-12)

> He who has been stealing must steal no longer, but must work, doing something useful with his own hands, that he may have something to share with those in need.
>
> (Ephesians 4:28)

Although Jesus and His followers seemed very relaxed about material things, this was because they placed their confidence in

God, not because they regarded work as unnecessary. Work is essential to man's well-being. This was true even before the Fall made work more difficult and necessary to man's survival. Material goods must be produced by work.

Those who do not work are taking unfair advantage of those who do. Affluent societies can afford to permit this. However, when affluence is coupled with state policies of redistribution of wealth, serious abuses can occur. These abuses tend to perpetuate themselves because the distributions are administered by bureaucrats who have a vested interest in maintaining dependency. Work is often discouraged, and the poverty level is adjusted upward to maintain the dependency on which the bureaucracy itself depends.

The "manna complex," the preference to remain in immediate dependency rather than assuming the responsibility of maturity, enables some Christians to be comfortable with permanent dependency on government programs as described above. This dependency is not only devastating to the individuals involved, but constitutes an abdication of our responsibility to each other in community.

A Right Attitude Toward Work
Work is a necessary responsibility, but it is also a privilege. The Israelites' experience in the wilderness was inferior to their experience in the Promised Land where they were privileged to assume responsibility and become coworkers with God in producing material goods and creating wealth. Work is a necessary and desirable part of our lives, and a number of scriptural admonitions show us the proper attitude toward it:

> Whatever you do, work at it with all your heart, as working for the Lord, not for men. . . . It is the Lord Christ you are serving.   (Colossians 3:23-24)

> Serve wholeheartedly, as if you were serving the Lord, not men, because you know that the Lord will reward everyone

for whatever good he does, whether he is slave or free.

(Ephesians 6:7-8)

Whatever you do, do it all for the glory of God.

(1 Corinthians 10:31)

Our people must learn to devote themselves to doing what is good, in order that they may provide for daily necessities and not live unproductive lives.   (Titus 3:14)

Paul himself exhibited a proper attitude toward work. In Acts 20:33-35 he says, "I have not coveted anyone's silver or gold or clothing. You yourselves know that these hands of mine have supplied my own needs and the needs of my companions. In everything I did, I showed you that by this kind of hard work we must help the weak, remembering the words the Lord Jesus Himself said: 'It is more blessed to give than to receive.'"

Work is a privilege that produces many benefits, not the least of which is the ability to give.

The sluggard's craving will be the death of him,
     because his hands refuse to work.
All day long he craves for more,
     but the righteous give without sparing.

(Proverbs 21:25-26)

A popular, negative attitude toward work is summed up in the phrase T.G.I.F! (Thank God It's Friday!) Our national productivity suffers because too many of us view our work only as the means to a paycheck. In addition to negative attitudes prevalent in the work place, Christians can also fall into patterns of erroneous thinking about work that they feel are based on "spiritual" attitudes. The artificial, "other-worldliness" attitude toward material things can affect our attitude toward work as well.

In a recent discussion about life's priorities, I challenged several statements that sounded good, but did not stand up under questioning. The first such statement was, "My priorities will always be God first, family second, business third." Only our Western tendency to think in categories prompts such distinctions. To analyze this statement, we must first consider how one serves God. As we have seen, two of the most scriptural and prominent aspects of service to God are service to family and other communities, and the exercise of stewardship. So how can one put family in second place when Paul says that the man who does not provide for his family "has denied the faith and is worse than an unbeliever" (1 Timothy 5:8)? How can we put family second when teaching God's truth to our children is not only a direct responsibility, but life's greatest opportunity? How can one put business in third place after considering the scriptural teaching on work and stewardship? These three aspects of life are not in conflict! The second two aspects are the only means to accomplish the first!

The second statement was, "This is God's business, I am only a steward." That statement may be true in the sense that God ultimately owns everything, but He transferred ownership to us and gave us the responsibility of dominion. The danger with this statement is that it can encourage us to become passive and expect God to do what we are responsible to do. We must remember that God is not in business. He lives and works within us. God does not bless businesses, He blesses His children. God is not our partner in business, as many Christians believe; He is our master and has given us specific responsibilities.

Work is essential to man's well-being, is commanded in Scripture, and is the means to fulfilling our responsibilities to God through service to others. Work is truly a privilege.

Establishing Moderation in Our Work

God plans for us to engage in productive labor. Work is mandatory, yet the Christian has other priorities as well. Even though we live in a world subject to the curse, and operate within a system that reflects man's fallen nature, God does not want us to be slaves to our work. He expects us to make room for other priorities. These priorities include seeking and serving God; serving our families, brothers, and community; and having adequate time to enjoy life.

Christians get out of balance in regard to their work and become "workaholics" for several reasons. Work may be an escape from reality or difficulties in other areas of life. The emphasis on work may be based on insecurity and fear, which result from too much dependence on the job and insufficient trust in God. But most often, an unbalanced emphasis on work stems from an inordinate desire for success—wealth—which is an expression of covetousness. Proverbs 23:4 specifically addresses this problem: "Do not wear yourself out to get rich; have the wisdom to show restraint." Jesus did not disparage material things, but He did tell us that we cannot serve both God and money. When we follow Him we can have no other master—not material possessions, not employment.

In unusual situations it may be necessary to concentrate almost exclusively on our work for periods of time. This need may arise in the early stages of a career or business. For instance, during the first three years of my career I gave priority to establishing my business to a degree that I would not consider doing on a permanent basis. Working our way out of a difficult circumstance is another situation that may require an unusual investment of time and attention. If we permit ourselves to get into financial trouble, we may have to pay a price to extricate ourselves. These out-of-balance times should be kept as short as possible, and under no circumstances should other priorities be abandoned entirely.

Moderation should be the rule for Christians. We should not avoid the responsibility of a fully productive job that utilizes our talents, abilities, calling, and opportunities. Yet we should not allow our job to dominate our lives. Something is wrong if we abandon other responsibilities in order to fulfill a job. The cause may lie within us if we are using our work as an escape, are dominated by insecurity, or if covetousness has made us too ambitious and greedy. The problem may be that we have over-reached our capabilities, and that the job is simply too big for us. The problem could also be that the demands of our employer (or business) are simply unreasonable.

As Christians we need to maintain control of our lives, including our work involvement. The best time to do this is before we find ourselves involved in an unfavorable situation. So we need to carefully evaluate the demands of our prospective employment or businesses.

At the time I was discharged from military service after World War II, the Veteran's Administration provided a career counseling service. This was quite extensive and included several days of psychological and aptitude testing. As a result of the tests, they advised me to prepare for one of two professional careers. However, I did not follow their advice because neither possibility seemed to fit with my life priorities. In retrospect, I realize that I made the right decision. Neither of the recommended careers would have offered the flexibility that I have experienced in my business, and the time demands they entailed would have prevented many of the most valued aspects of my life and service from taking place.

A good friend of mine is a successful franchisee in a nation-wide business chain. He was a leader in his trade association as well as a successful businessman. The parent corporation recognized his ability and offered him the job of president—a very significant position. He made several trips to another state to negotiate the employment and the prospects appeared excellent. He left home one day to make the final arrangements and his wife was surprised to see him return later the same day. On the outgoing trip he had spent time in prayer and realized that the position would conflict with his life priorities. So he turned around at the distant airport and returned home. He was simply not willing to sell himself to the corporation.

If you find yourself trapped in an unfavorable work situation, it is necessary to take action. The first thing to do is negotiate. If you are a valuable asset to the company, you may find your superiors surprisingly reasonable in allowing you the freedom for other priorities. Another solution is to make yourself indispensable. Gain irreplaceable knowledge and experience about your job and company. Then arrange to be paid on the basis of your knowledge and your contribution, rather than the number of hours you put in. If all else fails, the final solution is to change your employment or business. There is really no other choice, because a Christian cannot abandon his or her God-given responsibilities.

One of my friends and his wife are in the process of a significant career change. One of their first steps in making this change was to call together six members (three couples) of their Christian community to help them consider the situation. During the discussion it became apparent that their career conflicted with what they felt were the most important things in their lives. Their earning capacity in a new career was not only uncertain, but would be fraction (possibly one-third) of the income they had been receiving. However, their conviction that a change was needed was so clear that in a matter of weeks they began transferring their clients to another professional, offered their house for sale, and began to function in their new role. They are an example of the willingness necessary to arrange our lives according to God's priorities.

Understanding Our Responsibility to Save

> In the house of the wise are stores of choice food and oil,
>   but a foolish man devours all he has. (Proverbs 21:20)

In the vernacular of *The Living Bible* this verse is translated, "The wise man saves for the future, but the foolish man spends whatever he gets."

Saving is natural in an agrarian society. From one crop the farmer saves seed for next year's planting, food for his family and lifestock and—if he is prudent—something for the lean years. In Genesis 41 we see that Joseph, under God's guidance, instructed Pharaoh to save for the famine years. In Leviticus 25:21, God instructed the Israelites to save for the Sabbatical Year. Even ants have the instinct to gather their food in summer (Proverbs 30:25).

If we couple the Old Testament encouragement to save with the advice in 1 Timothy 5:8, "If anyone does not provide for his relatives, and especially for his immediate family, he has denied the faith and is worse than an unbeliever," we have a strong incentive to provide for the future. If we take this responsibility seriously, a reserve margin—or savings—is absolutely necessary. According to the *Random House Dictionary,* a margin is "an amount allowed or available beyond what is absolutely necessary." If we do not have a margin to provide for unforeseen family needs, someone else will have to meet those needs.

Christians who have the "manna complex" feel that a margin as described above is "unspiritual" and indicates a lack of faith. This is not true at all, because God actually provides the margin. A margin does not prevent us from living by faith and being dependent on God, for we are still dependent on God for everything! Health, continuing employment, wisdom in conducting our business—all of life—comes from God.

God desires that we grow into maturity, moving into new frontiers of faith. Romans 1:17 tells us that our righteousness is to be "by faith from first to last" or from faith to faith. We can move from immediate dependence into the experience of thanksgiving and praise for continual blessings. Our faith can progress to higher levels in our hierarchy of needs. We can begin to be responsible stewards, using our capital to provide for our future needs and the needs of others. It is unwise to limit God's provision.

There are several distinct kinds of saving. The first is a reserve for unforeseen needs, for emergencies. This saving enables us to fulfill our responsibilities to provide for ourselves and loved ones. The concept may be extended to include meeting the emergency needs of others by setting aside a portion of our giving.

Another kind of saving is the accumulation of capital to produce continuing future benefits. As we have previously mentioned, this saving will vary in relationship to our calling, gifts, abilities, and convictions.

The third kind of saving is accumulation for the purpose of making a purchase. This actually is not true saving, but is a form of spending. Saving for a future purchase is an excellent way to avoid the use of credit. (We will talk about this in part three of the book.) Such saving is highly recommended, but is not to be confused with a genuine margin for emergencies. A financial counselor told about encouraging a couple to begin saving. The wife was reluctant to give up any immediate purchasing power, but suddenly decided that saving was a good idea if she could use the money to purchase a new refrigerator! Of course this was hardly what the counselor had in mind.

Insurance, within reasonable limits, is also an acceptable way to provide for future contingencies. But we need to maintain a balance in our saving, for it is not possible to provide for everything. The sufficient margin or amount of insurance will be different for each of us. When determining our need, we must ensure that greed is not disguised as provision for the future. Saving should not be utilized as an excuse for unwarranted acquisition. Each of us must determine what is enough. Categorical rules regarding saving would make our stewardship simpler, but would not produce maturity. God has given us freedom and responsibility, and always takes the risks that will allow us to mature.

Avoiding Entrapment
We have pointed out the desirability of being in control of our financial situation in order to free ourselves for other priorities of

life. Many things can prevent us from progressing to financial maturity. If Satan can trap us on the elementary level of finances, he limits our effectiveness. However, most of our financial difficulties originate from within. James reveals the primary source of temptation: "When tempted, no one should say, 'God is tempting me.' . . . But each one is tempted when, by his own evil desire, he is dragged away and enticed" (James 1:13-14).

Difficulties in our financial affairs can originate in several ways. One is to have a distorted understanding of material things, which we considered in our discussion of syndromes of false assumptions (chapter 2).

The most significant trap is that of materialism, which we have discussed at length. It is an attitude of the heart that elevates material possessions to a position of supremacy, thus constituting idolatry. Materialism is expressed in covetousness and possessiveness, and if unchecked leads to more overt acts associated with the selfish acquisition of wealth.

In this section we will consider two secondary traps. It is possible for us to avoid doctrinal distortions and the ideological trap of materialism, and still become entrapped on practical financial levels.

The most common, practical trap is that of indebtedness. The use of credit in biblical times was limited, but the subject is dealt with briefly in Scripture. The book of Proverbs points out some of the potential disadvantages of indebtedness, emphasizing the nature of the debtor-creditor relationship. "The rich rule over the poor, and the borrower is servant to the lender" (Proverbs 22:7). There is also a sense in which debt puts us under bondage, which is an undesirable condition. If we find ourselves in debt, Scripture indicates that we must meet our obligations. "Let no debt remain outstanding, except the continuing debt to love one another" (Romans 13:8).

In Scripture we do not find a flat prohibition against debt, but the tenor is that of warning and caution. Since society today is based on the extensive use of credit, entrapment is a much greater possibility—and often a reality—for Christians. Christian debtors are to meet their obligations, and in fact should place such obligations at the top of their list of priorities for the utilization of money.

In extreme situations there may be exceptions to this rule. God did not want His people in Israel to be in perpetual slavery or debt. On the Sabbatical Year Israelite slaves were to be freed and all debts were to be cancelled. The basic principle here is the provision of a way out of impossible situations. Our society deals with impossible financial situations through bankruptcy laws. This provision is often abused, but in its proper application it can serve the same purpose as the sabbatical forgiveness in the Old Testament.

It is not wrong for Christians to avail themselves of the bankruptcy option if the situation is impossible. Our first responsibility, though, is to meet our obligations. If this is not possible due to immediate pressures, but will be possible over a longer term, the bankruptcy laws provide a special arrangement in which all creditors are eventually paid. In completely hopeless situations, a bankruptcy and new beginning are justified. If Christians lived in true community, our interest in each other's welfare would help prevent such difficulty and provide the resources for resolution if the need arose. The prevention would be provided through the giving and seeking of financial counsel, and resources to resolve a problem would be provided through giving and receiving.

Other scriptural principles do not speak directly to the matter of credit, but definitely apply to its use:

> If we honor God with our finances as the Philippians did, there will be little need for credit because God will honor His promise to supply all our needs. (See Philippians 4:19.)

> If we really learn the secret of contentment—of being satisfied with our situation and with what we have—there will be very little need for credit. (See Philippians 4:11-12.)

If we learn to be patient and exercise the discipline of self-control, there will be very little need for credit.

If we ask God for wisdom in financial matters and exercise our common sense, there will be very little need for credit.

If we want to avoid the bondage of indebtedness, there will be very little use of credit.

My recommendations regarding consumer credit, given in part three of the book, are extremely restrictive. This is because every Scripture reference regarding debtors is negative. Indebtedness is described as slavery.

Common sense tells us that interest charges add to the cost of goods and substantially reduce our purchasing power. Credit often limits our options and reduces our opportunity to buy advantageously. Essentially, consumer credit enables us to have today what we really cannot afford. Credit's main function is to serve materialism.

Another secondary trap is to become obligated for the debts of others. This trap carries all the disadvantages of the personal use of credit plus additional ones. Here are a few of the scriptural warnings given about accepting obligation for others' debts:

A man lacking in judgment strikes hands in pledge
    and puts up security for his neighbor. (Proverbs 17:18)

He who puts up security for another will surely suffer,
    but whoever refuses to strike hands in pledge is safe.
                  (Proverbs 11:15)

My son, if you have put up security for your neighbor . . .
    if you have been trapped by what you said. . .
    do this . . . to free yourself.   (Proverbs 6:1-3)

Do not be a man who strikes hands in pledge
    or puts up security for debts;

if you lack the means to pay,
> your very bed will be snatched from under you.

(Proverbs 22:26-27)

From the language used in the *New International Version,* we would conclude that there is a flat prohibition against being a guarantor. *The Living Bible* modifies these statements somewhat. It refers to the poor judgment of countersigning another's note, not countersigning unless you have the extra cash on hand, and being sure you know the person well before you guarantee his obligation. So from the warning in *The Living Bible* we would learn to exercise extreme precautions: recognizing that guaranteeing another's debt is poor policy, agreeing to never guarantee for a stranger, and deciding to never guarantee more than we could afford to pay.

If we are to avoid credit for ourselves, it would certainly be poor policy to guarantee others' credit. We are instructed to meet the needs of our brothers in community by generous giving. If we are not able to give, we certainly are not able to be responsible for others' debts. There may be occasions, however, when we are able and willing to give, but it would be better to guarantee a loan for that person. So I believe it would be acceptable to guarantee a loan if we are completely willing to pay the debt in the spirit of generosity toward a brother.

Accepting Diversity

Diversity is acceptable in God's Kingdom. Men are created as individuals in God's image, but with great differences. As this individuality is expressed, differences are amplified; the results of choices build on each other. Nowhere is this more obvious than in the economic realm.

Scripture carefully describes our Christian conduct in certain matters. Certain things are morally right, others are morally wrong. These areas of life are black and white. But most of life is not so clearly defined. Most of our decisions regarding Christian conduct fall into the gray area where individual differences come into play. Thus we must make many decisions regarding morally neutral matters on which Scripture gives no clear teaching as to what is right or wrong.

In 1 Corinthians 8 and 10 and Romans 14 Paul deals with the matter of individual liberty in areas of optional standards and disputable judgments. In Romans 14:1-4, he defines the over-scrupulous as weak Christians, and those who recognize the relative nature of these scruples as strong Christians. He instructs the Church to accept the weak, and to avoid being drawn into arguments or forcing judgment on such matters. In verse 5, Paul goes on to say that each person should be free to develop his own convictions. Diversity is to be accepted! Neither the weak nor the strong should judge each other (verses 3,10,13), and the strong should thank God for their clear conscience (verse 22). In another letter Paul says that we are to refuse to let anyone judge us on our convictions (Colossians 2:16).

Many Christians follow a different pattern than what is seen in Scripture. We tend to reverse the definitions of "weak" and "strong" and not only engage in disputes over scruples, but permit the weak to set the standards for the entire body. We resist the idea of diversity, insist on conformity, and judge each other on these matters.

Elisabeth Elliot deals with this problem. She writes, "Sin is sin . . . says the man who sees all things in black and white. There is no question in his mind about right and wrong. He knows. He knows not only what he must do, but what his brother must do . . . or at least what his brother must not do. Does the Scripture teach that sin is sin, in the sense that what is sin for one man is always sin for all? It does *not*. In fact it shows that what may be sin in one man may glorify God in another."[7]

This thought is expressed in 1 Corinthians 8:1-2, and is particularly well stated in the Phillips version: "It is easy to think that we 'know' over problems like this [eating meat sacrificed to idols], but we should remember that while knowledge may make a man look big, it is only love that can make him grow to his full stature. For whatever a man may know, he still has a lot to learn."

The matter of finances is certainly one area where Scripture does not give all the answers in black and white. Instead it gives principles that we are to apply in our progress toward maturity. The results of Scripture's teaching may be different for each of us. The writer of Hebrews describes the mature as those "who by constant use have trained themselves to distinguish good from evil" (Hebrews 5:14). The growth process is often more important than the action itself. The process requires freedom to exercise discernment—even to make mistakes. Enforced rules of conformity do not permit such growth.

We need to help our brothers mature in financial matters, not judge them. The New Testament soundly condemns judging between brothers. Paul directly condemns judgments regarding disputable conduct in Romans 14. Other passages condemn judging on a broader scale.

> Who are you to judge someone else's servant? To his own master he stands or falls. And he will stand, for the Lord is able to make him stand.   (Romans 14:4)

> Each one should be fully convinced in his own mind.
>   (Romans 14:5)

> You then, why do you judge your brother? Or why do you look down on your brother?   (Romans 14:10)

> Therefore let us stop passing judgment on one another.
>   (Romans 14:13)

> You, therefore, have no excuse, you who pass judgment on someone else, for at whatever point you judge the other, you are condemning yourself.   (Romans 2:1)

Judging is dangerous because we ourselves are vulnerable. It is easy to see the "speck" in our brother's eye and to ignore the "plank" in our own, a tendency Jesus warns against in Luke 6:41. We seldom have enough information on which to make a valid judgment on another, even if we were entitled to do so. In the financial area, it is easy to be blind to our own mistakes and extravagances while those of our brother seem so apparent.

If we are to accept diversity in economic matters, it follows that we will respect our brothers regardless of their financial situation. The old delusion that poverty is a sign of God's disapproval and wealth is a sign of moral worth is being displaced by the opposite view. Both are equally wrong, and wealth should have no role in the assessment of a person. We have a tendency to defer to wealth, fame, and power by our actions. James warns against this: "Don't show favoritism. . . If you show special attention to the man wearing fine clothes . . . have you not discriminated among yourselves and become judges with evil thoughts?" (James 2:1-4).

The scriptural principles we have discovered about material things will apply differently to each of us. We are responsible to apply those principles to our own lives, keeping our consciences clear. We need to help and encourage our brothers to apply the same principles in their lives, not condemn them as they struggle toward maturity.

The Role of Investment and Speculation

One use of the term "speculation" indicates the commitment of money in expectation of an abnormally high return. The unusual return may be expected from fortuitous market factors; from the success of a new concept, idea, or invention; or from a company's rapid growth. Speculation is invariably coupled with a high degree of risk.

Another aspect or definition of speculation is that given by Dr. Richard Chewning, of the Chair of Christian Ethics at Baylor

University. "Technically speaking, to 'invest' in something means you are looking for income through the inherent operation itself. To 'speculate' is to look for a change in the value through something that happens externally to the operation itself."[8] Buying bonds for their income would be investing, buying them for an expected dramatic change in interest rates that would increase their selling price would be speculating.

Investment and speculation are not the same. In an investment, the return is expected to fall within a normal range for the type of investment made. This expectation is based on experience, earnings, and ordinary market fluctuations. The risk is reduced to an acceptable level. However, even the most conservative investments involve some risk. A savings bank may fail, and government bonds can change dramatically in liquidation value. For instance, I have a very conservative associate who regarded municipal bonds as the ultimate in after-tax return and safety. But during a period of high interest rates his bonds were worth approximately fifty percent of what he paid for them. Investments usually produce long-term gain, while speculation more commonly yields short-term profit.

None of these distinctions between investment and speculation are precise, because every venture involves both risk and the expectation of profit. There is a continuum rather than a sharp line of distinction. It is easy to differentiate between the most conservative investment such as a guaranteed savings certificate, and a highly leveraged futures contract that depends entirely on correct forecasting to produce a return. Most investment/speculation opportunities fall into the gray area between these extremes. Each of us will make our own distinctions. Something that may be speculation for one person might not be for another who is an expert in the particular field.

While there may be nothing inherently wrong with speculation, there are several aspects to speculation that we need to weigh carefully. Any particular venture is wrong if it causes us to violate our understanding of the scriptural principles regarding money and wealth. In the final analysis, the individual's motivation may be the determining factor for what is right or wrong.

Speculation is dangerous if it is motivated by any of the following spiritual considerations:

A desire to be wealthy.

"People who want to get rich fall into temptation and a trap and into many foolish and harmful desires that plunge men into ruin and destruction. For the love of money is a root of all kinds of evil." (1 Timothy 6:9-10)

A desire for quick wealth, in contrast to faithful stewardship.

"A faithful man will be richly blessed,
but one eager to get rich will not go unpunished."
(Proverbs 28:20)

"He who works his land will have abundant food,
but he who chases fantasies lacks judgment."
(Proverbs 12:11)

"Dishonest money dwindles away,
but he who gathers money little by little makes it
grow." (Proverbs 13:11)

"The plans of the diligent lead to profit,
as surely as haste leads to poverty." (Proverbs 21:5)

A desire to avoid the responsibility of work.

Dissatisfaction with God's present provision. Lack of contentment and thanksgiving. (See Philippians 4:11.)

In addition to these spiritual considerations, we must consider the practical aspects of stewardship. Capital is to be preserved to produce continuing benefit over a long time period. Speculation involves a high probability of the loss of capital.

Scripture offers no exhortations encouraging speculative investments that compare to the exhortations regarding work. There are no promises of reward for speculation similar to the promises of reward for diligence. There is no scriptural basis on which we can expect God to bless us with wisdom for speculation. And I can tell you from experience that speculation does not work. The odds are too great.

From the Scriptures and my own experience, I have discovered one pattern of investment that God invariably blesses. This is our faithful stewardship of the capital He has entrusted to us—the human capital of our gifts, talents, and abilities; and material capital as well. Success is realized by persevering in diligent employment, using the resources God has given us. I have never experienced or observed God's blessing on speculation. He has promised to bless *us* so that He might bring us to maturity. The idea of earning money for God is ridiculous. He does not need the money we can give. It is *we* who need the discipline of work, stewardship, and the privilege of assuming responsibility and expressing God's nature within us through generosity.

Since work is God's appointed way for us to provide for our needs, and we are to curtail our desire for wealth, practice contentment, and be responsible stewards of the capital entrusted to us, speculation is questionable. Wise investment, however, is prudent and constitutes good stewardship.

Special Instructions to the Rich

The first principle that we found in the book of Genesis was that the material universe is good—not evil—and is God's provision for us. We also saw that for the patriarchs, wealth was a sign of God's blessing. In the rest of Scripture we found no general condemnation of wealth, just profit, or wealthy people.

However, Scripture totally condemns injustice. Those who obtain wealth by oppression, exploitation, cheating, stealing, robbery, or murder are harshly condemned. God is against them and on the side of the oppressed and exploited. He is always on the side of justice and against injustice. He is not against the rich, on the side of the poor, although He is certainly sympathetic to the poor, as He is to all human suffering. In Scripture, oppression of the poor does not refer to individual inequality, but to the injustice of reducing people to poverty through corrupt legal systems, oppressive laws, and false measures.

Those caught up in the "guilt syndrome" that we talked about in chapter 2 would not agree with this view. Some have simply failed to make any distinction between unjustly gained wealth and capital as God's provision. Others are convinced that *all* possession of wealth is invariably wrong. But the "guilt syndrome" is not consistent with scriptural examples of wealth as God's blessing, the absence of scriptural denunciation of wealth, Jesus' attitude toward the wealthy He encountered, or the individuality and diversity of man as God created him.

The Bible does deal thoroughly with our attitudes toward wealth, our acquisition of wealth, and our use of wealth. The Bible never condemns wealth itself or those who enjoy it. The Scriptures we have studied regard wealth as evil only under certain conditions: when it is gained through exploitation, oppression, and injustice; when it is excessive and in surfeit; when we depend on wealth instead of God; when our attitudes are materialistic (covetous and possessive); or when our greed deprives others.

While wealth is not condemned, the Scriptures recognize that its possession involves additional challenges and problems, along with opportunities and responsibilities. Paul summarizes both the positive and negative aspects of wealth in 1 Timothy 6:17-19:

> Command those who are rich in this present world not to be arrogant nor to put their hope in wealth, which is so uncertain, but to put their hope in God, who richly provides us with everything for our enjoyment. Command them to

do good, to be rich in good deeds, and to be generous and willing to share. In this way they will lay up treasure for themselves as a firm foundation for the coming age, so that they may take hold of the life that is truly life.

The dangers of wealth are that we might fall victim to the materialistic attitudes of pride, possessiveness, conceit, arrogance, and selfishness. We can place our reliance on riches like the rich farmer in Luke 12, basing our hope on material things rather than on God. We can forget that God has provided everything that we enjoy. These spiritual failures can pave the way for the overt actions of the oppressively wealthy people that are described in James 5.

In contrast to these dangers are the benefits that God intends us to realize from material possessions. They include increased responsibility in stewardship, a greater opportunity for generosity, enhanced brotherhood through giving, and the opportunity to build up treasures in Heaven. Material wealth can be used for eternal purposes. God intends and desires that our possession of wealth will provide all of these benefits.

NOTES:
1. Herbert Schlossberg, *Idols for Destruction* (Nashville, Tennessee: Thomas Nelson, Inc., 1983), page 88.
2. Schlossberg, page 7.
3. Michael Novak, *The Spirit of Democratic Capitalism* (New York: Simon & Schuster, 1982), page 53.
4. Jeremy Rifkin & Ted Howard, *The Emerging Order* (New York: G.P. Putnam's Sons, 1979), page 20.
5. Archibald Thomas Robertson, *Word Pictures in the New Testament* (New York: Harper & Brothers, 1930), Vol. II, page 174.
6. Schlossberg, page 107.
7. Elisabeth Elliot, *The Liberty of Obedience* (Waco, Texas: Word Books, 1968), page 53.
8. Richard Chewning, "Scripture Is Filled with Economic Principles," *Spiritual Fitness in Business*, Vol. 3, No. 4, April 1985.

EIGHT

The Privilege of
Giving and Receiving

In Acts 20:35, Paul quotes words of Jesus that were not recorded in the Gospels: "It is more blessed to give than to receive." We teach this principle to our children in Sunday school, but often we personally view giving to be an obligation rather than a blessing. Yet it is a marvelous experience to learn to see every need as an opportunity, even though we can't personally meet every need.

For most of us, learning to give in this manner takes discipline at first because it runs contrary to our natural selfishness. It takes very little practice, however, for the experience of giving to stimulate our hearts' generosity that comes from God's image within us. When this happens, giving becomes a privilege—one of the most satisfying of all spiritual experiences.

The Blessing of Giving
Paul taught about the blessing of giving, and some of his followers learned the lesson well. In 2 Corinthians 8:2-3, he recorded the

generosity of the Macedonian Christians. "Out of the most severe trial, their overflowing joy and their extreme poverty welled up in rich generosity. For I testify that they gave as much as they were able, and even beyond their ability." Apparently they were in such great poverty that Paul had declined to ask for their help when he was collecting money to help the struggling Christians in Jerusalem. But they heard about the need, and "entirely on their own, they urgently pleaded with us for the privilege of sharing in this service to the saints" (verses 3-4). The Philippian church, the only church that assisted Paul financially, had previously experienced the joy of giving (see Philippians 4:10-19). As we see in 2 Corinthians 8, their vision and habit of generosity had extended throughout Macedonia.

Lydia of Philippi was so generous in welcoming the Apostle Paul that I cannot help but believe she was a motivating force behind the Philippians' generosity. At any rate, Paul said, "Moreover, as you Philippians know, in the early days of your acquaintance with the gospel, when I set out from Macedonia, not one church shared with me in the matter of giving and receiving, except you only" (Philippians 4:15).

I have never read a statement that produces such an ambivalent emotional response as this particular one. Only the Philippians gave to Paul! I rejoice at the privilege of the Philippians in showing their generosity toward the one they had come to love since he had brought them the gospel. I rejoice in the Philippians' privilege of participating in the first, and perhaps the greatest, thrust of the gospel! But my response is sadness when I think of the other Christians who missed the opportunity through selfishness, ignorance, or insensitivity.

Why is giving so satisfying to us and so pleasing to God? I believe it is because giving relates directly to God's image within us and satisfies a need of our essential nature. God is love and expresses His love nature through generous giving. We are created in His image and are most fulfilled when we act in accordance with His loving nature.

This explains why giving is satisfying even to nonChristians. God's image in man has not been completely obliterated. Of course it is true that giving can be motivated by selfish reasons and can be self-serving. But it is also true that much giving, even by nonChristians, is an unconscious expression of God's nature within us. We can be generous because we were created in God's image.

Many passages in Scripture emphasize God's loving nature as expressed in giving.

> For God so loved . . . that he gave his one and only Son."
> (John 3:16)

> He who did not spare his own Son, but gave him up for us all—how will he not also, along with him, graciously give us all things? (Romans 8:32)

> Each of you should look not only to your own interests, but also to the interests of others. Your attitude should be the same as that of Christ Jesus: Who, being in very nature God . . . made himself nothing. (Philippians 2:4-7)

These verses directly tie God's giving of His Son and the Son's willingness to be given to the attitude that we should have toward the interests of other Christians.

Giving is not only satisfying to us and pleasing to God, it greatly enhances community. By giving we participate in the life and ministry of others. We were not created to live alone, but in relationship to others in community. Giving of material things is the economic aspect of community. God's image in man includes both individuality and community, and both are essential to man's nature. God's statement in Genesis 2:18, "It is not good for the man to be alone," can be too narrowly interpreted. Although it primarily refers to marriage as the basic form of community, its implications go much further: leading to the New Testament's strong emphasis on brotherhood and the body.

I believe one reason God established individual property ownership was to make giving possible. Our participation in others' lives extends to participating in their ministries. Paul revealed this aspect of God's accounting system in Philippians 4:17, "Not that I am looking for a gift, but I am looking for what may be credited to your account."

The "indescribable gift" mentioned in 2 Corinthians 9:14-15 has often been interpreted as a reference to Christ: "In their prayers for you their hearts will go out to you, because of the surpassing grace God has given you. Thanks be to God for his indescribable gift!" However, I believe the "indescribable gift" refers to the privilege of giving, which is the subject of the context for verses 14 and 15. I know that the words describe the joy of giving. Thanksgiving is the proper response to the inner satisfaction that comes as generosity in giving expresses the love-nature of God's image within us. Thanksgiving is our response as we realize that giving brings pleasure to God Himself, and as we experience enhanced community through our giving. I have prayed the following prayer hundreds of times:

> Dear God, I thank You for arranging Your economy in
> such a way that I can participate in the lives and ministries
> of others through the simple mechanisms of giving and
> praying.

I'm overwhelmed by this "indescribable gift!" God has expressed His generosity by allowing us to participate in it!

Giving and Receiving in Community

The concept of giving implies ownership; we can give only if something is ours to give. Giving is based on man's individuality and personal ownership of property. The necessity of community reveals another aspect of giving. Since we are complete only in community, giving to enhance community is beneficial to the giver as well as the receiver.

One possible definition of giving is that of an owner who voluntarily gives to others. A more complete definition of giving would emphasize the spontaneous, natural, nearly inevitable sharing that can take place within close community. (And nothing will more surely produce close community than giving!) In genuine community, the individual as the giver is de-emphasized while the concept of a community of sharers is emphasized. In true community, giving becomes sharing.

I believe that voluntary giving in the context of community is seen in the example of God's giving, which was a voluntary act from an individual God to man. He gave voluntarily because of love. Since love is the essence of God's nature, its expression in generous giving was inevitable. Having created man to fellowship with Him in community, it became a necessity that God should give, even to the extent of giving Himself.

The Incarnation was the ultimate expression of giving in community. These two aspects of giving are based on God's nature as individual and as community. This is to some degree as inscrutable as the concept of the Trinity.

Maturity in giving occurs as we move from emphasis on the individual as the giver to the spontaneous sharing in community. The first aspect is always present, but the second aspect can become predominant. Let me share an example of this.

A very close friend of mine returned from twenty-five years of missionary service and settled in the city where I live. As is often the case, neither my friend nor his missionary organization had made any provision for his relocation to this country. My friend's income had not been sufficient for savings, and the organization had not provided for this need. As a builder, I was able to put him into a new house and give substantial assistance during his career transition. It was only after my friend expressed his appreciation that I thought of those transactions as giving. The sharing had been so natural and spontaneous, and our identification in God's Kingdom so complete, that I had never perceived the relationship as one of an individual giving to another.

On another occasion, a missionary friend returned home without savings, and two of us agreed to provide funds for a down payment on a house. I was aware that another missionary who lived in the same city was going overseas and desired to sell his house. I thought the house would be perfect for the returning family, so I suggested that my friend consider purchasing it. He wondered whether the asking price would be equitable. I replied that it really did not make any difference. If the price was low, my friend would benefit. If the price was high, the departing missionary would benefit and put the proceeds to good use in God's Kingdom. The returning missionary followed my advice and purchased the house at the first mentioned price. (Incidentally, the price was more than fair, and the outgoing family left many of their personal effects with the house.)

I believe this must have been the spirit of sharing that existed in the Jerusalem church when "no one claimed that any of his possessions was his own" (Acts 4:32). I believe this type of sharing is what Paul had in mind when he used the Incarnation as an example to encourage us to "look not only to your own interests, but also to the interests of others" (Philippians 2:4). In this kind of brotherhood, where sharing in community is the norm, receiving is as natural as giving.

Our society's emphasis on extreme individualism makes it difficult for many people to receive. One obstacle to gracious receiving is pride. Our natural selfish nature, which does not understand giving and is therefore uncomfortable with receiving, is also an obstacle to gracious receiving.

Another obstacle to receiving is of a more positive nature—the desire to be on the giving side of the equation. Scripture encourages this desire. Jesus directly stated that giving is better than receiving. Paul said, "These hands of mine have supplied my own needs and the needs of my companions . . . by this kind of hard work we must help the weak" (Acts 20:34-35). He instructs Christians to work in order to "have something to share with those in need" (Ephesians 4:28), and to work "so that your daily life may win the respect of outsiders and so that you will not be dependent on anybody" (1 Thessalonians 4:12).

When the occasion arises, we should not be reluctant to receive. In spite of his admonitions on giving, Paul joyfully received from the Philippians. Our need to receive may be temporary because of circumstances, or may be permanent because of calling. In fact, the only situation in which receiving should be long-term or permanent is when the receiver's calling justifies it. For the rest of us, the need to receive should be temporary. Paul makes it clear that we are to manage our financial affairs in a way that enables us to be on the giving side of the transaction. With this understanding, we are free to graciously receive, whether our need is temporary or permanent.

An exception to man's general reluctance to receive is found among Christians who have fallen prey to the "dependency syndrome"—the desire to remain in immediate dependence on God's emergency provision. These Christians are unwilling to become productive members of the body, to assume responsibility for their own welfare, and to be able to help others. I have observed that these Christians tend to relate their dependency to God, rather than to the brothers who help them. In testimony of God's wonderful provision, they say very little about the giver— the person God uses to make the provision. Instead, the emphasis is on the receiving as though it were better than giving. Among these Christians, any reluctance to receive—whether it stems from pride or the scriptural encouragement to be responsible—is sublimated to an exaggerated dependency on God.

When giving becomes spontaneous sharing in community and each member of the community meets his or her responsibility, there is no need for any reluctance to give or receive. Reluctance is superseded by the recognition of the great diversity and different gifts within the Body. Those who live in such community also recognize that roles are subject to change. For example, when asking for help for the afflicted Christians in Jerusalem, Paul said, "At the present time your plenty will supply what they need, so that in turn their plenty will supply what you need" (2 Corinthians 8:14). In Christian community, "This is mine, I will give it," becomes, "This is God's provision, we will share it."

Earlier in this chapter I gave an example of spontaneous sharing between individuals. Such sharing can also occur between Christian communities. When I first became acquainted with the dynamic, young Christians in Brazil, many of them were students and only a few had begun their professional careers. Their funds were extremely limited, but they recognized the need to build upon a Brazilian cultural and financial base without becoming dependent on outside help. This was very commendable although it was partially based on Latin pride and a fear of being under the influence of "America do Norte." The real basis of their desire, however, was the determination to build indigenously and responsibly.

A group of us in Minneapolis had provided the financial base for Jim and Marge Petersen, the Americans who began the work among these Brazilian intellectuals. After six years, Jim invited two of us to visit Brazil, informing us that the "turma" (Body) there was now mature enough to cope with "gringos." Our bond as brothers in Christ was virtually instantaneous. It was not long until they regarded us as members of the "turma." They decided that distance was not a barrier to unity in Christ, and that the national origin of our money was secondary to our identification in God's Kingdom. They concluded that there were times when our financial assistance could be helpful, provided that it was done in ways that would not create dependency or make them less responsible.

On one occasion the "turma" decided that one of their members in a university city should spend all of his time working with students and new Christians. The "turma" committed themselves to his monthly support, a commitment that resembled the Macedonians' generosity. They were, however, unable to provide an automobile that was necessary for the work. Deciding that this was an instance when the brothers in Minneapolis could help, they located a good used Volkswagen and informed us of their project. I replied that they should proceed with the purchase because we would provide the funds. Their reply was extremely satisfying to me. They informed us that they had purchased the car the day they sent the letter, since they had no doubt about our response. This was not giving! This was sharing in community!

The Privilege of Giving Is for Everyone

In 2 Corinthians 8 and 9, Paul writes to all the Christians in Corinth and refers to an act of giving by the Macedonian churches. He says the latter responded with generosity in spite of their "extreme poverty" and "great trial." This passage alone should make it clear that the grace of giving is a privilege intended for all of us.

> And now, brothers, we want you to know about the grace that God has given the Macedonian churches. Out of the most severe trial, their overflowing joy and their extreme poverty welled up in rich generosity. For I testify that they gave us much as they were able, and even beyond their ability. Entirely on their own, they urgently pleaded with us for the privilege of sharing in this service to the saints. . . . So we urged Titus . . . to bring also to completion this act of grace on your part. But just as you excel in everything . . . see that you also excel in this grace of giving. . . .
>
> For you know the grace of our Lord Jesus Christ, that though he was rich, yet for your sakes he became poor, so that you through his poverty might become rich.
>
> (2 Corinthians 8:1-9)

In addition to describing giving as a grace, Paul describes it as a service. As a grace, it is compared to the grace of Christ who gave Himself. As a service, it is related to other Christians.

Often those who have limited means feel they cannot give because they have so little that their gifts will amount to nothing. The story of the widow's offering in Mark 12:42 should dispel this concern, as well as Paul's statement that "if the willingness is there, the gift is acceptable according to what one has, not according to what he does not have" (2 Corinthians 8:12).

On the other hand, the wealthy—and those who would criticize them—tend to feel that their gifts are not sacrificial enough. Giving from abundance is different from giving out of poverty. It presents an entirely different set of stewardship considerations. We have noted the warnings to the rich about the dangers of wrong attitudes toward possessions and the special instructions given to the wealthy. We have also observed Jesus' attitude toward wealthy individuals. Nowhere have we found an indication or a general instruction that they should reduce themselves to poverty. The one exception to this was the special situation of the rich, young man who came to Jesus.

Mark 14:3-7 gives us insight into Jesus' attitude toward gifts from the wealthy. He accepted an expensive gift of perfume, allowed it to be poured on His head (wasted, the disciples thought), and commended the giver.

God looks at the heart of the giver, not at the cost of the gift: at the spirit, not the amount. So the privilege—the grace of giving—is intended for everyone. As such it should be desired and cultivated.

Giving as a Special Gift

The special gift of giving is a gift over and above the grace of giving that all Christians should desire and cultivate. The teaching about special gifts within the body is introduced in the New Testament in connection with its elevated concept of community. The special gift of giving is an extension of the diversity that is part of man's nature as God created him. In the following quotations we see that all Christians are encouraged to help each other. We also see references to a special gift of giving:

> Share with God's people who are in need. Practice
> hospitality.   (Romans 12:13)

> There should be no division in the body, but . . . its parts
> should have equal concern for each other.
>   (1 Corinthians 12:25)

> Therefore, as we have opportunity, let us do good to all
> people, especially to those who belong to the family of
> believers.   (Galatians 6:10)

> We have different gifts, according to the grace given us. If a
> man's gift is prophesying, let him use it in proportion to his
> faith. If it is serving, let him serve; if it is teaching, let him
> teach; it if is encouraging, let him encourage; if it is contrib-
> uting to the needs of others, let him give generously.
>   (Romans 12:6-8)

> Now you are the body of Christ, and each one of you is a
> part of it. And in the church God has appointed . . . those
> able to help others.   (1 Corinthians 12:27-28)

Since we are all to have "equal concern for each other" and are to place each other's interests equal to our own, everyone should help others. But some people within the Christian community have a special ability to meet others' needs. So when we refer to giving as a special gift, we're talking about the degree of involvement, a God-given ability to specialize in giving.

Those who exercise the gift of giving have a special ability to discern genuine needs and a special sensitivity to identify with another's situation. They also have the capacity to relate to those with needs and to offer help graciously, in an understanding way that truly benefits the recipient. They also have the resources to meet needs. This does not necessarily mean they have great wealth, but they have a willingness to use what they have in the service of others.

The majority of those with the gift of giving have very ordinary means. But they are observant, sensitive, thoughtful, discerning, and willing to use what they have. They are alert to opportunities and quick to seize them. Their discernment enables them to offer assistance before they are asked, putting the relationship between the giver and receiver on a level not otherwise possible.

The biblical references I quoted in relation to the gift of giving all refer to helping other individuals, which is undoubtedly the most neglected aspect of giving today. The impulse to help others can be expressed through contributions to humanitarian causes, but that is not the tenor in the New Testament. The New Testament refers to individuals who relate and give to other individuals within the Body, the community, that is their normal sphere of influence. Humanitarian philanthropy, giving to organizations or causes, and supporting churches or the missionary enterprise are all worthwhile. I'm not demeaning these outlets for giving, but I am simply pointing out that they are not mentioned in the New Testament in connection with the gift of giving.

In some cases, the gift of giving involves the production of wealth. Wealth certainly facilitates the gift of giving, but having a great deal of money to distribute does not in itself constitute the gift of giving. It is my observation that individuals demonstrate the gift of giving before God entrusts them with great amounts to give. This is implied in 2 Corinthians 9:8-11:

> And God is able to make all grace abound to you, so that in all things at all times, having all that you need, you will abound in every good work. . . . Now he who supplies seed to the sower and bread for food will also supply and

increase your store of seed and will enlarge the harvest of your righteousness. You will be made rich in every way so that you can be generous on every occasion.

A person with the gift of giving has learned the lesson of Philippians 2:4 well: "Each of you should look not only to your own interests, but also to the interests of others." Since giving itself is so pleasing to God and so satisfying to us, it is indeed a privilege to be a specialist who has the gift of giving!

NINE

Characteristics, Results, and Rewards of Giving

If giving is a privilege and is the natural expression of God's image within us, we would expect to find that His revelation in the Scriptures describes giving extensively. This is true, even though the subject is not treated exhaustively in any one place. We will find, by looking at numerous portions of Scripture, that together they present a comprehensive picture of God's view of giving.

Most of the characteristics of giving relate primarily to the giver rather than the gift. Similarly, the results and rewards of giving affect the giver. This is consistent with God's purpose in permitting us to give. His objective is not the gift, but the maturity of the giver as he expresses God's image. So when we talk about giving in this way, we are not talking about the act of giving as much as we are about the nature of the giver.

Characteristics of Giving
When the scriptural characteristics of giving are present, our

giving is truly an expression of God's image within us. We have discussed some of these characteristics previously, so I will just review them briefly here.

Giving must be voluntary. By definition, giving is voluntary. The only compulsion for true giving stems from the nature of the individual giver: God's nature within us, the nature of love.

We are sometimes confused about this because certain Old Testament requirements were mandatory. The tithe was mandatory, but this tithe did not actually belong to the individual. God had reserved it for Himself. Similarly God reserved the firstborn and the first fruits for Himself. The firstborn were God's because God had destroyed all the Egyptian firstborn, but spared the Israelites. The first fruits were God's because God had given them the covenant land and brought them safely into it. The Israelites' real giving consisted of freewill offerings and vows to God, and generous giving to poor and needy brothers, widows and orphans, the Levites, and strangers and travelers. The Israelites were taught to do these things, but did them on a voluntary basis.

Voluntary giving demonstrates love, which Paul compares directly with Christ's love. "I am not commanding you, but I want to test the sincerity of your love by comparing it with the earnestness of others. For you know the grace of our Lord Jesus Christ, that though he was rich, yet for your sakes he became poor, so that you through his poverty might become rich" (2 Corinthians 8:8-9).

Giving must be cheerful. We have seen that God is primarily interested in our attitude toward money, and our attitude toward money is clearly demonstrated through our giving. In both the Old and New Testaments, the proper attitude of cheerfulness is contrasted with giving that is done grudgingly:

> Do not be hardhearted or tightfisted toward your poor
> brother. Rather be openhanded and freely lend him what-
> ever he needs. Be careful not to harbor this wicked thought:

> "The seventh year, the year for cancelling debts, is near. . . ." Give generously to him and do so without a grudging heart.   (Deuteronomy 15:7-10)

> Each man should give what he has decided in his heart to give, not reluctantly or under compulsion, for God loves a cheerful giver.   (2 Corinthians 9:7)

The Macedonians had urgently pleaded with Paul for the privilege of giving, and Paul had reminded the Corinthians of their eager willingness to give. If we join those New Testament Christians in recognizing that giving is a privilege, we will have no trouble maintaining a cheerful attitude in giving.

The amount of our giving is to be proportionate and generous. God has never suggested a set percentage for giving. The tithe was common in the ancient world prior to, and independent of, its biblical usage. Abraham and Jacob voluntarily gave or promised a tenth of their increase in certain situations. The tithe for the Levites was a portion God had reserved for Himself, and God was the One who gave it to the Levites. The Law was clear that if the Israelites used this tithe for themselves, they were actually stealing it from God. Jesus used the word "tithe" only once—when speaking to the Pharisees—and Paul, in spite of his very extensive treatment of giving, never used the word.

I am not at all opposed to an individual decision to give ten percent. In fact, this is an excellent place to begin the habit of giving. I am, however, opposed to the idea that a ten percent tithe is a scripturally imposed, mandatory standard. If it is mandatory, it obviates the voluntary essence of giving. Nothing in the New Testament indicates that there is a scripturally imposed, mandatory standard. Also, if we regard a certain percentage as God's definition of adequate giving, it is easy to conclude that that amount is sufficient. For most of us in an affluent society, this is not the case; ten percent should be just the beginning of our generosity.

Our proclivity to teach tithing is just one aspect of our tendency to prefer rules to freedom. It is much easier to memorize the rules than to exercise our senses to determine what is right. In matters of giving, as in all matters of liberty, we are reluctant to give our brothers the freedom to determine God's will for themselves; we prefer regulations that establish uniformity. The New Testament concept of giving is so beautiful and its standards are so high that it is difficult to understand why we resort to legalism. It appears that we feel God made a mistake in this area, and fear that our organizations would be in financial difficulty if we followed the biblical pattern.[1]

Instead of following legalistic standards, the amount of our giving should be based on two New Testament principles. The first is proportionality. "On the first day of every week, each one of you should set aside a sum of money in keeping with his income, saving it up" (1 Corinthians 16:2). The *King James Version* says, "as God hath prospered him." What a perfect opportunity for Paul to remind the Corinthians of the tithe if that was an essential part of his teaching. In this passage he could have told them that this sum of money could be a part of their tithe, that it must be in addition to their tithe, that it should be alms to the poor and did not really count as part of their giving, or that it should not interfere with their "storehouse tithing." The fact is, Paul avoided any mention of a fixed percentage. He desired that the Corinthians' gifts be voluntary, proportionate to their income and ability to give, and in proper relationship to other factors.

Proportionate giving, rather than tithing, is the consistent New Testament standard. In Antioch, for example, "The disciples, each according to his ability, decided to provide help for the brothers living in Judea" (Acts 11:29). The Macedonians gave "as much as they were able . . . entirely on their own" (2 Corinthians 8:3). The Corinthians were encouraged to give "according to [their] means. For if the willingness is there, the gift is acceptable according to what one has, not according to what he does not have" (2 Corinthians 8:11-12). Later Paul instructed the Corinthians that "each man should give what he has decided in his heart to give, not reluctantly or under compulsion" (2 Corinthians 9:7). The tithe may be proportionate for someone making $10,000 per year, but not at all proportionate for someone making $100,000. In the New Testament, the individual determines the proper proportion for giving before the Lord. As we have seen, there is a good deal of scriptural teaching that will lead each individual to make the correct decision.

Generosity is the second principle that should determine the amount of our giving. Generosity is pleasing to God. Even relatively obscure habits of generosity are noted in Scripture. A disciple named Dorcas had the reputation of "always doing good and helping the poor" (Acts 9:36). The message to Cornelius was that "God has heard your prayer and remembered your gifts to the poor" (Acts 10:31). The Israelites were instructed to be generous, an admonition that is continued throughout Scripture:

> One man gives freely, yet gains even more;
>> another withholds unduly, but comes to poverty.
> A generous man will prosper. (Proverbs 11:24-25)

> A generous man will himself be blessed,
>> for he shares his food with the poor. (Proverbs 22:9)

> Remember this: Whoever sows sparingly will also reap sparingly, and whoever sows generously will also reap generously. (2 Corinthians 9:6)

> Command them [the rich] to do good, to be rich in good deeds, and to be generous and willing to share.
>> (1 Timothy 6:18)

God is generous and takes every opportunity to express His generosity. He is pleased when we reflect His character. So we need to be generous and look for every opportunity to be generous. The selfish man has tunnel vision that is focused entirely on his own interests; the generous man has peripheral vision that enables him to observe others' needs. I appreciate two verses that tie this concept together:

> The liberal soul shall be made fat; and he that watereth shall be watered also himself.   (Proverbs 11:25, KJV)

> But the liberal (generous) deviseth liberal things; and by liberal things shall he stand.   (Isaiah 32:8, KJV)

This last verse implies planned generosity!

Giving should be regular and systematic. In his instructions to the Corinthians, Paul suggested that they set aside their gifts each week (1 Corinthians 16:2). He was aware of the discrepancies that develop between our intentions and actions, so he suggested a weekly discipline. Although there is nothing universal about the weekly arrangment he suggested, it is necessary to plan our giving. Paul emphasized planned giving in 2 Corinthians 9:7, "Each man should give what he has decided in his heart to give." The Corinthians were to decide the amount of their giving, set it aside, and complete the gift when Paul arrived. Our human weakness reveals the need for advance decision and planning, even without scriptural commandment.

Perhaps the best policy is to set money aside for giving when we receive our income. I strongly recommend establishing a special account into which we make regular and proportionate deposits for giving. With such a system, our gifts will be available for distribution as needs arise and as God leads. We can also meet our regular obligations such as church and missionary support out of this account.

Remember, we are the stewards of our gifts. If we follow the scriptural pattern, much of our giving will be to meet others' needs. Our giving account will enable us to give immediately when opportunities arise. We should not abdicate the privilege and responsibility of stewardship by giving everything to an organization. When we give solely to organizations, we miss the joy of personal participation in the lives and ministries of others.

Giving should be without display.

Be careful not to do your "acts of righteousness" before men, to be seen by them. If you do, you will have no reward from your Father in heaven.

"So when you give to the needy, do not announce it with trumpets, as the hypocrites do in the synagogues and on the streets, to be honored by men. I tell you the truth, they have received their reward in full. But when you give to the needy, do not let your left hand know what your right hand is doing, so that your giving may be in secret.

(Matthew 6:1-4)

Jesus linked ostentation with hypocrisy, both in this passage and in Matthew 23:23, where the Pharisees made sure everyone knew that they gave a tenth even of the spices from their gardens—but abrogated justice, mercy, and faithfulness. Their ostentation in giving was a deliberate attempt to appear righteous when they were the opposite. As usual, the important thing in God's eyes was the motivation, not the action. The motivation behind their giving was not to be righteous, but to be applauded as righteous. Since that was their motivation, they received their reward on earth, but would receive no reward in Heaven.

If our desire is to build treasure in Heaven rather than to receive the acclaim of men, we need to be conscious of both our motivation and our actions. Our giving should not be publicized, but if our motivation and attitudes are right, I do not believe that our giving must always be completely secret.

Paul motivated both the Corinthians and the Macedonians by telling each about the other's willingness and eagerness to give. In Hebrews 10:24 we are told to "consider how we may spur one another on toward love and good deeds." I have often been motivated to give through the action of a generous brother, and I trust that I have been able to encourage others to do the same. But this encouragement cannot be accomplished through the kind of ostentation Jesus condemned. The only thing that such ostentatious giving could possibly stimulate would be the attempt to outdo others. Paul did not want to run the race of life in vain. Neither should we want to compromise our giving by doing it with improper motivation or action.

The Results of Giving

Giving produces many positive results. These results are often mentioned in Scripture, so I have listed some of the results and the corresponding Scriptures.

Giving causes thanksgiving and praise.

> Through us your generosity will result in thanksgiving to God. This service that you perform is not only supplying the needs of God's people but is also overflowing in many expressions of thanks to God. Because of the service by which you have proved yourselves, men will praise God for the obedience that accompanies your confession of the gospel of Christ, and for your generosity in sharing with them and with everyone else.   (2 Corinthians 9:11-13)

> The gifts you sent . . . are a fragrant offering, an acceptable sacrifice, pleasing to God.   (Philippians 4:18)

> I thank my God every time I remember you.
>   (Philippians 1:3)

Giving causes rejoicing.

> I rejoice greatly in the Lord that at last you have renewed your concern for me. . . . [Your gifts] are a fragrant offering, an acceptable sacrifice, pleasing to God.
>   (Philippians 4:10,18)

Giving causes prayer.

And in their prayers for you their hearts will go out to you, because of the surpassing grace God has given you.

(2 Corinthians 9:14)

I thank my God every time I remember you. In all my prayers for all of you, I always pray with joy because of your partnership in the gospel from the first day until now.

(Philippians 1:3-5)

Giving produces maturity.

We want you to know about the grace that God has given the Macedonian churches . . . see that you also excel in this grace of giving. (2 Corinthians 8:1,7)

[God] . . . will enlarge the harvest of your righteousness.

(2 Corinthians 9:10)

Giving encourages others to give.

And now, brothers, we want you to know about the grace that God has given the Macedonian churches. . . . Entirely on their own, they urgently pleaded with us for the privilege of sharing in this service to the saints. (2 Corinthians 8:1-4)

For I know your eagerness to help, and I have been boasting about it to the Macedonians, telling them that since last year you in Achaia were ready to give; and your enthusiasm has stirred most of them into action. (2 Corinthians 9:2)

The Rewards of Giving

God blesses the giver in many ways. There are many specific returns to giving, but these must be understood in a larger context of living in obedience to God. It is not possible to isolate giving from the whole flow of obedience and discipleship. God looks on the heart and judges according to its intent. It is dangerous, then, to extricate a promise from its context and apply it universally.

An example of such a promise is found in Malachi, where God describes the nation Israel as totally corrupt. The Israelites have despised God's name and offered Him no honor or respect. He accuses them of profanity, contempt, and breaking their vows. The Levites have violated their covenant and caused stumbling. The people have been guilty of partiality in law, of breaking faith with the wives of their youth, and of divorce. They have become sorcerers, adulterers, perjurers, defrauders of laborers, and oppressors of the widows and fatherless. They have deprived aliens of justice, have said that serving God is futile, and have robbed God of the tithe He reserved for Himself. In Malachi 1:10 God says, "I will accept no offering from your hands." In 3:10 He promises that if they bring their whole tithe into the storehouse He will bless them abundantly. In 3:12 He continues, "Then all the nations will call you blessed, for yours will be a delightful land."

Is God saying that the Israelites can bring the tithe, continue with all the other abominations, and still receive His blessing? No! Such an interpretation would be a classic example of removing a text from its context. The very idea of God trading His blessing for a ten-percent tithe from a rebellious people is repugnant. God's promise is related to the total repentance called for by Malachi. The likelihood that they would bring the tithes when they had totally rejected God is remote indeed. If they did so, in a crass attempt to buy God's favor, I do not believe He would accept it, for He had told them that He would accept no offering from their hands.

In Matthew 5:23, Jesus insists on our reconciliation with any alienated brother before we make an offering to God. Maturity in giving is usually the result of maturity in other areas. So generous giving is invariably linked to discipleship, and the disciple who gives generously will receive many benefits of God's blessing.

Giving produces a spiritual return. When we give, God promises to direct the fullness of His grace toward us. With a generous measure of blessing, He will make us rich in every way—meeting all of our needs, which will result in the fullness of our souls. Here are some examples of His blessing:

> And my God will meet all your needs according to his glorious riches in Christ Jesus.   (Philippians 4:19)

> Give, and it will be given to you. A good measure, pressed down, shaken together and running over, will be poured into your lap. For with the measure you use, it will be measured to you.   (Luke 6:38)

> And God is able to make all grace abound to you. . . . You will be made rich in every way.   (2 Corinthians 9:8,11)

> The liberal soul shall be made fat.   (Proverbs 11:25, KJV)

Giving can produce a material return. The promises of reward for giving are primarily spiritual. The promises quoted above include material blessings, but each in a very special way. The "all your needs" of Philippians 4:19 should be interpreted in light of 2 Corinthians 8:14, where Paul wrote, "At the present time your plenty will supply what they need, so that in turn their plenty will supply what you need." The reference is to basic needs in time of need. The "having all that you need" of 2 Corinthians 9:8-11 has a specific objective in that it would enable them to "abound in every good work . . . so that you can be generous on every occasion." In a similar manner, Jesus' teachings contain broad promises of reward for following Him that could include material blessing, but which could hardly be interpreted as the emphasis of His teaching.

The only specific promises of material prosperity as a result of giving were made to the nation Israel. These promises were part of the special arrangement between God, the nation Israel, and the Promised Land He had given to them. Here are some of the promises:

If you follow my decrees and are careful to obey my commands, I will send you rain in its season, and the ground
will yield its crops and the trees of the field their fruit. . . .
You will eat all the food you want and live in safety in your
land.   (Leviticus 26:3-5)

Give generously to him [your poor brother] and do so
without a grudging heart; then because of this the LORD
your God will bless you in all your work and in everything
you put your hand to.   (Deuteronomy 15:10)

Honor the Lord with your wealth,
     with the firstfruits of all your crops;
then your barns will be filled to overflowing,
     and your vats will brim over with new wine.
                                           (Proverbs 3:9-10)

In the absence of similar promises in the New Testament, it
does not seem justifiable to extend these conditions and their
rewards beyond the nation of Israel. Garry Friesen, in *Decision
Making & the Will of God,* summarizes this point: "The Old
Testament pattern is no longer operational . . . the promise of
material blessing for obedience is no longer applicable."[2]

In the area of expecting material rewards for our giving, we
need to guard against compromising our motives. Recently a
businessman told me that he was "getting into tithing this year, to
see if it works." His further comments revealed that he expected
God to see to it that he would have a very profitable year, since
God would benefit from the ten percent he planned to give. In
response, I attempted to explain to him the true nature and
privilege of giving as giving.

The saying, "You can't outgive God," is absolutely true, but
God does not always reciprocate according to our timetable or in
exactly the way we expect. My father often told the story of the
atheistic farmer who bragged that his crops were better than those

of the Christians whom he saw at church every Sunday while he worked his fields next door. His Christian neighbor replied, "God doesn't always settle His accounts in October!"

I'm afraid that the more we expect God to pay us back with material blessings, the less likely He is to do so. We need to remember that *giving is giving;* it is not trading or bartering for blessings. Giving is not "the best financial investment you will ever make" if it is done as a financial investment.

I received a book recently that contained a chapter entitled, "The Giver is the Getter." My worst suspicions were aroused by the title and confirmed by the content: "So, if you're basically greedy, take heart. You have every reason to become a hilarious giver. The more you give, the more God gives back to you. Giving is not only a no-risk investment, the returns are great."[3]

God is not interested in making financial deals, in guaranteeing a "no-risk investment," or in rewarding "basically greedy" manipulators of His generosity. He is interested in our spiritual maturity, and is looking at our thoughts and the intent of our hearts. How can we think that He will reward greed and selfishness that is thinly disguised as giving? "God cannot be mocked. A man reaps what he sows" (Galatians 6:7).

In Acts 4, we see the spontaneous generosity of some of the Jerusalem Christians who sold their property and gave the money to meet the needs of others. I'm sure that God rewarded them for their generosity, but the result was not prosperity. In fact, things became so difficult for them that Paul collected funds from the Gentiles to help meet their needs. He in turn did not promise prosperity to the Gentiles who gave, but assured them that the assistance would be returned when they found themselves in need. "At the present time your plenty will supply what they need, so that in turn their plenty will supply what you need. Then there will be equality" (2 Corinthians 8:14). In both cases, the reward for giving was the experience of the grace of giving and the promise of future receiving rather than prosperity. Stanley C. Baldwin summarized the point this way: "'God wants you to prosper' is less accurate than 'God wants you to learn the grace of both giving and receiving.'"⁴

The Apostle Paul says that for the sake of Christ, "I have lost all things" (Philippians 3:8). Baldwin asks the question, "Can we honestly assure people today that the same thing won't happen to them?"⁵ Paul had not been guaranteed prosperity, but had learned how to handle either prosperity or poverty (Philippians 4:11-12). It seems that in Paul's case, "'God wants you to prosper' would seem to be less accurate than 'God wants you to learn how to handle both abundance and being in need.'"⁶

God wants to be generous to us because that is His nature. He wants us to give as an expression of His nature within us. If we give as an expression of Christ's love in our hearts, and not with the expectation of financial return, God is free to bless us in any way He chooses. When He blesses us with material things, He has a specific sequence in mind: "He . . . will also supply and increase your store of seed and will enlarge the harvest of your righteousness. You will be made rich in every way so that you can be generous on every occasion" (2 Corinthians 9:10-11).

Giving enhances community and brotherhood. The most immediately gratifying reward of giving and receiving is found in enhanced relationships. In 2 Corinthians 9, Paul promised that the service of giving would overflow in "many expressions of thanks to God" and that men would praise God for their obedience and generosity. Then, in verses 14-15, he continues, "Their hearts will go out to you, because of the surpassing grace God has given you. Thanks be to God for his indescribable gift!" It is indeed an indescribable privilege to express the grace of God to another Christian. Through giving and receiving, brotherhood and community are realized in a unique way.

Giving brings shared rewards. It is wonderful that God has set up His economy in such a way that we can participate in the ministry of others through giving. God is entirely capable of providing directly for our brothers' needs, but He has chosen to give each of us this privilege by making us interdependent in community. He also promises that, because of our contribution, we will share in the reward for our brothers' ministry! It is as though He is looking for excuses to be generous. This expression of God's generosity is made clear in several verses:

> The share of the man who stayed with the supplies is to be the same as that of him who went down to the battle. All will share alike.   (1 Samuel 30:24)

> And how can they preach unless they are sent? As it is written, "How beautiful are the feet of those who bring good news!"   (Romans 10:15)

> In all my prayers for all of you, I always pray with joy because of your partnership in the gospel from the first day until now.   (Philippians 1:4-5)

> In the early days of your acquaintance with the gospel, . . . not one church shared with me in the matter of giving and receiving, except you only.   (Philippians 4:15)

> Not that I am looking for a gift, but I am looking for what may be credited to your account.   (Philippians 4:17)

Jesus' exhortation to lay up treasure in Heaven takes on new meaning in this context. What a privilege to enter into the ministry of others. God's generosity is overwhelming!

Giving brings a future return. Since we are specifically told to use material wealth to build treasure in Heaven, it is obvious that the most important reward for our giving will be in the future. Jesus promised that those who suffered loss for the Kingdom's sake would receive a hundredfold in this life and the future reward of eternal life (Mark 10:29-30). We will each "receive what is due him for the things done while in the body, whether good or bad" (2 Corinthians 5:10). Several portions of Scripture make it clear

that this future accounting will include a reward for our stewardship of material things:

> Do not store up for yourselves treasures on earth, where
> moth and rust destroy, and where thieves break in and steal.
> But store up for yourselves treasures in heaven, where moth
> and rust do not destroy, and where thieves do not break in
> and steal. For where your treasure is, there your heart will
> be also.   (Matthew 6:19-21)

> I tell you, use worldly wealth to gain friends for yourselves,
> so that when it is gone, you will be welcomed into eternal
> dwellings.   (Luke 16:9)

> Not that I am looking for a gift, but I am looking for what
> may be credited to your account.   (Philippians 4:17)

> Command them [the rich] to do good, to be rich in good
> deeds, and to be generous and willing to share. In this way
> they will lay up treasure for themselves as a firm foundation
> for the coming age.   (1 Timothy 6:18-19)

God will reward us for our stewardship of the material things
He has entrusted to us. We can use worldly wealth to realize
eternal blessings. We can do this by direct investment in God's
Kingdom and can share in our brother's eternal reward by giving
and receiving.

One of the most significant rewards of giving will be the
eternal extension of everything we talked about regarding brotherhood and community. The process of giving and receiving
establishes a sharing relationship between us and our brother. As
that brother serves, others in turn receive, and some enter the
Kingdom through that brother's ministry. Through giving, the
sphere of our service and its accompanying reward is expanded far
beyond our comprehension. I believe the faithful Christian will be
amazed to see the extent of the influence of his or her service in

eternity. The earthly relationships with our brothers and sisters and the visible results are highly rewarding, yet the eternal returns will be of even greater significance.

NOTES:
1. For a very concise discussion of the biblical teaching on tithing, please refer to chapter 22 of *Decision Making & the Will of God* by Garry Friesen. This is an excellent book with a solid biblical base.
2. Garry Friesen, *Decision Making & the Will of God* (Portland, Oregon: Multnomah Press, 1980), pages 358, 360.
3. Russ Johnston, *God Can Make It Happen* (Wheaton, Illinois: Victor Books, 1976), pages 78-79.
4. Stanley C. Baldwin, "The Prosperity Fallacy," *Eternity,* October 1979, page 46.
5. Baldwin, "The Prosperity Fallacy."
6. Baldwin, "The Prosperity Fallacy."

TEN

Where to Give

In chapter 7 we looked at the New Testament priorities for the utilization of income:

Providing for family.
Providing for the needs of brothers in difficulty.
Providing for widows and orphans who have no families.
Providing for the poor.
Providing for spiritual leaders.
Showing hospitality to travelers and strangers.
Giving for the extension of the gospel.

The majority of these priorities consist of giving. Actually only one of these priorities—the provision for one's family—is not entirely giving. Yet even this priority involves the sharing of income and possessions in the family community, and in practice involves significant giving.

Although we will consider slightly different categories of

giving priorities in this chapter, all of the previously mentioned categories will be included in our study.

Giving to God

The idea of giving to God is present in the Old Testament, even though this concept was applied to only a small portion of the Israelites' giving. The terminology "giving to God" is most likely to be used in connection with freewill offerings and vows. The verb "give" is rarely used in connection with the tithe that God reserved for Himself and gave to the Levites, except to clearly designate that *God* gave it to the Levites. The people "brought," "paid," or "took" the tithe to the designated place. Similarly the first fruits that God reserved for Himself were "brought" to the priest and were "offered" or "presented," but not generally described as "given."

The New Testament has no equivalent to the Old Testament gifts that were presented directly to God, and even in the Old Testament gifts could only be presented to God through the priests and the temple services. Under the New Covenant there is no temple, and we as Christians are priests unto God. There is also nothing similar to the Old Testament tithe or the first fruits that God explicitly reserved to His ownership. These were highly symbolic within the special relationship between God, the Israelites, and the land.

Since God is the ultimate owner of everything, the idea of giving to Him is a bit absurd. David recognized this when he and the leaders of Israel gave so freely and wholeheartedly to construct the Temple. "But who am I, and who are my people, that we should be able to give as generously as this? Everything comes from you, and we have given you only what comes from your hand . . . as for all this abundance that we have provided for building you a temple for your Holy Name, it comes from your hand, and all of it belongs to you" (1 Chronicles 29:14,16). Paul quoted from Job to remind his readers of the same thing. "Who has ever given to God, that God should repay him? For from him and through him and to him are all things" (Romans 11:35-36).

The concept of giving material things to God does not appear in the New Testament. Jesus talked about giving to the needy; instructed the rich, young man to dispose of his wealth and give it to the poor; and motivated others, such as Zacchaeus, to distribute a portion of their wealth to the poor. Apparently gifts to the poor were regularly made from the disciples' common purse, which was administered by Judas. In the story of the good Samaritan, Jesus encouraged giving to brothers who were in distress or need. Paul strenuously encouraged the believers to be generous in helping each other, and responded favorably to the help he received from the Philippians. So the New Testament has a great deal of teaching on giving, but says nothing about giving to God.

While our service of giving is directed toward our fellowman, all of it is, in a sense, giving to God. Jesus told the Twelve that "he who receives you receives me" (Matthew 10:40), even in something as small as offering water to drink. In reference to meeting the needs of the hungry, thirsty, and homeless, Jesus said, "Whatever you did for one of the least of these brothers of mine, you did for me" (Matthew 25:40), and "Anyone who gives you a cup of water in my name because you belong to Christ will certainly not lose his reward" (Mark 9:41). In that sense, all of our material giving is to God.

The New Testament reveals that our real giving to God is giving of ourselves: "Therefore, I urge you, brothers, in view of God's mercy, to offer your bodies as living sacrifices, holy and pleasing to God—which is your spiritual worship" (Romans 12:1). In our new, intimate relationship in Christ in the New Covenant, all of life and all that we have becomes dedicated to God. The Holy Spirit's indwelling presence makes all of life sacred. Since God is within us, we direct our attention in giving to others. God, then, gives to others through us. In the matter of giving, God's will for us is to be generous to our brothers.

Giving to the Poor

Generous, charitable giving is a biblical imperative. Giving is voluntary in the sense that no set pattern is prescribed, but it is such a consistent emphasis throughout the Bible that it cannot be considered optional. I estimate that ninety percent of what the Bible says about giving refers directly and explicitly to giving to the poor. We are instructed to generously meet the needs of the poor, and specifically to meet the needs of widows, orphans, travelers, and strangers. Commands to this effect are so numerous that I mention only a few:

> Do not be hardhearted or tightfisted toward your poor brother. Rather be openhanded and freely lend him whatever he needs. . . . Give generously to him and do so without a grudging heart. . . . I command you to be openhanded toward your brothers and toward the poor and needy in your land.   (Deuteronomy 15:7-8, 10-11)

> If a man shuts his ears to the cry of the poor, he too will cry out and not be answered.   (Proverbs 21:13)

> Now this was the sin of your sister Sodom: She and her daughters . . . did not help the poor and needy.
>   (Ezekiel 16:49)

We saw that Jesus and the disciples gave to the poor from the common purse, and He encouraged those who responded to Him to give to the poor. In Acts, Dorcas and Cornelius were commended for their habit of giving to the poor. This emphasis on giving to the poor continues throughout the New Testament.

How can we fulfill this instruction today? Poverty in the world is so widespread and structural that there is no simple solution. However, I believe we have a responsibility to do our part in humanitarian causes when we are assured of positive results. We need to be sure that the money is not dissipated in excessive administration, that real needs are being met in constructive ways that lead to permanent solutions, and that the funds or products are not diverted into personal gain. Projects controlled by churches located in the needy area are perhaps the most meaningful ways for a Christian to give.

Our most direct responsibility, however, is within our own sphere of influence. When we give assistance on a personal basis, we can ensure that it is constructive. We should meet needs in ways that provide permanent solutions rather than perpetuate dependency. The best way to do this is to provide capital—not in the form of money, but in the form of training, education, jobs, and other means that encourage the needy to discover and develop their aptitudes and abilities. If we awaken the awareness of an individual's potential and help that individual to realize his or her potential, our financial assistance can be temporary.

The welfare system makes it easy for us to feel that we are released from responsibility to the poor. I do not believe that welfare programs release us from our responsibility because they often do not produce constructive, permanent solutions. Rather, they tend to establish permanent dependency, thus making poverty hopeless. Artificial needs and arbitrary definitions of poverty are tools that help to create permanent dependency. Biblical poverty, however, is defined as a lack of the necessities of life; it does not mean to fall below an established level of income.

In Israel God established elaborate rules to avoid perpetual poverty. With that system, assistance was often designated as a loan, which implied the hope of recovery and repayment. It also indicated that those needing help viewed their situation as temporary. Interest on these loans was prohibited, and the debts were forgiven and slaves were freed on the Sabbatical Year. Land was returned to the original owner on the Year of Jubilee. All of these regulations were designed to prevent perpetual poverty and hopelessness. The poor could maintain hope and dignity in the midst of their poverty. Our personal assistance to the poor today should be directed to accomplish these same objectives.

Giving to Other Christians

Much of the New Testament teaching on giving is in connection with giving to the needy Christians in Jerusalem. First Corinthians 16, 2 Corinthians 8-9, and Acts 11 all relate to this. The idea of helping brothers in need, however, extends beyond this one situation.

> Share with God's people who are in need. Practice hospitality. (Romans 12:13)

> Therefore, as we have opportunity, let us do good to all people, especially to those who belong to the family of believers. (Galatians 6:10)

> If anyone has material possessions and sees his brother in need but has no pity on him, how can the love of God be in him? . . . Let us not love with words or tongue but with actions and in truth. (1 John 3:17-18)

In a way, giving to meet the needs of needy Christians is an extension of giving to the poor. But it is different because of the special bond we have with our brothers as members of the Body of Christ. It differs also in that our responsibility to other Christians goes beyond meeting their needs for life's necessities. We are to be vitally interested in our brothers' welfare. Doing good to our Christian brothers goes beyond giving alms. This is expressed in the verses I have quoted so often, which to me are the ultimate expression of brotherhood with a direct application to material things:

> Make my joy complete by being like-minded, having the same love, being one in spirit and purpose. Do nothing out of selfish ambition or vain conceit, but in humility consider others better than yourselves. Each of you should look not only to your own interests, but also to the interests of others. (Philippians 2:2-4)

I have found the application of this principle to be extremely rewarding, both in results and relationships. Years ago I met a brother who was a professor and scholar with a special interest in a certain scholastic field. He came from a different part of the world and from a totally different religious and cultural background than my own. We became the best of friends, and I found the relationship to be extremely stimulating in many ways. On one occasion, he informed me of a financial problem in one of his scholastic pursuits. I really had no interest in that project as such, and it was not related to my involvements in God's Kingdom, but I did have an interest in my brother. So I made a financial contribution that proved to be quite strategic in the project's long-range success.

Not only did I experience my brother's gratitude through my gift, but I found the project itself to be very stimulating. My involvement has led to a profitable learning experience in a new area, and has opened the door to new understanding and new relationships. The whole process began when I deliberately looked not only to my own interests, but also to the interests of others.

On another occasion, a brother came to me for advice concerning a very critical situation in his profession. Unless a miracle occurred he would eventually face bankruptcy, the loss of his professional licenses, great disruption to his and his family's life, and severe economic loss to many of his clients. It was even possible that the regulatory agencies of his profession would consider his conduct to be technically illegal. The problem was far beyond my financial capability, so I suggested that we ask other Christians for assistance. I was privileged to be one of several Christian men who worked together for more than a year to put together a package of outright gifts, loans, the formation of a new corporation, and other assistance to reach a satisfactory solution.

The financial and time investment of each of these men was substantial. Through their commitment, a miracle took place that salvaged a man's career, reputation, family, and ministry. None of us had any interest in our brother's business, but we did have an interest in his life.

Our concern for the interests of other Christians should not be limited to difficult situations. It should be commonplace in our Christian communities.

Giving to Family

This is perhaps the most natural and widely accepted aspect of giving. The scriptural admonition to provide for our families is easy to understand. Giving to our families is simply an extension of this privilege. The Scriptures accept the inheritance of wealth as desirable. In the Old Testament we read, "A good man leaves an inheritance for his children's children" (Proverbs 13:22); and in the New Testament, "After all, children should not have to save up for their parents, but parents for their children" (2 Corinthians 12:14).

While an inheritance is a good thing to give to our families, we could perhaps realize greater benefits through lifetime giving. Money invested in our children's education is an example of this. This is a capital investment (because it produces continuing benefit over a long period of time) and is therefore the most valuable contribution we can make. Other transfers of capital can be equally advantageous if made earlier in a son's or daughter's maturity rather than after we are gone. One advantage of earlier transfers is that we are still around to give advice and to determine our heir's ability to manage and conserve the capital we have given.

In American society, assistance in home ownership can be an extremely valuable gift. An early start in this capital item can be a tremendous boost to our children's long term financial stability. There are other strategic giving opportunities too, most of them pertaining to capital items and the use of credit. Let me give a hypothetical example.

Let us say that a young man has completed his education and

has become established in his first career job. One of his first ambitions will be to purchase a decent automobile because he has either been doing without one or has been driving something quite dilapidated. If he follows the normal pattern in our society, he will line up a bank loan and purchase a car.

As I write this, a $10,000 loan for three years at eleven percent would cost him $327.50 per month. The best advice you, if you were his father, could give him would be to drive the junker until he could pay cash for a better car. Although monthly automobile payments are a permanent feature of the majority of family budgets, you should be reluctant to see him begin what often is a lifetime habit of buying on credit.

There is an attractive alternative. It is to give your son $10,000 to purchase the car in return for several promises. The first promise would be that he would never purchase an automobile on time payments. The second promise would be for him to set aside the $327.50 per month on a permanent basis (since his car payments would, in all probability, have been permanent). Of that $327.50, $166.67 (or $2,000 per year) should be invested in an Individual Retirement Account, with the remaining $160.83 deposited into an account toward the purchase of his next car. At the conservative return rate of eight percent, he would have $11,896 for a new car, plus $12,238 in the IRA in five years! Since he can pay cash for his next car, he will be able to continue making the deposits. In 30 years, the IRA would contain $241,292, which is quite a return on a $10,000 gift! More important than the dollar amount you have given are the money management lessons that you have communicated to your son.

While this particular concept may not appeal to you personally, it illustrates how we can creatively give to family members and achieve significant financial results.

When I was young I was the recipient of the most generous gift I have ever seen a person give. My father and I had been building a few houses during my college years, and we decided to go into business together. He informed me that since I had decided to go into business, he wanted me to have a good financial start. So the entire profit from the first year of our partnership would be mine! He would not even accept wages for the carpentry work he contributed.

My father's offer was not made from a position of affluence. His entire net worth was less than the profit we made that first year. He had a house to live in, a pickup to drive, and very few living expenses except groceries for himself and my mother. Yet his concern for me superseded his concern for his own finances.

Our profit that year far exceeded what my father had expected. When we reviewed the statements at the end of the year, I persuaded him to accept a nominal amount for his work. Our business prospered and his generosity was rewarded. In a few years, he was able to retire without financial concerns. I have had many opportunities to be involved in giving, but never on a scale of generosity that compares with my father's example.

Giving to Spiritual Leaders
If any principle of giving is clearly established in Scripture, it is that we should support those who minister to us. We have a special responsibility to the sources of our spiritual help. God directly gave ten percent plus certain cities and the land around them to the Levites, but the Israelites were to give other support to both the priests and the Levites. A group of women supported Jesus and the disciples. As they traveled, the Twelve and the seventy were provided for by those to whom they ministered. Paul and his coworkers, as well as the other apostles, were entitled to support (see 1 Corinthians 9:14-18). Elders were worthy of support (see 1 Timothy 5:17-18), as well as traveling leaders (see Titus 3:13-14, 3 John 6-7).

> If we have sown spiritual seed among you, is it too much if we reap a material harvest from you?   (1 Corinthians 9:11)

Those who preach the gospel should receive their living
from the gospel.   (1 Corinthians 9:14)

Anyone who receives instruction in the word must share all
good things with his instructor.   (Galatians 6:6)

Not one church shared with me in the matter of giving and
receiving, except you only; . . . you sent me aid again and
again when I was in need.   (Philippians 4:15-16)

This principle of supporting those who minister to us con-
tains lessons for both givers and receivers. Many times people we
have never seen before ask us to give. Appeals for money have
become so common in my own Christian circles that it is impossible to respond—even with minute amounts—to all of them. I
believe this is because we have adopted our society's fundraising
standards rather than following biblical principles. We need to
remember that our first responsibility is to support those who have
ministered to us. Just as God's leading in our lives is in relationship
to our gifts and abilities, His leading in our giving is usually in
relationship to our normal sphere of influence and its expansion.

Those who depend on others for financial support need to
keep this principle in mind. I remember a situation some years ago
when a missionary friend returned to the United States for a
three-year assignment after fifteen years of very successful work
overseas. After so many years of service, it was quite normal that
he needed to expand his support base. We had difficulty understanding why our efforts to involve new people were not very
successful until we realized that we were approaching people who
were not familiar with the missionary, his ability, or his qualifica-
tions, and who had not enjoyed the benefits of his ministry. Those
of us who were supporting him agreed to meet his financial need
for two years to give him a chance to minister to people in the
United States. That decision made further efforts to increase his
support unnecessary, because during that time his sphere of minis-

try expanded and the financial support automatically followed.

The most specific application of this principle is our obvious responsibility to provide for those who minister to us on a continuing basis, primarily our church leaders.

Giving to the Church

There are a number of facets to our church giving. Giving to support the leaders who serve us was referred to above. In New Testament times this was a simple matter, since all the leaders were selected from within the churches and most served while remaining in their regular occupations. When the leaders were asked to devote all of their time to the ministry, they were supported. With today's emphasis on professional rather than indigenous leadership, our situation is quite different. However, this does not alter our obligation to support those who serve us.

In today's churches a primary emphasis is serving the membership. As church members, we desire many benefits for ourselves and our families, so much of our money is spent to enhance our worship, education, comfort, convenience, entertainment, and aesthetic enjoyment. It is only reasonable that we pay for our share of these expenses.

It is difficult for me to regard this responsibility as giving. Paying my share of the gas bill so that my family and I can be comfortable hardly strikes me as a charitable contribution. I have to pay my share of such expenses at the country club or health spa. We are fortunate that our government in the United States lets us deduct these expenses as contributions. (It is difficult to understand how this constitutes separation of church and state, but this is a significant privilege that we enjoy.) Christians in the rest of the world have never had such consideration.

Some similarity exists between what we give to the church and the Old Testament tithe because both are to support the religious establishment. The similarity stops there, however, because God reserved the tithe for Himself and our contributions to the church are voluntary giving. Also, the tithe was a fixed amount, while our contributions vary to meet the need. In the New Testament churches, where house meetings and a basically nonprofessional leadership were the norms, the financial needs of the church were minimal. With our expectations today, the financial needs of the church are much greater, and perhaps contributing ten percent of our income is not sufficient to meet them. We need to be willing to contribute our share of the money required to provide the buildings, programs, and professional leadership that we demand.

Another aspect of the church that relates to giving is the charitable and missionary function. Giving to charities and missionaries is genuine giving. To exercise our stewardship in this area, we must examine the benevolence and missionary programs of our churches to see if they are worthy of support. God has given us the responsibility of stewardship as individuals. We cannot abdicate that responsibility to corporate decision making. Our individual stewardship responsibility does not mean that we must wholeheartedly approve of every budget item. But we can expect the thrust of the budget to be in the direction of profitable enterprises that communicate the gospel and further God's Kingdom. Exercising stewardship by making designated contributions within a budget that doesn't meet our approval does very little good. It simply frees up funds for other budget items.

I have mentioned three aspects of giving to our churches: the support of spiritual leaders, the provision for church facilities and programs, and the church's financial outreach through missions and charity. The first type of giving is scripturally mandated; the second is a responsibility that varies greatly with each society, culture, and situation; and the third is established in Scripture by example, and is necessary to carry out the scriptural commands that we will study in part three of this book.

Scripture makes it clear that we need to be involved with other Christians in the Body of Christ. When we choose a church as a vehicle for brotherhood and community, we need to be generous in assuming our share of its support. Giving to our church should have all the characteristics of giving that we previously mentioned. It should be voluntary, proportionate to our ability, regular and systematic, done without display, cheerful, and—above all—generous.

Giving to Other Organizations

This is giving for the purpose of extending God's Kingdom, and includes giving to missions. The local church's direct sphere of influence is limited to a specific locality. Many worthy opportunities throughout the world can be met only through a mobile function. This was true even in New Testament times, where we see both the established churches and the mobile, apostolic function. The churches supported those involved in the mobile function, appointed some of their number to join it, and thus became involved in extending God's Kingdom beyond their immediate sphere of influence. Many worthy organizations today are involved in a mobile ministry beyond the sphere of local churches.

The best illustration of this is the Apostle Paul. Acts 13:2-3 tells of the appointment of Paul and Barnabas to a special ministry: "While they were worshiping the Lord and fasting, the Holy Spirit said, 'Set apart for me Barnabas and Saul for the work to which I have called them.' So after they had fasted and prayed, they placed their hands on them and sent them off." After establishing churches in Cyprus and Asia Minor, they returned to Antioch "where they had been committed to the grace of God for the work they had now completed . . . and reported all that God had done through them and how he had opened the door of faith to the Gentiles" (Acts 14:26-27). The mobile group increased when Paul and Silas, and Barnabas and Mark formed separate ministry teams (see Acts 15). Timothy later joined Paul and Silas, and Apollos, Priscilla, and Aquilla are also mentioned in the context of this mobile ministry. When Paul returned to Asia on his second journey, seven others were in the missionary party.

Direct financial support of the missionary enterprise is illustrated by the relationship between Paul and the Philippians. We have quoted Philippians 4:15-16, in which Paul reminds the Philippians that they were the only church that contributed to him, and that they had done this on numerous occasions. This giving and receiving established the "partnership in the gospel" that Paul mentions in Philippians 1:5. We have already talked about the principle of shared reward that comes into play when we support others in ministry (see Philippians 4:17). Other verses also refer to the support of mobile leaders:

> Do everything you can to help Zenas the lawyer and Apollos on their way and see that they have everything they need. (Titus 3:13)

> Dear friend, you are faithful in what you are doing for the brothers, even though they are strangers to you. They have told the church about your love. You will do well to send them on their way in a manner worthy of God. It was for the sake of the Name that they went out. (3 John 5-6)

All of this giving and receiving is part of carrying out the general charge Jesus gave to His disciples to proclaim the good news of the gospel throughout the earth:

> Go into all the world and preach the good news to all creation. (Mark 16:15)

> You will be my witnesses in Jerusalem, and in all Judea and Samaria, and to the ends of the earth. (Acts 1:8)

> "Everyone who calls on the name of the Lord will be saved."
>
> How, then, can they call on the one they have not believed in? And how can they believe in the one of whom they have not heard? And how can they hear without

someone preaching to them? And how can they preach
unless they are sent? As it is written, "How beautiful are the
feet of those who bring good news!"   (Romans 10:13-15)

How wonderful it is to have the privilege of participating in
the extension of God's Kingdom by sending His laborers out! God
is generous in giving us this privilege. He has arranged for us to be
co-laborers with Him and the mobile teams that serve Him. We
have the privilege of participating in the lives and ministries of our
brothers, and have the promise of sharing in their rewards. We are
involved in God's great purpose in history. Our hearts should be
full of thanksgiving and praise at God's generosity in arranging His
economy this way!

Selecting Recipients of Our Giving

As stewards of what ultimately belongs to God, we should seek
God's guidance in our giving. We need to be sensitive to His
leading, but should carefully avoid making decisions on an emotional basis. We need to pray about our giving and keep our hearts
open to His guidance.

The most profitable request we can make concerning our
giving is that God will give us wisdom, which He has promised to
do. "If any of you lacks wisdom, he should ask God, who gives
generously to all without finding fault, and it will be given to him"
(James 1:5).

Our giving is an expression of God's nature, and if there is
any area where we can expect His guidance, it is in wisdom for
giving. However, He is more likely to guide us as we use the
wisdom He gives us and apply our intelligence guided by scriptural principles, than He is through mystical experiences. Remember, our first responsibilities lie within our normal sphere of
influence. God's leading will usually be natural to our circumstances and our customary relationships. As we are faithful and
generous in meeting the needs that arise within our sphere of influ-

ence, God can open up unusual situations and new opportunities.

Giving to our families is an example of immediate responsibility and serves as a good illustration of this principle. Our first responsibility in giving to those in need is to give to those within our normal relationships. As these needs are met, we are free to give on a broader scale as opportunities come to our attention. Our giving to other Christians, whether they are in need or because of our brotherly interest in the things in which they are involved, is within the normal sphere of our lives. We are free to choose our church and spiritual leaders, but once we make that choice, the recipients of this portion of our giving are obvious. We have a wide range of choices when we give to other organizations and individuals who serve in them. But even in these situations, most of our introductions to areas of need are made through our normal contacts.

Whenever we give—whether it be to our church where we assume our proportionate share of its operation and support of its leaders, to our church's mission and benevolence programs, or to other organizations and individuals—we need to evaluate whether or not we should give for that purpose. The following questions will help us make that decision:

Is the message true to Scripture?
Is God blessing the ministry with spiritual fruit?
Do the lives of the individuals involved conform to the
     message?
Are there reasonable standards of efficiency? (Standards of
     excellence, freedom from waste, proportionate
     results.)
Are associates and personnel treated equitably, fairly, and
     with consideration?

Finally we must ask ourselves a subjective question, *Am I convinced that God wants me to have a part in this ministry?*

We are the stewards of our giving. We need to cultivate the

habit of being open to God's leading and ready to generously respond. Every opportunity to give within God's Kingdom is a privilege, but it is impossible to participate in every opportunity. If there is any area in which we can expect God to lead us, it is in the area of giving.

Partnership in the Gospel

A very special relationship existed between the Apostle Paul and the Christians at Philippi. The nature of this relationship is revealed in the tone and content of the book of Philippians. His ministry to the Philippians was the bright spot in Paul's career. This church did not begin in the synagogue, but through Paul's contact with a group of women at a place of prayer. Lydia—the first convert at Philippi—was apparently an outstanding, influential, and wealthy woman. Her enthusiastic response to the gospel and her hospitality to Paul and his companions set the tone of Paul's relationship with all the Philippian Christians. From the very beginning they shared a genuine relationship of love.

Paul's letter to the Philippians differs from his letters to other churches. It is a spontaneous expression of his love and appreciation for them. There is no structure or logic, no sin to rebuke, no doctrinal error to correct. It is like a letter one would write to his dearest friends. Look at some of the phrases:

> I thank my God every time I remember you . . . because of your partnership in the gospel from the first day until now.
> (Philippians 1:3,5)

> It is right for me to feel this way about all of you, since I have you in my heart.   (1:7)

> God can testify how I long for all of you with the affection of Christ Jesus.   (1:8)

> Through my being with you again your joy in Christ Jesus will overflow on account of me.   (1:26)

My brothers, you whom I love and long for, my joy and
crown . . . dear friends!   (Philippians 4:1)

I rejoice greatly in the Lord that . . . you have renewed your
concern for me . . . you have been concerned, but you had
no opportunity to show it.   (4:10)

In the early days of your acquaintance with the gospel . . .
not one church shared with me in the matter of giving and
receiving, except you only.   (4:15)

You sent me aid again and again when I was in need. (4:16)

The gifts you sent . . . are a fragrant offering, an acceptable
sacrifice, pleasing to God.   (4:18)

Paul had this kind of a relationship only with the Philippian
Christians. He said that "no other church" showed concern for his
material needs, but the Philippians ministered to him "again and
again." In fact, Paul engaged in tentmaking rather than accepting
gifts from other churches because he feared that in their immaturity they would misconstrue his motives.

Paul's relationship of mutual privilege with the Philippians
was ideal. Paul received gifts from the Philippian Christians that
facilitated his determination to take the gospel to others, enjoyed a
warm love relationship with the Philippian Christians, saw this
love expressed in tangible ways, and related to the Philippians as
equals in the partnership of the gospel and its rewards. In turn, the
Philippians not only experienced the privilege and joy of giving,
but expressed their love for him and participated in extending the
gospel throughout the world. It is possible to enjoy this kind of
partnership in the gospel in the twentieth century. The kind of
intimate relationship Paul had with the Philippians can, and
should, be copied and cultivated.

A leader in a worldwide mission organization observed my
relationship with one of their missionaries. Since this leader was

interested in encouraging others to develop similar commitments, we discussed how to develop such a relationship, and the special commitment on the part of both the missionary and the supporter that it requires. Missionaries too often treat their supporters simply as donors, but the partnership I am talking about is based on a personal relationship.

Developing a personal relationship and genuine partnership requires adjustments from the twentieth-century norm. For the missionary, professional superiority, status, and aloofness must be replaced with equality and openness. Honesty must replace communication that is designed to impress and demonstrate cost effectiveness. Failures and difficulties, as well as successes, must be shared. A casual contact must become a genuine relationship. The missionary must open up his life and ministry to those who would become his partners.

The donor-partner must also exhibit characteristics of equality, openness, and honesty mentioned above. He must open up his life to a genuine relationship. In addition, he must be willing to make a firm commitment. The interests of his brother—especially the financial—must equal or supersede his own. His attitude cannot be, "If it is financially convenient I will help out." It must be, "I will meet my partner's need at any cost." That is why the Philippians were willing to give to Paul's project "out of their deep poverty and affliction."

I have been stimulated and encouraged by Christians' generosity toward their brothers in God's service. But I have also sometimes been appalled by the shallowness of their commitment—even after lifelong relationships and involvement. We have a long way to go in following Paul's instruction to look not only to our own interests, but also to the interests of our brothers.

I believe that any of us—whether donor or recipient—could develop a partnership in the gospel relationship with a brother. I have had this privilege more than once. As demonstrated by the references I have made to the ministry in Brazil, a partnership in the gospel opens up opportunities and involvements far beyond our expectations. During the past fifteen years, my most significant opportunities for ministry and most enjoyable relationships with my brothers—both in this country and in Latin America—have developed from such a partnership. This book is itself an example. I strongly encourage you to pray for and work toward such a relationship.

PART THREE
The Beginning of Practical Application

Our objective has been to discover principles that have broad application to man's relationship to material things. These principles will have varying applications for each of us because of our different gifts, abilities, and callings. In addition, our situations will be different due to the culture and the subculture in which we find ourselves. These statements are in themselves applications of one of the principles—that of diversity.

Principles need to be applied in specific situations, not in abstract settings. In this practical section dealing with application we must continue to avoid suggesting rigid formulas or patterns that can be copied. Please remember that it is not my intention to present a system, or even a pattern, that can be followed. My intention is rather to stimulate your personal application of principles. Look upon the illustrations as simply illustrations, not as prototypes. Find the principles that you can accept and begin to work out their application in your life.

I chose the title for this section of the book very deliberately. This is simply a beginning—for me as well as for you who are reading it.

ELEVEN

Creative Giving

I have a special concern relating to these ideas on creative and strategic giving. I fear that many readers will not attempt any personal application of these principles because they think the amounts they can give are not large enough for these considerations. Others may feel that these principles apply only to those who have the gift of giving. I feel the application of these principles is for all of us.

I believe anyone can learn to exercise creativity in giving— even in giving small amounts. In fact, the suggestions that follow are more important for those who are able to give average amounts than for those who have great resources. This is because one of the functions of creative and strategic giving is to increase the amount available to give; another function is to multiply the effectiveness of giving. Both functions are important for small gifts as well as for large gifts. I believe that God will multiply what is available to us as we exercise good stewardship of our resources.

Some of the illustrations I will use involve larger amounts of money with complex applications, but please don't let those things distract you from the applications you can make in your own giving.

In Isaiah 32:8 (KJV) we read, "But the liberal [generous] deviseth liberal things; and by liberal things shall he stand." A generous person will conceive generous ideas. He will look for opportunities to be generous and will devise ways to make his generosity more beneficial. This is accomplished by multiplying the resources available, applying them creatively, and devising ways to consciously use material things for spiritual objectives.

The Process and Results of Creative Giving

The first factor in giving creatively is to apply the intelligence God has given us. In a context other than giving, Jesus instructs the Twelve to be "as shrewd as snakes and as innocent as doves" (Matthew 10:16). In Luke 16, we see the parable of the steward who was commended for acting shrewdly. Jesus' application of this parable is that we should intelligently and deliberately use material possessions for spiritual objectives. In James we find God's promise to give wisdom generously to those who ask for it. Proverbs is full of exhortations to seek after wisdom and diligently apply our intelligence. We can conclude that God expects us to use our intelligence in connection with stewardship, and is willing to give us the wisdom we lack.

The second factor in creative giving is that God will multiply the effectiveness of our giving. God "will also supply and increase your store of seed and will enlarge the harvest of your righteousness. You will be made rich in every way so that you can be generous on every occasion" (2 Corinthians 9:10-11). Righteousness here refers to the grace of giving, and the metaphor is that the seed represents our gifts and the harvest represents the results of our giving. So God promises to enlarge (other translations use the words "increase" and multiply") the harvest!

A generous God enjoys seeing His generosity reproduced in His children. As we demonstrate a pattern of generous giving, He makes it possible for us to increase in the grace of giving. He does this through the Holy Spirit's work in our hearts and minds to enhance and increase our abilities and talents. God can also increase our giving by enhancing the effectiveness of our gifts.

Sometimes this multiplication happens without any conscious effort or planning on our part. All we do is release the "seed" of our gift into the Kingdom and the multiplication process begins. Let me illustrate this from my own experience, in which I simply responded to and capitalized on the opportunities that were presented, and God did the multiplying.

A missionary friend of mine wrote that he would be returning to the States for a six-month furlough. I had made it clear to him that he could count on me for any special need. This time the need was for an automobile suitable for extensive traveling with his wife and two children.

Nothing fell out of the blue concerning the car, so shortly before his arrival I purchased a new, mid-sized car. At $100 over the dealer's cost, the car cost $4,200. My friend was living in Iowa and traveled to California and Texas, and made several trips to Colorado. After six months and 15,000 miles of reliable, enjoyable transportation, he returned the car to me. He insisted on giving me a check for $900, the amount he had budgeted for minimal transportation.

I now had only $3,300 invested in the car. No immediate need for the car turned up, so I offered the car to my daughter who was in college. She took the keys, drove around the block, and returned them to me. She thought that her older, smaller, slightly beat-up car was more appropriate for her needs.

In a short time, another missionary friend called from Colorado. He had returned to the United States the previous year after two overseas assignments. He had leased a used auto for one year, but a new leasing arrangment would be more than he could afford.

I suggested that he come to Minneapolis and said we would have something for him. I then transferred the car to his organization as a tax-deductible contribution. The manufacturer had raised prices on that model since I had purchased it and the car was still a current model, so the appraisal came in high enough to reduce my income tax by $2,350. I now had only $950 of my money invested in the car.

My friend, like most missionaries, had been unable to accumulate any cash reserves during his seventeen years of service overseas. When he arrived in Minneapolis, I informed him that he could take the automobile on one condition: that he deposit the amount of his prior lease payments into an investment plan for a specified period of time. We decided to invest in a conservative mutual fund. During the next few years, just as we had agreed, he deposited $3,000 into this and another investment. Since this was only a fraction of the money he would have spent on lease payments, it was in reality "free" money. The remainder of what he would have spent for leasing was available for other purposes. When the odometer on the car reached 175,000, we decided it was time for a change. The organization then sold the car for $625, which was used to meet another need in which my friend and I had an interest.

What a return I received on my $950 investment! The first brother and his family enjoyed 15,000 miles of comfortable travel. The second, 160,000 miles, plus—for the first time in his Christian experience—a small accumulation of capital. The $625 from the sale of the car was invested in another worthwhile project in the Kingdom.

This entire sequence was not planned, and demonstrates one thing to me: *God is still in the business of multiplying our loaves and fishes!* In the biblical narratives of Jesus' feeding of the multitudes by the miraculous multiplication of the loaves and fish, John is the only one who mentions a source. "Here is a boy with five small barley loaves and two small fish" (John 6:9). I consider my role in this sequence to be similar to that of the lad with the lunch.

The second story I want to share with you about creative giving involves more deliberate planning. Most of the time, the multiplication of our giving results from the active application of our God-given intelligence. Just as we are co-laborers with God in the creation of wealth in bringing the earth under our control, we can work together with Him to multiply the benefits of our resources.

A missionary friend in Latin America shared two problems he was facing. One was the matter of housing for the missionaries under his supervision. In many areas, rental housing suitable for an American family in ministry was hard to find. Since their ministry was centered in the home and family, this need was especially critical. When housing was available, moves were frequent because evictions to circumvent rent control were common. In the absence of control, rents could be raised exorbitantly, which was often done because the owners tended to believe that all Americans were wealthy. (I received a letter from a family in Mexico whose rent was being increased from $400 per month to $1000 per month at the expiration of the lease!) My friend said it was not uncommon for his people to spend fifty percent of their budgets for housing.

The frequent moves and uncertainty were difficult for the missionary families and their ministry. School changes and other changes in family life were detrimental to the psychological well-being of all family members. Uncontrolled inflation and artificial exchange rates added to the problems. A great deal of time, mental energy, concern, and concentration were being expended on the housing problem.

Home ownership by the missionaries would solve all of theseproblems, but this was not possible because mortgages as we know them were not available in Latin America.

Home ownership would have the additional advantage of

more closely identifying the missionary with the culture. This would change the people's perception of the missionary, since he was making a tangible investment in the country and in effect becoming one of them. Home ownership would help the missionary and his family fully integrate into the culture in which they lived, and direct their focus away from the culture that sent them. A missionary is rarely successful until he not only overcomes the normal culture shock, but identifies with the new culture. A successful missionary must cease to feel like an outsider, and no longer think in constant reference to his native culture.

The second problem that concerned this missionary leader was the provision for retirement. Many of his people were at the age when they should consider this need, yet most of them had been unable to make any provision for retirement or for returning to their home countries. This is a widespread problem among missionaries and those who serve in Christian organizations. It is too difficult to meet immediate needs, much less to be concerned about the distant future. Missionaries invest their lives in their field ministries. When financial needs are either great or overwhelming, it is natural for them to apply any available resources to meet those needs. I have seen missionary families return home after thirty years of service overseas with no financial provision other than a partial social security benefit. I'm afraid that this situation is the norm rather than the exception.

To meet these two concerns, my missionary friend and I developed a plan for the missionary families to purchase houses. To illustrate how this works, I will use an actual situation—a missionary family in Buenos Aires, Argentina, faced all of the problems outlined above. They had savings of $4,000, which we supplemented by securing another $4,000 of outright gifts. They found a house that could be purchased for $58,000, which required $50,000 of financing. For the sake of simplicity, let us say that I approached five of their supporters and each responded with a $10,000 contribution to the charitable organization sponsoring the program. This contribution was fully deductible and would cost the donor as little as $5,000, depending on his marginal tax bracket. These five gifts were used to fund a $50,000 mortgage to the family in Argentina. Interest was eight percent, and the monthly payments were $500 per month. The mortgage would be paid off in 168 months, or just under fourteen years.

This was a great benefit to the family because the $500 payments were considerably less than they were paying for rent. Equally important was the permanent stability they achieved. Rents that could escalate astronomically with inflation and exchange rates would no longer affect them. Their budget was stabilized, family disruptions were eliminated, and the ministry location was made permanent. The time and mental energy previously spent on housing concerns could be profitably used. The missionaries had taken a significant step toward permanent identification with the culture and the people. In addition, they were building equity in the house that would assist them in their relocation or retirement.

I have been privileged to assist in a number of similar opportunities that uniquely contribute to the lives and ministries of missionary families. The results have met all expectations. In reference to the family in Argentina, their supervisor wrote to me a year after the transaction. He said, "Because of inflation and the exchange rates, this family has suffered the loss of purchasing power of their U.S. dollars at the rate of 8.7 percent per month for the first eight months of this year. It suddenly occurred to me that it would be impossible for us to keep them there had we not stabilized the housing portion of their budget."

It is difficult for those of us who enjoy a relatively stable economy to fully realize the effects of inflation. The house in Argentina was purchased for $58,000. Within six months, it was worth $90,000, and within a year was valued at $130,000. Within two and one-half years, it would have required $250,000 to purchase the house. Six months later, after the Falkland Islands war, its value had fallen fifty percent. During those years, rents would have followed housing values, and the effect on the family budget would have been disastrous.

In my mind, there is absolutely no doubt that this is an example of an excellent investment in God's Kingdom. But so far we have seen only half the story. The $500 monthly payments that return to the foundation that sponsors the loans are in reality free money because they constitute only a fraction of what would have been paid for rent. The foundation permits the original donors to designate how the payments will be used for the first 100 months of the loan, providing their designation is a worthwhile project in God's Kingdom. So a donor who contributed $10,000 would designate the use of $100 per month for 100 months, or a total of another $10,000. The remaining sixty-eight payments, totaling $6,800, will be retained by the foundation to build a fund for future mortgages. Let me graphically illustrate the results.

Cost:		Benefits:	
Original check	$10,000	To missionary family	$10,000
After tax cost	$ 5,000 (±)	To designated causes	$10,000
		To permanent fund	$ 6,800
		Total Benefit	$26,800

At a cost of $5,000 (or a little more or less depending on the tax bracket) $26,800 is available for use in God's Kingdom. This is one example of what I mean by creative giving.

There is another significant factor to consider in this giving equation. The contribution becomes capital to the missionary recipient. The house produces continuing benefits over a long period of time. This will continue for the missionary's lifetime since the equity in the original house will be transferred into one for retirement.

This kind of creative giving opportunity is not limited to extremely wealthy Christians. If you have currently committed fifty dollars per month to a missionary or a project, you could make a $5,000 contribution to a similar housing project. Due to tax benefits, this contribution would cost you less than $5,000. Then you could designate the return payment of fifty dollars per month to meet your original pledge. Both the housing gift and regular support could be given to the same missionary. The housing need would be met, your pledge would be taken care of for 100 months, and an additional $3,400 would eventually accrue in the mortgage fund. The fifty dollars you have originally promised to give could replenish whatever source you used for the $5,000 contribution.

I am constantly amazed at the results accruing from financial investments in the Kingdom. The only thing required of us is a spirit of generosity and a willingness to release some of our resources to God's Kingdom. When we do this, He starts the multiplication process. Sometimes God works through the active application of our intelligence; sometimes He works in more mysterious ways. When we give on the basis of scriptural principles, we can be sure that God's purposes are fulfilled—usually in ways beyond what we can imagine.

Principles of Strategic Giving

When I speak of strategic giving, I'm not implying any grandiose strategy for giving to God's Kingdom, but I simply mean that we should have a strategy for giving. We should give with an objective—with a purpose or multiple purposes in mind. In order to give strategically, we need to adopt some principles to govern our financial involvement. I will highlight six principles that I have found helpful.

Select recipients carefully. It is a privilege to be involved with those who are making significant contributions to the Kingdom. Such ministries are not always the most popular or glamorous, but they are on the cutting edge of what God is doing. By contemporary standards, these ministries may seem insignificant and out of touch with the times and the popular themes of the Christian community. But God is never impressed with popularity or trendiness. The greatest giving opportunity of a lifetime can occur when this kind of a person or organization comes within your circle of contacts. Be ready to recognize and seize the opportunity!

Discernment is necessary when selecting missionaries to support. We need to avoid sentimentality here because fifty percent of those sent out do not return for a second term, and the first term is rarely productive because of the language barrier and cultural adjustments. Failure on the field usually occurs because the missionaries were not qualified or equipped for cross-cultural ministry. (Mission organizations have been notably lax in developing adequate screening. The scope of need in the world is so great that it is tempting to accept almost anyone who claims to have been "called" and is able to raise financial support.)

We can look for sensitivity, discernment, adaptability, flexibility, and awareness of cultural differences when selecting missionaries to support. We can determine if they have previously had a productive ministry in their own culture. If so, we can find out what kind of people they ministered to: those from their own sub-culture. It would be a good assignment for prospective missionaries to demonstrate their ability in cross-cultural ministry by crossing the lines that separate the sub-cultures within their own country.

I once attended a fundraising luncheon for a young man who was going to another country as a missionary. Having no knowledge of that country—even of the language—he had employed someone in the United States to translate his "materials" into that language. He planned to have his materials printed here for use upon his arrival in the foreign country. This represented a total lack of cultural understanding. He is now back in this country.

I met another young man who was accustomed to working on large university campuses to recruit students for fulltime Christian service. He felt that there was no possibility of profitable ministry among those of us involved in normal employment, businesses, or professions. He was unable to adjust to his brothers here who did not fit his pattern, yet expected to be supported in a cross-cultural ministry! Such lack of preparation and understanding reminds me of Jeremiah 12:5: "If you have raced with men on foot and they have worn you out, how can you compete with horses? If you stumble in safe country, how will you manage in the thickets by the Jordan?"

A poor relationship between a husband and wife and the lack of family discipline will almost certainly cause failure on the mission field. Learning the language, attempting to make a cultural adaptation, going through culture shock, and beginning a new ministry in a strange culture are significant challenges. When family instability is added to these challenges, the burden is simply too difficult. Firm family support is absolutely necessary to a successful missionary experience.

We need to exercise all of our discernment and ask God for more in selecting those to whom we give. This does not mean that we look for superstars or feel that our gifts are so important that they must be reserved for someone outstanding. It does mean that we want to be certain that those we support are following God's leading and are attempting to do something that is within the scope of their talents, abilities, and potential.

Give in a way that encourages others to give. This is simply a matter of sharing the opportunity. In a few giving situations, my relationship with the recipient was of such a nature that I personally wanted to assume full responsibility for the need. I realize that this was selfish. On other occasions, I have selected only a few individuals with whom to share a giving opportunity—just as Paul selected the churches from which he received support. But usually I encourage everyone within the natural sphere of an individual or a project to give. Rarely, if ever, would I approach those who were strangers to the recipient. Never have I approached the general Christian public.

I sincerely believe that the privilege of participating in the lives and ministries of our brothers, or in worthwhile projects in God's Kingdom, through giving are genuine opportunities. So without apology I can encourage other Christians to participate in giving situations within their normal sphere of interest. To the extent that I ask them to give, I do so because giving is better than receiving. But I do not ask them to give, as much as I offer them an opportunity to participate in the work of God's Kingdom. If they fail to perceive this truth, it is because they have not understood and participated in the grace of giving. It is a worthwhile endeavor to encourage others to participate in the grace of giving. Paul wanted his readers to excel in giving.

Our purpose in sharing giving opportunities with others is not to publicize our own giving, but to encourage others to give. On occasion I have felt free to promise to contribute the final portion of a need if others contributed to a certain point, or to match the contribution of others. Sometimes I did this to stimulate the other givers, sometimes to stimulate both the giver and the receiver to work on a specific project. If our giving encourages others to give, we have not only multiplied the resources available, but have led our brothers to more fully exercise the grace of giving.

Multiply the money available to give. There are several ways to do this. Those of us who live in the United States enjoy tax laws that encourage charitable contributions. Our giving should always be motivated by the desire to give, but there is nothing wrong with taking advantage of tax provisions that enable us to increase the amounts we give.

Most of us would be surprised to compare our marginal tax rate to the overall percentage of our income that goes for taxes. The marginal rate is the percentage we pay in federal and state taxes combined on the highest portion of our income. The marginal rate is the level at which our contributions are effective in reducing our taxable income. It does not take a millionaire's income, or anything close to it, to put us in the 33 to 50 percent marginal bracket. In the 33 percent bracket, for example, one third of the money we give would otherwise go for taxes.

In addition, the tax laws enable us to contribute property instead of cash. If our gain on this property were to be classified as long-term capital gain, we would avoid the tax on the contributed property.

With a little effort, many of us can make contributions that in reality cost us only fifty cents or less per dollar. In other words, we can choose to have fifty cents in our own pocket after taxes, or contribute one dollar to God's Kingdom. Many of our contributions ultimately accrue to the benefit of individuals. An example of this is the housing program I explained earlier. Long ago I absolutely determined that I would choose one dollar for my brother's welfare rather than one half of that for my own.

I have mentioned only the elementary aspects of the tax advantages of giving. There are more if we make the effort to understand and apply them. However, our objective should be to use the tax laws to increase our giving rather than to save taxes for ourselves. By that I mean to apply the advantage of beneficial tax laws to God's Kingdom rather than to ourselves. For example, if we are willing to give $1,000, we can either use the tax laws to give $2,000, or we can use them to have $500 of our $1,000 returned to us as a tax reduction. I believe we should choose the former.

Some of us employ methods such as tax shelters to reduce our taxable income. If we do, we should calculate our giving at the highest bracket, using the highest level of tax savings to increase our giving. Our analysis of other investments that produce tax benefits should then be made at the lower brackets. Personally, I cannot see the need for a Christian to have any other form of tax shelter. We have the best one ever devised—investment in God's Kingdom! Our government permits us to invest up to fifty percent of our income in this shelter—where the rewards are eternal, and the principal and interest build up tax-free treasure in Heaven!

Giving to a project early—if possible before the financial need arises—is another way of increasing our giving. Income from the gift that would otherwise be taxable can accumulate tax free within a charitable organization. An example would be to contribute $1,000 worth of a utility stock yielding twelve percent with a semiannual dividend. If the stock were contributed just before a dividend payment, the charity would have $1,180 at the end of thirteen months. If the contribution were made six years in advance of the need, the $1,000 gift would have increased in value to $2,000.

This kind of income accumulation is one of the advantages of a private foundation. Another advantage is the foundation's freedom to accumulate larger sums of money for special projects. If the foundation is a public charity, it can receive and manage gifts of property (such as real estate) that are often difficult for a church or other organization to handle. Too often we make the mistake of thinking that these advantageous giving opportunities are available only to the wealthy. The truth is, all of us can multiply our giving by taking advantage of these opportunities.

Taking advantage of tax benefits to increase our giving is good stewardship. I have only touched on the possibilities available to us. Some of us will be able to employ these advantages to the maximum, and anyone who gives can benefit by using them at his or her personal level of involvement.

Have resources available for strategic opportunities. We studied the concept of saving to have a margin for our personal finances. Here I would like to explain the importance of having a margin for God; setting aside a part of our giving to meet the emergency needs of others who do not have their own reserve, and to take advantage of unusual opportunities in the Kingdom. We also need to have our own finances in order so that we can increase our giving when special opportunities arise.

We need to position ourselves to be ready to give. This does not happen by accident. It must be accomplished deliberately. On many occasions, I have seen people with adequate resources and the willingness and desire to give who were unable to do so because they had not organized their financial affairs to allow this flexibility. Some people prefer to tie up all of their assets because it provides an excuse for their unwillingness to be generous.

If we want to be ready to give, we cannot always be fully invested or overextended in our businesses. We have to avoid a standard of living that consumes every bit of our income and the use of credit that artificially increases our standard of living. When we exercise discipline in these areas, we can begin to build the financial reserves that will enable us to take advantage of strategic giving opportunities.

Some people do not have a reserve for giving because they lack an understanding of personal stewardship. Christians have often been taught that their stewardship responsibility is solely to give a percentage of their income to the church, which in turn administers their giving. There is nothing wrong with voluntarily giving a certain percentage of our income, or giving to the church. In fact, both are desirable. But our giving cannot stop there. We are the stewards of our giving, and our responsibility does not end when we give a fixed percentage to someone else to administer. For most of us in our affluent society, the tithe is a cop-out if it is the full extent of our giving. If we give a tithe (or any certain percentage) to our church, we must also be ready to meet our scriptural responsibilities in giving beyond that amount.

A giving reserve opens up new possibilities for the giver and the receiver. For many years I have offered an option to the individuals I have agreed to support. I will either regularly contribute a fixed sum, or I will meet special, larger needs as they develop. I have also told them that they should never pass up strategic opportunities in God's work because of finances. With this understanding, none of these people have ever chosen to receive monthly support from me! They realized that others were willing to give monthly, but they had no one else they could fall back on to provide for special needs.

In a good number of cases, the special need was the provision of an automobile during their furloughs. A new, but modestly priced, automobile can provide reliable and comfortable transportation for their time in the United States. At the end of their furlough, the car can be sold. The proceeds can be used to purchase another vehicle on their field of service, or to meet other needs. Over the years, my contribution has been about the same whether I give $100 per month for four years, or $4,800 at one time to meet their special needs.

Give direction along with your contributions. If God has helped us understand the proper relationship between a Christian and material possessions, we can pass this understanding on to others along with our contributions. If we have learned to think creatively, we can encourage those we help to broaden their perception. My assistance to missionaries that enabled them to buy houses communicates the idea that capital is desirable, has a legitimate place in a Christian's life, and produces continuing benefits over a long period of time. It communicates the need for responsible stewardship of that capital. The gift of the automobile that I told you about introduced a missionary brother to the idea of setting aside a reserve for the future. That lesson was more valuable to him over the long term than the automobile itself. Both of these efforts demonstrated and communicated biblical truth about giving and receiving, and our relationship to material possessions.

I have suggested that the giver should carefully select the recipients to assure that his or her gifts will be used to accomplish the purposes for which they were given in an advantageous and efficient manner. However, we should never try to control others through our gifts. Giving is giving. It involves "letting go" and releasing what we give. While there is a fine line between proper stewardship and improper control, it is quite distinct. We should exercise discernment when we select recipients. When we give to those recipients, we must respect their individuality and the fact that they, too, are God's servants. He will not always lead them in the same way He leads us.

Some churches have withdrawn their support of certain missionaries because they disagreed on a minor issue or cultural adaptation. Apparently these churches had more confidence in the universal nature of their particular standards than they did in God's ability to direct the missionaries. One of my friends had invested fifteen years in a very difficult culture, was confident of God's leading, and was encouraged by recent results. He received a letter from a supporter telling him that he was wasting time and money where he was, and that he should move where results were more promising. I have heard organizational leaders threaten to withdraw logistic support of a ministry because the men working in certain countries were not following the sending country's policies or cultural standards.

We need to follow God's leading in directing our giving. Then we need to respect our recipients as equals in God's Kingdom. We need to have confidence that God is able to lead them and that they will respond to His leading. Giving to others does not give us the right to exercise control over them. Our giving should never be designed to impose our ideas or force conformity upon a brother. We should not attach strings to our contributions although it is proper to suggest the opportunities they present. Our objective should be to communicate truth and stimulate growth, not to control.

Giving in the form of capital. If our gifts are in the form of capital they will produce long-term, permanent results. The homes that others and I have helped missionaries purchase are a perfect example of this. It is unlikely that the equity the missionaries accumulate in those homes will ever be converted to consumption. When the home is sold, the proceeds will eventually be used for a retirement home. We inform the missionaries that we desire our gifts to provide a permanent addition to their capital.

One mission organization recently began to permit their

overseas personnel to set aside an amount in their budgets to purchase a home and meet other relocation expenses when they return to this country. Without such a program, their people were virtually without resources when they returned home. The mission's stateside personnel had fared much better financially, primarily because they had built up equity in houses. I was very pleased when the organization made this opportunity retroactive, which enabled donors to contribute to those with many years of service overseas.

This giving opportunity is an exciting prospect, because the contributions are gifts of capital, which will provide for our brothers' needs for the rest of their lives. I am pleased to see many supporters of these missionaries respond generously to this opportunity. I am saddened to see some supporters who want to respond, but have not arranged their financial affairs so that they are able to make a larger contribution. I am most disappointed that many supporters fail to see the significance of this unique opportunity. It is a chance to make a once-in-a-lifetime, major contribution—in the form of capital—to families who have dedicated their lives to God's service.

There are many ways to give in the form of capital. I have focused on housing because it is a capital item that everyone needs. Giving our children a head start in accumulating housing capital can be the foundation of lifelong financial stability. Providing their education is another capital contribution—the most important financial investment we can make for our children. We can apply these gifts of capital to others as well. I work with a foundation that makes scholarships available to missionary children. This offers the double benefit of providing an education and relieving the missionaries of this major expense.

The concept of giving capital is perhaps the most significant aspect of creative giving. It is giving more than money; it is helping someone become self-sustaining. Tuition at a vocational school is more valuable to an unemployable young man than groceries. A gift of capital provides the potential to move an individual beyond dependency into the responsibility of stewardship.

Giving capital also has significant implications for the mission enterprise. Too often, the missionary leaders hold the strings on available resources, making the national Christians (those native to a country) dependent on them. Much of what we do in this regard violates man's nature. So when we consider financial involvements overseas, we need to ask whether our action will set free or bind the national Christians. We should begin to think in terms of providing the right "seed money" (capital) with appropriate assistance. Giving capital makes it possible to preserve the personal dignity and responsibility that God has given every Christian. A mission leader recently expressed his feeling that "giving capital is a new exercise in Christlikeness in giving everything, the practical application of lordship in a new dimension."

Our giving to others should always be constructive. It should contribute to permanent solutions to their need. If our giving is made in the form of capital, it can accomplish that goal.

Personal Involvement in Creative Giving

Creativity, strategy, and faith can work together in transforming our giving into an exciting enterprise. This will not happen without effort on our part, but I can assure you from experience that the rewards make the effort worthwhile. Following are a few steps that we can take to help develop our talents in giving.

Develop your giving talent. If you are involved in giving, especially if your gift is giving, take time to develop your talent. Be willing to pay the price in time and effort to maximize your giving and its results. This development should involve praying, discussing, observing, listening, thinking, analyzing, and experimenting.

Developing your giving talent involves work. Studying the tax laws and working with accountants and attorneys is hard work, but it is worth it. Setting up a foundation to facilitate giving is a great deal of trouble and involves some expense, but it can be very valuable. Traveling to the mission fields (this only sounds glamorous!) to study situations and work out solutions to problems is hard work, but it produces results. Studying Scripture to discover the principles involved in our relationship to material possessions, and our giving and receiving takes time, but it is very rewarding.

Deliberately cultivate creativity. Cultivating creativity involves the willingness to challenge traditional patterns. Don't be hypnotized by tradition. Be willing to let God lead you into new approaches.

God does not lead everyone in the same way. I have no doubt that God led George Müller to live and operate his orphanages in day-to-day dependence on God's provision through other Christians. Hudson Taylor followed a similar pattern of prayerfully counting on God's provision. In contrast, William Carey found God's leading to be entirely different. He was fully involved in the missionary enterprise and leadership, yet used his unusual linguistic ability to teach at the university. He also translated more of the Scriptures into a greater number of languages than most people could do in a lifetime. After a few years in India, he instructed his supporters to send no more money. He explained that his teaching salary was sufficient to support the four couples then in India, and suggested that his supporters use the money to send more missionaries. Each of these men lived by faith, yet God's leading for each was different. We need to shed our preconceptions and, in faith, let God lead us into new pathways of creativity.

Piet Hein is a contemporary Danish poet, designer, and engineer—a truly versatile person. When asked about an unusual accomplishment, he replied, "The trick is not to let yourself be hypnotized by traditional solutions and present solutions, but to see the whole wide manifold of possibilities, to generalize the problem, to scan the whole field with all the possible dimensions and degrees of freedom and then pick the best possibility."[1] Hein gives us the theory, and Carey provides the example of deliberately exercising our creativity to further God's Kingdom.

Recognize your unique calling. The lives of Müller, Taylor, and Carey illustrate that God does not lead each of us in the same direction.

Jesus cautioned Peter to focus on God's leading for himself, not on God's leading for John. In sharp contrast to His leading for the other apostles, God led Paul into ministry to the Gentiles. God's pattern for the priests and the Levites in Israel regarding their relationship to material possessions was entirely different than it was for Israel in general. This contrast persists in the New Testament. Paul vigorously defended the right of those who serve the gospel to receive their living from the gospel. Although he chose not to exercise this privilege, Peter took advantage of it. In contrast to this dependence, Paul instructs Christians in general to provide for their own needs and to be able to give to others. We each need to determine God's leading for ourselves, and be obedient to that calling.

Understand the nature of faith in giving and receiving. While we recognize differences in calling, we often glamorize what we refer to as "the life of faith" and minimize the life of responsibility. As I mentioned earlier, this may be because those who receive their support "by faith" are in church leadership and missionary positions. Stories of God's provision are central to their experience and are often repeated so the rest of us begin to regard their experience as the norm rather than the exception. My illustrations of how God has provided automobiles and housing for missionaries do not instruct most of us about receiving, because we are the ones God uses to do the providing.

Receiving is no more an act of faith than is giving, and perhaps less so. How could we possibly conclude that asking and receiving is more of an act of faith than responsible stewardship, planning, and giving? Hebrews 11 describes faith and its involvements. Noah, Abraham, Joseph, Moses, Joshua, and the others demonstrate that faith involves belief, action, determination, and perseverance. Faith includes all the actions of stewardship, giving, and receiving.

Give by faith. Hebrews 11:6 says that "without faith it is impossible to please God." The writer is speaking of an active faith; "faith by itself, if it is not accompanied by action, is dead" (James 2:17). If our stewardship is to be pleasing to God, both our giving and receiving must be acts of faith; a faith that assumes the responsibility to take action.

Conclusion

Giving is a natural result of God's image within us. It is a very tangible, physical manifestation of love, and as such it represents an expression of God's nature. That is why giving is so satisfying to us and so pleasing to God.

Giving is a great privilege and a great enhancement to Christian community. All of us can give, and some of us have the gift of giving. Whatever our ability, means, or calling, making the effort to increase in the grace of giving is a significant and worthwhile endeavor. We have looked at some of the aspects of doing this. Our ability to fully participate in the grace of giving depends on our stewardship—mastering the financial aspects of our lives.

NOTES:
1. Jim Hicks, "A Poet with a Slide Rule," *Life Magazine*, Vol. 61, October 14, 1966, page 55.

TWELVE

Principles of Money Management

In this chapter I will present elementary principles that will lead to control of your financial situation. I will not go into details such as budget preparation, investment choices, short- or long-range planning, or any of the topics commonly regarded as financial planning. That specific advice must be tailored to your individuality, diversity, variety of gifts, and calling. Instead, I will focus on a few ideas that have broad application.

The objective in applying principles of money management is to realize financial freedom. Although this term is often used to indicate an abundant supply of resources, I am talking about being in control of your finances. We have already studied the bondage of materialism, the slavery to material things that can entangle both the rich and the poor. Here, however, I am not referring to the trap of materialism, but to the lack of mastery of your financial situation. A lack of financial control can vary in intensity from constant anxiety and concern, to actual financial difficulty, to the severe limitations of continuing poverty.

Throughout most of man's history, financial bondage meant literal bondage—either slavery or debtor's prison. Today's suffering from financial bondage is more mental than physical, consisting of constant worry and concern about financial needs, the embarrassment of being unable to meet obligations, and the limitations of financial inadequacy. These are the characteristics of financial bondage:

> Constant worry and concern about financial matters. Preoccupation with financial concerns.
>
> Excessive obligations. Even when we are not delinquent, our financial demands are burdensome and limit our freedom.
>
> Delinquency. This is true indebtedness: the inability to meet our obligations as agreed.
>
> An inability to extricate ourselves from a situation. Frustration, discouragement, and guilt related to finances. The opposite of confidence.
>
> Continually being on the receiving end of the giving-receiving scale. Inability to exercise the grace of giving.
>
> No freedom to live in accordance with our priorities. Financial considerations control our lives.

In contrast, the following characteristics demonstrate financial freedom:

> Confidence in financial matters. Finances in proper place and perspective.
>
> Few or no obligations.
>
> Current in all existing obligations.
>
> Having a margin.
>
> Praise, joy, and thanksgiving related to finances.
>
> Ability to grow in the grace of giving.

Freedom to realize established priorities. In control rather than in subjection.

Financial freedom is a wonderful experience! There are a few simple rules that will help all of us experience it. The first is the most important!

Live Below Your Income

This is the "first commandment," the golden rule of finances. It is basic to all other considerations because it makes everything else possible. Living below your income is absolutely essential to financial health. By this I simply mean that total expenditures—for whatever purpose—must be less than total income. The amount coming in must exceed the amount going out.

In order to live below your income, you must control your standard of living. This requires a philosophy of life that puts material things in their proper place. It cannot be a materialistic philosophy based on a greedy desire for more; it need not be an ascetic philosophy in which you deny yourself the enjoyment of material things. It should be a balanced philosophy that sets an appropriate standard of living for your circumstances. Most important, your standard of living must be established at a level *below* your income.

If this rule is violated, there is no way to escape the consequences. Even little violations are deadly. They not only establish a precedent, but always add to the difficulty of tomorrow's situation. Therefore the rule to live below your means must be applied rigidly. Make no exceptions to this rule, regardless of the situation.

Establish Your Priorities

Notice that the basic rule of financial freedom is to live *below* your income, not *at* your income level. Living below your income implies a surplus, however small it may be. This surplus presents the opportunity for financial planning according to priorities.

Proper, scriptural priorities provide a foundation for God's continuing blessing. Here is a suggested sequence of priorities:

Taxes and Debts (Automatic responsibilities)
Basic Giving (Putting God first)
Basic Family Needs (Food, housing, education, medical)
Saving for a Margin (Insurance a partial option)

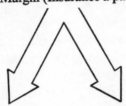

Increased Giving   Secondary Family Needs
                         (Clothing, transportation,
                         recreation)
Increased Giving   Saving for Capital
Increased Giving   Family Amenities
                         (Convenience and comfort)
Increased Giving   Personal Amenities
                         (Travel, luxuries, etc.)

The first four priorities are basic essentials. Giving is included in this category because there seems to be a correlation between basic giving and financial discipline. Entirely apart from any reward is the subjective aspect of giving; it does something for us.

Beyond the first four essentials are two tracks, both of which need to be pursued. Establishing the priority for these items is a personal matter. Balance must be achieved at the discretion of the individual and family.

I would like to make one point regarding the last four secondary items on the right-hand side of the diagram. When given the proper place in our order of priorities, there is nothing wrong with these items. They are desirable aspects of our utilization of material things. God "richly provides us with everything for our *enjoyment,*" (1 Timothy 6:17). The Israelites were encouraged to use the tithe that they set aside for the special celebration to purchase "whatever you like . . . anything you wish" (Deuteronomy 14:26). So God is generous—often more generous than we sometimes realize—in regard to our enjoyment of the material universe He has provided for us.

These priorities generally reflect our financial responsibility as indicated in Scripture. Though some of them are quite mandatory, they are not absolute in every situation. Their application will vary at different times in our lives. Ecclesiastes 3:1 reads, "There is a time for everything, and a season for every activity under heaven." Even our giving has a "season." It varies greatly at different phases of our lives. For example, someone in severe financial difficulty may find it necessary to give priority to meeting his obligations, even if this means he must temporarily curtail his generosity. Or, a student who is investing in his education may not be able to give the same proportion of his resources as when he moves into his productive employment years.

Master Your Credit
We have already talked about the bondage of indebtedness. Although the Scriptures do not prohibit all borrowing, every reference to it from the borrower's standpoint is negative. The borrower is described as the lenders' servant. We quoted Proverbs 21:20: "The wise man saves for the future, but the foolish man spends whatever he gets" (TLB). And more!

In our society, credit is not only readily available, it is thrust on us through intense merchandising. This is because lending is an extremely profitable business. And if it is profitable to the lender, it is expensive to the borrower. Even if Scripture had nothing at all to say about it, common sense would tell us that consumer borrowing should be avoided.

The first requirement of creating financial order is to live below our income. Buying on credit is actually living beyond our income, using tomorrow's income to purchase what we want today.

A little analysis reveals how expensive consumer credit can be. A revolving credit account is the ultimate trap. Many people use these accounts to the maximum of their approved credit, and charge new items as they make payments against their unpaid balance. This practice automatically adds the interest charge (usually eighteen percent or more) to everything they purchase. In addition, the buyer becomes to some extent a captive customer. Without available cash to shop for bargains, the revolving credit buyer makes purchases wherever his account happens to be.

Many people who use credit extensively feel that their basic financial problem is their income level. But this is not the case. The basic problem is that they have a higher standard of living than their income will support, and that they use credit to achieve it.

For many years, my firm has worked with families that are purchasing homes. This has involved credit checks and detailed investigation of their finances. We have learned that the level of income is a very poor indicator of financial status. Some financially disciplined families with annual incomes of $15,000 have more financial stability and savings than financially undisciplined families that earn $40,000! Some individuals use a financial windfall, such as an unexpected bonus, to get themselves deeper in trouble by using the money as a down payment on a consumer item. The level of income is secondary to the ability to manage it.

I recognize that there are proper uses of credit. Perhaps that is why there are no flat prohibitions against using credit in Scripture. The acceptable uses of credit fall into several categories.

Capital items that appreciate. These are major items that would otherwise be virtually impossible to purchase without credit. They would include major capital items for a business, land and buildings for a farmer, or a house for the consumer. Since the purchase of a house affects nearly all of us, it is worthy of some discussion here.

If we are certain of future appreciation, it seems logical to extend our credit to the utmost in the area of housing. This is almost unquestionably true in regard to our basic housing requirements. The benefits of ownership over renting are significant. They include building equity in a home plus the personal benefits of home ownership. In addition, there are other financial benefits to home ownership such as the homestead exemption on real estate taxes, and other tax benefits and deductions. Beyond the level of basic housing, we move to the luxury level where we need to exercise more discernment. There is nothing wrong with enjoying a comfortable, beautiful home if we can afford it without sacrificing other values. Here we need to carefully determine the actual cost of home ownership and balance it against our other priorities.

People are often unaware of their housing costs, especially if their equity in their home is large. Putting income tax and appreciation considerations aside, the cost of interest, taxes, insurance, and maintenance expenses is usually a *minimum* of one percent of the value of the house per month. A $100,000 house, for example, costs $1,000 per month; a $300,000 house costs $3,000 per month. We often fail to understand that this expense exists even if the house is completely paid for. The interest needs to be taken into account whether we pay it or not, because the money invested in our house could be earning income through other investments.

This means that a couple whose children are no longer in their home, who lives in a $200,000 house, could sell it, invest their equity, pay $1,000 rent, and have $1,000 leftover for other uses (taxes not considered). I am not advocating that all Christians own minimal housing or pay rent, but I am emphasizing the need to realistically analyze our housing costs so we can make choices according to our priorities. As a builder and designer, I personally take great pleasure in attractive housing. I have no intention of reducing the level of enjoyment my wife and I receive through our home. But I am aware of the cost, can afford it, and have made the personal decision that it is worth the cost.

The main issue here is the degree to which we should use credit to enjoy housing beyond the basic level. Credit is so readily available for housing that we can easily become overextended. Another thing to keep in mind when we consider housing beyond the basic level is the long-term cost of financing its purchase. When added to a mortgage, $10,000 in the additional purchase price will cost $31,592 if paid over thirty years on a ten percent mortgage. In the United States, we need to consider the tax deductions for home interest expense and weigh the entire cost against our needs and the home's potential appreciation.

Deciding what level of housing we need becomes very complex as we consider its cost; tax, investment, and appreciation factors; plus our personal preferences. I would not presume to give any guidelines for this very personal decision, but I encourage careful analysis and deliberation in this use of credit.

Capital items that depreciate slowly. For businesses, this includes machinery, equipment, vehicles, etc. For consumers, it may include major appliances and automobiles. I believe credit should be used for these personal purposes cautiously and rarely, if at all. I am strongly inclined to advise against using credit for personal purposes. Forgoing the immediate benefits and saving for these personal items is by far the best policy. Let me give you some personal illustrations of this.

The most important financial decision I have ever made in my life involved a small amount of money. I have made decisions regarding the use of hundreds of times the amount of money involved in that decision, but can state without hesitation that it was the most important.

My first ambition after being discharged from the Navy in 1946 was to purchase an automobile. Every young man wants a car, and I was no exception. New automobiles were in very limited supply because of wartime shortages, and used ones were very expensive. If you made a substantial cash deposit, dealers would put your name on a waiting list, but the estimates for delivery were several years in the future. Price controls were still in effect on new automobiles, so "black market" purchases were common. If you were fortunate enough to purchase a new Chevrolet from a dealer for the list price of $800 to $900, you could immediately and legally sell it for three times that amount.

I had saved $1,000 during my three years in the Navy. After much searching, I located a 1946 Pontiac with 20,000 miles that was available for a little more than $2,000. It was plain and had all plastic trim because of the wartime shortage of metals, but it looked attractive to me. The bank was very willing to loan me the additional money I needed for the purchase. Just before making the purchase, I realized that it was not wise to spend all of my savings and go into debt to purchase a car that was somewhat inferior, not new, and not absolutely necessary. So I promised myself that I would get along without an automobile until I could purchase one in cash from a dealer at list price. In the meantime I would use my father's prewar pickup. If the young ladies were not satisfied with my transportation, they would have to walk. Three years later, I purchased a new Ford under the conditions I had established. This was the beginning of a good habit, for I have never purchased an automobile or a vehicle through credit for personal or business use.

A few months after that automobile purchase, a Navy friend attended my wedding. I knew that he had used credit to buy an automobile right after our discharge. In discussing various aspects of our lives, he asked about my new car. He commented that if he could only be free from his automobile payments, he would be able to get ahead financially. In contrast, I had saved enough money to have a new house under construction and nearly completed.

Except for housing, automobiles are our major consumer purchase. My advice is to be satisfied with whatever car you can purchase with cash. An old automobile is only a temporary inconvenience, which is far outweighed by the long-term benefits of financial discipline.

When we were married, my wife desired two items that would enable her to continue the interests she had enjoyed in her parents' home. One of them was a piano, and the other a sewing machine.

The state of Minnesota declared an unexpected bonus for veterans, which we earmarked for the piano. Three months before the bonus was to be paid, a local music store offered an unusual bargain on a piano. The piano could be purchased on a finance plan, but if the balance were paid within ninety days, all finance charges would be waived. We purchased the piano and paid for it in ninety days with the bonus proceeds. With the exception of our home financing, I believe this has been our only use of credit.

Early in our married life, my bride showed me a local department store's full-page advertisement for a domestic sewing machine that met all of her requirements. It was available for a $10 down payment and $10 a month for twenty-four months, resulting in a total cost of $250. Although we wanted to purchase the machine, I was not comfortable with the method. Instead of purchasing the machine at that time, we began to set aside $20 per month toward its future purchase. Five months later, we purchased the machine for $106 at a wholesale outlet that sold only for cash.

These illustrations demonstrate that the cost of credit often goes far beyond the finance charges. The finance charges are always expensive—and sometimes exorbitant—but other factors can be even more significant. Cash gives the buyer a wider choice of suppliers and can be used to leverage advantageous purchases. So I make a strong recommendation to avoid using credit to purchase an automobile, and recommend that credit never be used to purchase other consumer items. There is no justification for using credit to make these kinds of purchases.

Consumable items. Up to this point we have explored the use of credit for purchasing capital items that either appreciate, or depreciate slowly. Credit is often necessary and acceptable for the first category and should be used with caution for the second category. But most of the things we buy fall into the category of consumable items—those things that will be consumed immediately or have a short lifetime. Consumable items include food, clothing, travel, entertainment, etc. Credit should *never* be used for these items. If we are unable to provide the basic necessities of life for ourselves and our families, we should ask our Christian community for temporary assistance. When we use credit for consumable items, we are deliberately living above our income—insisting on enjoying today the things that tomorrow's income must pay for. Only one word accurately describes the use of credit for consumable items: *never*.

Credit as convenience. In this instance, I am not really talking about credit, but about charging for convenience. There is a distinction between a credit card and a charge card. A charge card that enables you to avoid carrying cash is a great convenience, especially when traveling. It also serves as automatic approval for things such as making hotel reservations or renting an automobile. In fact, it is often very difficult to rent a vehicle without a major charge card.

When charging for convenience, you pay your bill in full when it is received. If credit is a temptation to you, then you should use a charge card that does not permit credit extension. Normally one charge card is sufficient for convenience. Since there is an annual charge for most cards, additional ones are an unnecessary expense. The reason many people have multiple cards is to have extended credit in many places, which is only asking for trouble.

Credit has legitimate functions as well as pitfalls. We need to always be in control of our use of credit. We need to master it. The use of credit, more than any other area of our finances can lead to financial enslavement.

Learn to Buy Wisely

I believe the cost of living for identical consumption can vary by as much as fifty percent between families, depending on their buying habits. Yes, I mean that literally! Purchases that cost one family $20,000 a year will cost another family $10,000. Here are the factors that bring about this discrepancy.

Avoid the use of credit. I have said enough about this, but I include it here because it represents a good part of the fifty percent savings.

Always purchase with cash. By this I mean not only to avoid using credit, but always use cash at the point of purchase. There are some situations when immediate cash payment can be used to realize a discount. This may not be applicable in department stores, but is often true with small merchants or when purchasing from individuals. I have offered merchants who accepted charge cards the choice of purchasing with the card or with cash at a five percent discount. Since they must pay a fee to the card company and may still wait thirty days for their money, the cash is often more attractive. On one occasion, I had agreed to purchase an item for $600, the best price I could negotiate. While the owner was filling out my charge slip I looked in my billfold and informed him that I had enough cash and would pay $550 instead. Without a word or a moment's hesitation, he tore up the charge slip.

This rule applies even if you are forced to use credit for a purchase. Arrange your credit elsewhere, usually at your bank, where credit is normally cheaper. Then, as far as the purveyor is concerned, you are a cash customer. Next, learn to leverage your ability to pay cash to the maximum.

Separate your needs from your desires. One of the reviewers who made suggestions during the writing of this book commented that this factor could be developed into an entire chapter. While this is undoubtedly true, I am going to leave the application of this principle up to you.

In our affluent society we are constantly exposed to a barrage of advertising designed to create artificial needs. This exposure increases our need for discernment in separating our needs from our desires. The principles we have already discussed—living below your income, establishing priorities, and mastering credit—make it easier and more necessary for us to separate our needs from our desires. Unless our resources are unlimited, mastering our credit will automatically limit our expenditures. This limitation forces us to make more disciplined choices. Let me emphasize that realizing our desires is not wrong if they have been subjected to scriptural principles and have a proper place in our priorities.

Don't permit anyone else to create a need for you! Learn to be immune to advertising and teach your children the same resistance. We do not best express our love for our children by granting every desire that is planted in their minds through advertising or peer suggestion. The parental example of doing without things that would be nice to have, which everyone else seems to have, is the place to begin. Openly discussing the family budget and determining priorities through family decisions will help separate artificially created needs from genuine needs.

Never buy on impulse. Obviously this applies to larger purchases, but it is important in smaller ones, too. Buying decisions should precede and be separate from the actual buying situation. Unless your resources are adequate, even the grocery list should be prepared in advance, and the purchases should be limited to the list. The problem with impulse buying is why many women seldom send their husbands grocery shopping!

Anticipate your needs and exercise patience. This concept should apply to all purchases. On larger items, this allows time for study, comparison, and price shopping. The need to purchase quickly limits your options.

When it came time to replace our original, low-priced living room furniture, my wife and I anticipated purchasing the major items for three years. We decided on the style we wanted, browsed at every opportunity, and became acquainted with several dealers who would special order what we wanted at ten percent over their cost. We finally found exactly what we wanted and paid fifty-five percent of the full retail price.

Sometimes temporary provisions enable us to exercise patience. In my home office I used an old desk that I obtained for virtually nothing until I found a brand-new walnut desk and credenza at a salvage house. The retail price was more than $1,000, the sale price less than $300. The majority of the items in our home were purchased this way without the slightest compromise in quality or style. The only requirement was our patience.

Clothing needs can also be anticipated and planned. I refuse to make any compromises on the quality of my clothing, but I seldom purchase any item at retail. There are too many opportunities to purchase my clothing at a fifty percent discount. Since my wife has more time to shop, she realizes an even greater savings on her clothing purchases.

This concept is equally important for smaller purchases. A reasonable stock of household items can be purchased on sale at savings up to fifty percent. Buying household items on sale also saves time and money spent on running to the store for minor things. If you find yourself without light bulbs; bathroom, kitchen, and cleaning supplies; or literally dozens of other items around the house, you not only have to purchase them at full price, but may make extra trips to the store. In the rare instance when we use the last of a household item, we immediately put it on the list of future purchases. Rarely do we purchase household items at regular prices. I'm certain that we save at least one third on every household item we use.

The savings on household items can be even greater through the use of coupons. My wife has the habit of clipping coupons and does so without much time and effort. It is not uncommon for her to show me a grocery store receipt that shows a twenty percent discount on her expenditures due to the coupons. In the case of nonperishable items, she realizes the maximum benefit by waiting until a store sale coincides with the coupon she has on hand. Our reserve supply of household items makes it possible to wait for this advantage. Many times the savings are fifty percent, and occasionally more.

One recent study found that families with incomes of more than $40,000 per year use the majority of coupons. Those families with the lowest incomes, who needed the savings the most, seldom took advantage of coupons. This demonstrates the effectiveness of good financial discipline habits.

Take time to compare. Compare quality, desirability, size-price ratio, etc. The small package on sale may cost more per unit than the large package at regular price.

Buy value—not exclusively price. We have discussed conserving dollars by careful shopping. However this should not be done at the expense of quality. It is foolish to waste dollars by paying too much, but even more foolish to pay too little for an inferior product. Sometimes careful shopping will result in a superior product that will not be cheaper at the time of purchase, but will save many dollars over its lifetime. If you anticipate your needs and exercise patience, you will be able to realize both quality and price advantage.

Repair instead of replace. It is almost always more reasonable to repair something than to replace it. This principle is true both in the immediate expense and the long-term cost. It is certainly true in the case of an automobile. The American Automobile Association annually publishes the per-mile cost of operating different age automobiles. Taking into full account the cost of repairs, their survey shows that the newer the car the more expensive it is per mile. This does not mean that you should not purchase a new car, because there are other advantages to consider. It does mean that you should be sure you can afford a new car and that its expense fits into your priority system. It is only rationalization to think that you will save money by having a more expensive automobile to depreciate. Although there are exceptions to this rule, such as an automobile that is a "lemon" and requires constant repair, the general rule still applies. It is usually more advantageous to repair than to replace.

Always buy at your initiative. The proper buying sequence is to realize a need, make a decision to purchase the item needed, and then take the initiative to find a supplier. Be suspicious of any situation that does not follow this sequence. Never let anyone *sell* you anything. If you find yourself in a situation that involves sales pressure, always wait. Defer the purchase until you have made an independent decision.

I recently spoke with a salesman who informed me that his offer would be void if I did not purchase during our appointment. I dismissed him by telling him that I never sign during an appointment, but insist on making the decision alone. I would call him if I decided to purchase. He suddenly found a way to extend his offer for another day! Although his proposal was acceptable, I did not call him. I refuse to reward that kind of pressure. Pressured decisions are almost always wrong.

In a door-to-door selling situation, every factor is wrong. The initiative is not yours. You have not had a chance to anticipate the need, evaluate available products, compare, or search for a favorable price. The door-to-door price is virtually always too high. This problem is best handled before you get into the pressure of the sales pitch. Simply refuse the interview, and never make exceptions.

Buying is important. Disciplined buying habits coupled with limited use of credit can greatly increase the buying power of financial resources we have available. In many instances, a wife can make a greater contribution to family finances by giving attention to disciplined buying than by working outside the home. When both parents work, extra taxes, childcare, clothing, and transportation are direct, additional expenses. There is often a tendency to pay for services that family members would otherwise provide, and to claim additional "entitlements" (such as extra meals away from home, special entertainment, and travel) as rewards for working so hard. If this also results in lessened efficiency in buying and other aspects of family finances, there can easily be a net loss due to the wife working.

We have all heard that "a penny saved is a penny earned." This is actually an understatement because earnings are subject to income tax at the marginal bracket (our highest). This means that the penny saved can be twice as valuable as the one earned!

Plan and Budget

Planning is absolutely necessary to financial control. Couples should carefully work out their plans together. The first step is to establish priorities: the things you want to accomplish and their order of importance. You must then plan in relationship to those priorities.

It is wise to seek counsel in planning, which can be done on several levels. You may need help on the basic organization of family finances, on the career planning level, or in regard to investments and estate planning. You may also need help on the elementary level of budgeting, although I do not believe this is necessary for everyone. If basic financial principles are applied there may be no need for detailed budgeting. A budget may be absolutely necessary for some, primarily those who are in financial difficulty or are unable to discipline themselves on the basis of principle. Often a budget is necessary to begin good financial management, but becomes less important as the financial situation improves, good habits become established, and sound principles are incorporated into one's life. There are innumerable sources of counsel available on this level, and as I promised, I will not go into details. Any bookstore can provide you with books that will help you set up a budget.

Seek God's Guidance and Help

Prayer is an essential part of each Christian's life, and should be the foundation for every aspect of our finances. As God impresses His basic principles on our minds and they become incorporated into our lives, our prayers will not always focus on every detail but will resemble Paul's admonition to pray without ceasing. We will be able to conduct our affairs in an attitude of prayer in accordance with the truth God has revealed to us. God will give us wisdom (James 1:5), will direct our steps (Proverbs 16:9), and will, on the basis of this wisdom and direction, bless the plans we make with success (Proverbs 16:3).

I believe it is important to have an understanding of how God works in our lives in order to pray properly. The belief that God is deliberately orchestrating every detail of our lives may be fine when things are going well, but often leads to problems when things are going badly. I have known Christians whose faith was severely shaken during times of adversity when their prayers were not answered in the way they desired. One example of this is a man who built an expensive, new house, then felt that God let him down when he was unable to sell the old one. He "spiritualized" a perfectly natural problem: many Christians (and nonChristians) have difficulty selling their houses. This man's concept of God needed to be corrected. I have known many others who were confused by some misfortune, illness, or accident and were forced by their concept of God's working to rationalize that He must have "sent" the problem to teach them something.

God has not promised to control every detail of our lives, either the good ones or the bad ones. He has promised to give us strength to endure our problems (1 Corinthians 10:13) and to utilize everything that happens for our good (Romans 8:28). The fact that most of our experiences are the natural result of life in our world is made clear in 1 Corinthians 10:13, "No temptation has seized you except what is common to man." God's primary work is to accomplish His purpose in our lives by bringing us to maturity. Paul's confidence is that God "is able to do immeasurably more than all we ask or imagine, according to his power that is at work within us" (Ephesians 3:20). Paul also says, "It is God who works in you to will and to act according to his good purpose" (Philippians 2:13). In the economic realm, God teaches us the disciplines of good stewardship, which make success possible. He does this in preference to manipulating our circumstances so that our success would be guaranteed.

Because of my understanding of God's work in my life, I do not make it a habit to ask Him to bless my business. I ask Him to bless *me*. I do not believe that God is willing to manipulate the marketplace so that customers come to me rather than to a competitor. I do believe that if I ask, He will give me the wisdom to make our product desirable. God is more pleased when customers purchase houses from us because we offer exceptional value with integrity than He would be to miraculously provide those customers.

God has given us the responsibilities of dominion, and will work in our lives to make our dominion a reality. He will lead us and instruct us, but does not do the job for us. I have seen businessmen attempt to guarantee success by promising God a certain percentage of their business or profits. I do not believe we can buy God's blessing by such a promise. The ventures I have observed that operated on this premise all ended in failure. God is our Father, not our partner.

This does not mean we cannot ask God for help when it is needed, or that we ever reach the point where we are not depending on Him. It does mean that the manna situation of unusual provision should not be permanent. We should not expect God to continually manipulate the details of our financial affairs, when He has given us dominion over the material world and has taught us the principles of its workings. He is willing to give us the ability to assume the responsibilities of maturity.

Seek Counsel from Others

"Plans fail for lack of counsel, but with many advisors they succeed" (Proverbs 15:22). This biblical principle is based on the fact of our individual weaknesses and the benefits of community. "The heart is deceitful above all things" (Jeremiah 17:9). In addition to asking God to search our hearts and reveal our weaknesses, we need to seek others' counsel. This can be effective on several levels. Our brothers can provide an objective view as well as helpful analysis and guidance. Our spiritual leaders can offer experienced insight and direction into God's Word. Professionals such as counselors, psychologists, and career planners can help us work through many of our problems. Accountants, attorneys, estate planners, and investment advisors can be invaluable in the more technical aspects of our planning. "As iron sharpens iron, so one man sharpens another" (Proverbs 27:17).

Several precautions are advisable when seeking counsel. Many advisors, especially professional ones, tend to protect themselves by giving ultra-conservative advice. Seek those who will help you analyze the problem, search for alternative courses of action, consider the advantages and disadvantages, explore the possible consequences, and let you make the decisions. The best counselors are those who can give assistance without becoming personally and emotionally involved.

Remember, counsel is giving assistance and advice. You should always be free to make the final decision. For this reason you should not seek counsel from those who would be offended if you did not follow their advice.

Making Financial Decisions

Financial decisions, whether large or small, must be made in a deliberate manner by taking all of the basic principles into consideration. These principles should be consciously applied to the immediate situation one by one. This can be done best by asking yourself a series of questions:

Have I invited God into the decision by praying about it?
Will this be a step toward financial bondage or financial

freedom?

Is this step within my income?

Is this expenditure or investment the most important step I can take to realize my objectives in accordance with my priorities?

Does this step involve the unnecessary or unwise use of credit?

Have I anticipated this need, or is it an impulse?

Is this step at my initiative, or is it someone else's idea?

Am I under pressure to do this?

Am I exercising patience?

Is this a genuine need, just a desire, or—worse yet—an artificial need created by someone else?

Have I thoroughly investigated and compared all possibilities?

Is this within my plan and budget?

Am I exercising all of the leverage available?

Have I sought applicable counsel?

Does this step involve rationalization in any way?

Are we in agreement (if this is a joint decision), or is it one-sided?

If your answer to *any* of these considerations violates the principles outlined in this chapter, the step is probably wrong. If there is any doubt, wait. Never rush into a financial decision. When you approach decisions in a rational manner such as this, any uneasiness is a good indication that something is wrong. If you pray about the decision, you should insist on the complete peace of mind that the Holy Spirit is capable of giving. It is very rare to lose a real opportunity by taking the necessary time to be certain the decision is right. As Proverbs 21:5 advises, it is much better to run the risk of losing an opportunity than to make the wrong decision:

> The plans of the diligent lead to profit
>   as surely as haste leads to poverty.

Increasing Your Capital

Capital needs are entirely relative to the individual's talents, gifts, calling, and circumstances. All of us possess the human capital of our education, abilities, skills, and experience. We should work diligently to increase these, both for the personal benefit of our growth and for the compensation we receive. Success is not getting, as much as it is becoming, so the key to our future success is the person we become. Someone has said that we should work harder on ourselves than on our jobs. The more we become, the more valuable we become, and compensation is related to our value.

Many of us have little need for material capital beyond what we require for our homes, retirement, and savings reserve for emergencies. For some of us, our callings are such that additional capital could even be a handicap. Paul expresses this in his advice to Timothy: "No one serving as a soldier gets involved in civilian affairs—he wants to please his commanding officer" (2 Timothy 2:4). This verse is often misinterpreted to mean that all Christians should avoid any involvement with material things. It may generally apply in the sense that none of us should become so involved that we neglect other responsibilities, but the verse's specific application is to Timothy in his special calling. For most of us, our responsibilities to God include our involvement with material things, and capital is necessary to fully exercise our gifts and function within our calling.

Capital can be acquired by inheritance, it can be saved, and it can be created. An inheritance or other windfall can be an excellent opportunity to increase our capital base. Saving is the slowest, but perhaps the surest way to accumulate capital. Accumulating capital through saving provides sufficient capital for many of us. Some of us have the ability to create capital. This usually requiries some capital as a base, or an idea that is good enough to entice others to provide the capital base. God's blessing through this ability gives us the opportunity to be co-laborers with Him in the creation of wealth. Using the physical resources God has provided and transforming them into benefit for mankind is dominion in the fullest sense of the word.

I would like to repeat one previously discussed warning here; the need for capital should not become an excuse for unlimited acquisition. Instead, it should provide the opportunity to transfer capital to those in need. The ultimate gift is the transfer of capital, because it will produce continuing benefits far into the future.

Escaping Financial Bondage

This section is for those who find themselves in financial difficulty. Again, I will not go into detail, but will outline some steps you can take to bring the problem into focus and begin to work toward a solution. You will need counsel at every stage of the process.

Understand yourself. It is rare, but not impossible, that financial difficulty is the result of circumstances. Far more often, financial difficulty is the result of personal weaknesses. Excuses for difficulty seldom coincide with its real reasons. Circumstancial reasons, however obvious they seem, can only be regarded as actual causes after eliminating personal factors. Nearly every person with bad credit has plausible excuses for it, but the actual causes are usually poor management and lack of foresight. So the place to begin resolution is with yourself.

The first thing to do is to write down everything you know about yourself in relationship to money. Write down your assumptions about material things and your situation. Include what you believe the Bible says about money. This effort will take some honest soul-searching. Dig up the attitudes that you have never expressed. One person I counseled discovered that his excessive spending was based on the fact that he felt he was deprived as a child and had subconsciously determined to make up for it by lavish spending for himself and his family. His compulsion was so strong that he had refused to let himself add up the total of his debts!

Next take a close look at your financial habits. How do you handle money? Is it planned or happenstance? Why do you handle money this way? Pray for insight, wisdom, and soul-searching by the Holy Spirit. If you are married, you and your spouse should do all of these things separately, and then together. When you have done your best to know yourself, you are ready for counsel.

Obtain others' insights about yourself. I suggest that you approach at least three different people—a Christian friend who knows you very well, one who is willing to help but does not really know you well, and one of your spiritual leaders. (You should be confident that each of these individuals is competent in his own finances.) Ask them for their observations concerning how you handle money. Show them what you have written down and ask for their insight. You must be entirely candid and open with these people. You will never receive good advice if you cover up part of your situation. Open yourself to frank observations and to the correction of your own conclusions.

Face reality. Remember the simple logic we quoted from Mike Vance's seminar on creative thinking: You must start from reality, from correct premises, if you desire to reach constructive conclusions. This may not be easy because you have probably been concealing the real problems from yourself. This is no time for rationalization. In most cases you will see that your problem is not so much circumstantial (although circumstances can aggravate it) as it is your own doing. Take plenty of time for your analysis. If some point in your analysis upsets you emotionally, you are probably on the track of a basic weakness. When you understand the causes of your difficulty and are willing to make the necessary changes, you will be ready to turn to the practical aspects of resolving your problem.

List all of your assets and liabilities.

Liquidate assets not absolutely necessary. If you are making automobile payments, sell the car and, if a car is absolutely necessary, buy one that is within your means.

Make a budget that is substantially below your income. Take the list of essential and nonessential expenditures that you prepared and cross off every nonessential item. Then be ruthless in paring down your list of essentials. In this emergency situation, you will have to obtain your clothing from one of the many free supplies of good, used clothing available. Cancel all subscriptions, memberships, and anything else that is not absolutely essential. You can see that I am thinking in terms of drastic curtailment. Be ruthless.

Your emergency budget will consist of two items: debt payment and minimal family living. If these measures do not reduce your expenses below your income, you could take other steps. You may be able to consolidate your debts for a longer term, or sell your home if you own one.

Live below your income! It is essential that you reach the point where you can follow the "first commandment" of finances—living below your income. This will leave a surplus, however small, with which you can begin to develop your other priorities.

Ask your brothers for help if necessary. Write down your plan and discuss it with your counselors. They may recognize that you need assistance at certain points and be willing to arrange it. If this is the case, receive assistance graciously.

Make prayer an integral part of the solution. When you are in a "manna" situation, it is certainly appropriate to ask God for help. God is more interested in your freedom from bondage than you are yourself! He will reveal the weaknesses of your heart (Psalm 139:23-24), give wisdom if you ask (James 1:5), and lead you to brothers who will provide direct financial assistance if it is needed. The most important aspect of God's help is what He accomplishes within us. His work within us is what brings us to the point of maturity where we can assume responsibility for providing for ourselves and for others' needs.

God is not pleased when the "manna" situation becomes permanent. As human parents, we are not pleased if our children continue in helpless dependency on us. We desire that they grow into maturity and begin to assume responsibility. We never become independent of God, but our dependency can mature to different levels. In regard to material things, we can mature to exercise responsible and productive stewardship, and can be used of God to provide for others.

In every situation, our role in solving our problems is active rather than passive. As God provides insight and wisdom, we can take initiative and expect His blessing.

> Commit to the LORD whatever you do,
>   and your plans will succeed. . . .
> In his heart a man plans his course,
>   but the LORD determines his steps.   (Proverbs 16:3,9)

> We constantly pray for you, that our God may count you worthy of his calling, and that by his power he may fulfill every good purpose of yours and every act prompted by your faith.   (2 Thessalonians 1:11)

Conclusion

Let us look at the things suggested in this section. Their benefits are more obvious when we look at them together:

> Live below your income.
> Establish your priorities.
> Master your credit.
> Learn to buy wisely.
> Plan your financial affairs.
> Seek God's guidance and help.
> Seek the counsel of others.
> Discipline every financial decision.
> Increase your capital.

To someone unaccustomed to financial discipline, these things may seem exceedingly difficult. It is true that substantial effort is required at the beginning, but when these principles become part of our thought patterns, they become automatic. An analogy would be that of a doctor who makes a complicated diagnosis in just a few minutes. Behind what seems so simple are his years of experience in applying his training. Our application of these ideas can also become routine. What at first sounds difficult becomes extremely easy because we can conduct our affairs on the basis of predetermined principles. The benefits of financial discipline are very much worth the effort.

Following these principles of money management will lead to financial freedom. This is true at every income level. Living below your income does not mean that you will not try to increase it. It does mean that you can always be in control of your financial situation.

Contentment is the opposite of covetousness, not the opposite of growth. Freedom is not realized by accumulating an impressive net worth, but by being in control of our finances. Material things are the "very little" mentioned in Luke 16:10. When we enjoy the freedom of financial control, we are free to progress toward greater maturity—not only in regard to material things, but in other areas of life as well.

THIRTEEN

Evaluating Contemporary Economic Systems

Economics is not static. It has been developing throughout history. In Genesis we found the basic principles governing man's relationship to material things and their application to a nomadic society. We saw the same principles modeled in Israel's agrarian society and found that these principles were confirmed in the more complex societies of New Testament times. Man's cultural, political, and economic systems, are constantly changing. Man has never produced a perfect economic system. Flawed by sin, man will never be able to establish and maintain a system that completely conforms to God's Law. All of man's systems are marked by sin.

Economic systems—in the sense that we think of them today—had not been conceived, developed, or articulated at the time the Scriptures were written. The word "capitalism" did not appear until the end of the eighteenth century, and was actually introduced into broad usage by Marx and Engels. Socialism and communism, according to their theorists, were developed in response to capitalism's weaknesses.

Man's economic systems are not only imperfect, but are in constant development and change. In contrast, scriptural principles are consistent and universal. So scriptural truth is just as applicable today as when it was written centuries ago. God has given us basic financial principles that we are to work out in our own lives and within our own systems. Through this book we have attempted to discover these principles.

At one point in history, God established an economic system for the nation of Israel. Man immediately distorted this system. The prophets constantly pointed out the evils and injustices resulting from this distortion. There is no record that even a single Year of Jubilee, an essential feature of justice in God's system, was ever held. By Jesus' time, the system was completely corrupt. So even if God established a universal economic system, it would certainly be corrupted by man.

The main purpose of the New Testament teaching on economics is to instruct Christians how to live as individuals and in community within any system in which they find themselves. Jesus' and Paul's objective was not so much to command the system as to instruct Christians in how to live. God's truth, however, is valid when applied within a system because God created man and the material universe to work best when in harmony with God's Law. The ultimate success of any system is determined by the extent of its conformity to God's purpose.

The Need to Evaluate Economic Systems

We need to evaluate the world's economic systems in relationship to biblical truth for several reasons. The world is in great ideological conflict. This conflict can be understood only in the light of biblical revelation. Smaller nations are pawns in the ideological conflict between the major systems, and are tempted to make decisions on the basis of expediency without understanding the consequences. As Christians, we can fail to recognize and correctly evaluate the significance of the issues if we do not understand and apply biblically based principles.

Paul makes it clear that we are to be responsible citizens, which we cannot be without evaluating our world according to biblical principles. So we need to ask several questions:

> To what degree do today's economic systems conform to man's nature and God's purpose in creation?
> How do these systems support or contradict basic, scriptural principles?
> What are the systems' essential strengths and weaknesses?
> Should Christians today take a position regarding the world's conflicting systems?
> To the extent that we can influence our society, what should be the direction of that influence?

My contention that God has not given a detailed blueprint for a universal economic system does not mean that systems are not important. We all live within an economic system that gives us freedom or places severe limitations on our economic behavior. Ideally the system should make it possible for us to be *communitarian individuals*. That is, it should give us freedom to live according to biblical principles governing our individuality and community. To do this, the system must conform to the principles we discovered in Scripture. Below are some characteristics of a system that would enable us to live according to God's order.

> The system should be founded on the recognition of God as Creator and the acceptance of His sovereignty.
> At the very least, the system must respect and protect those who recognize and serve God.
> The system should preserve the dignity of individuals as God has created them in their individuality, freedom of choice, personal responsibility, and diversity.

The system must not be coercive in enforcing conformity, but respectful of individuality: neither denying freedom nor enforcing conformity. (Each individual's freedom of choice extends to economic matters. Each person either structures his economic life in compliance with God's principles or violates them. Each will realize the consequences of his choices.)

The system must accept man as being in God's image, with great potential for good; and sinful, with great tendency toward evil.

The system must permit and encourage community. Only the voluntary association of free individuals can meet the requirements of both individual freedom and the need for interdependence in community. The society itself cannot be the only community, because this would remove freedom of choice.

The motivational structure must be in line with man's nature. Man must be free to provide for himself, his family, and his freely selected communities.

The system must provide for private ownership of property, including the right to own and manage capital. This is essential to man's nature (individuality, freedom of choice, personal responsibility, and diversity) and to his obedience (responsibility, stewardship, and generosity).

The system must provide a stable monetary system in which money can function as a store of value and medium of exchange. Inflation is a violation of this responsibility.

The system must be pluralistic. Society cannot be constructed to accommodate only certain individuals or classes. There must be freedom for diverse individuals and diverse communities.

The system must preserve order. Individual freedom does

> not mean libertarianism. Society must protect itself
> and its individuals against those who violate the rights
> of others.

The system must establish and maintain justice. Exploitation, oppression, and injustice must be controlled.

Up to this point, our attention has focused on biblical principles that pertain to material things. Some of these principles are
directly related to our material possessions, but the most basic of
them are related to man's nature and the nature of the material
universe. As such, these principles have application far beyond the
field of economics.

In the same way, any analysis of systems must go beyond the
technical aspects of economics and deal with the basic underlying
principles. Pennington Haile refers to the "few, great, basic ideas"
that underlie our systems. "These ideas are not political or economic in their nature; they are truly philosophical, for they deal
with man's basic concepts about his own nature. Were we to
search through all the pages of history, we should find that only a
few concepts as to man's nature and proper function have been
compelling enough to shape men's thoughts, or to mold the sort of
society formed to accord with them."[1]

To move from the biblical principles we have discussed to
contemporary economic systems is to skip over a great deal of
man's history, but it is acceptable for our purposes. Haile points
out the three world views that have dominated Western man's
thinking during recent centuries.

> First, the sustaining dream of the dark medieval period, in
> which man's hopes were centered in heaven, his fears in
> hell. In revolt against this, with the "Age of Enlighten-
> ment," came the bright exciting vision of a society founded
> on personal freedom. In such a society, man, guided by the
> light of reason, and freed from any pre-ordained authority
> of church or state, could decide on the amount and kind of

political control needed to protect his freedom. Later there came a third vision . . . the dream of a life of security underwritten by the state for the well-being of a classless society.[2]

The medieval view was based on the philosophies of Aristotle and Thomas Aquinas. The works of Isaac Newton and John Locke contain the basis for the dream of freedom. Kant, Fichte, and Hegel laid the foundation on which Marx began to construct his socialist theory.

In addition to the major ideologies of capitalism, communism, and socialism, one encounters a great number of combinations, degrees, and shadings of each. It is not an exaggeration to say that there are no pure systems in any category. All socialists agree that their objective of pure socialism has never been even remotely approached. *Laissez-faire* capitalists decry the fact that all capitalistic systems are adulterated, and refer to even the purest, current systems as "interventionist" rather than capitalistic. Even proponents of a particular system do not agree on their definitions, and words themselves have different meanings and connotations to different people. In addition, societies in each category exhibit great diversity. Characteristics of the past often do not correspond to the present. Distinctions are not as clear as we imagine or would like them to be.

Evaluating competing systems is rendered difficult by all of these considerations. In the absence of any pure systems, comparative analysis of existing systems presents problems as well. This is complicated by the tendency to evaluate one's own system in terms of its ideals, while judging competing systems on the basis of examples. This gives the polemicist a distinct advantage, since all actual systems are flawed by man's sin. Proponents of all systems evaluate according to this tendency, but the tendency is built into socialist doctrine through the belief that socialism will be fully realized and the state will disappear only in the final stages of progress.

Joseph A. Schumpeter's *Capitalism, Socialism, and Democracy* is commonly regarded as a classic work on the comparison of economic systems, although he decidedly favors socialism. He devotes the major portion of the book to giving a negative answer to the question, "Can capitalism survive?", which is based on observed weaknesses and theoretical projections. He follows this evaluation with the question, "Can socialism work?" and begs the question in the next sentence, "Of course it can!" His subsequent "proof" is based on socialist theory, not its realization. Schumpeter admits this weakness himself: "We have now to guard not only against the dangers that lurk in any attempt to compare a given reality with an *idea*, but also against the error or trick inherent in any comparison of a given reality with an *ideal*."[3] I do not believe he guards against either. So I interpret this statement not so much as a warning as an admission.

All of these problems leave us with only one valid method of evaluation: the comparison of each system's accepted tenets with the biblical standards. Therefore we limit our evaluation to one simple question: "Do the underlying principles of the system conform to those taught in Scripture?"

The success of any system will be directly correlated with its conformity to the nature of man and the universe as God created them. If the basic principles conform we can work toward perfecting their application. If they violate scriptural truth, there is no possibility of realizing man's potential as God created him. This does not mean there cannot be "success" as defined outside of God's standards. It does mean that man cannot be fully man as created in God's image.

I will list briefly the principles, doctrines, and institutions of each system, covering the major systems in the order of their historic appearance. At the risk of being pedantic to my readers who are familiar with these subjects, I will begin with simple definitions. I do this to prevent emotionally charged connotations from prohibiting our focus on the basic meanings.

Capitalism

The simple definition of capitalism is "an economic system in which investment in and ownership of the means of production, distribution, and exchange of wealth is made and maintained chiefly by private individuals or corporations."[4] A more elaborate description reads:

> Capitalism, the economic system characterized by private ownership of property, production of goods for profit, and the institution of bank credit. Capitalism stresses freedom of individual economic enterprise, but the ultimate right of the state to supervise and regulate industry and trade (is) questioned by few.[5]

A popular economics textbook extends the definition somewhat, speaking in terms of the institutional arrangements that characterize capitalism. "These arrangements provide a set of basic beliefs that define how a society should be organized and how goods and services should be produced and income distributed. These beliefs are incorporated into the institutional arrangements that so typify a capitalist system."[6]

What follows is a summary of these beliefs or concepts, with a summary of the textbook description of each one.[7]

Private property. Land, labor, and capital—the agents of production—are held in private ownership. Individuals have the right to acquire property and to consume, control, buy, sell, give, or bequeath this property. This ownership encourages the thrift, accumulation, individual initiative, and industry that produce economic progress. Social groups or governments may impose limitations and restrictions on ownership. Corporations and governments can also own wealth.

The profit motive. Individuals or corporate managers are responsible for converting resources into products and deciding what to produce as guided by the marketplace. Profit is the motive of this process, and is necessary for the producer's economic survival. Profitability is the test that determines production and quantity, although the marketplace is the ultimate authority.

The price system. Decisions are made through the mechanism of prices, which are determined by supply and demand conditions. Prevailing prices determine production, distribution, and allocation of resources. The market is coordinated as millions of decentralized producers and distributors respond to supply and demand signals acting through the price mechanism.

Freedom of enterprise. Each individual has the right to choose any economic activity in any location. The institution of private property makes this possible. The welfare of society is advanced as the individual chooses the field in which he will be most productive.

Competition. Private property, freedom of enterprise, and the price system result in competition, which is indispensable to the system. This results in efficient use of resources and the elimination of waste, making cost reduction possible. To increase competitiveness, product innovation and improvement are emphasized. The increased number of producers results in a more equitable distribution of income and a greater variety of supply sources for the consumer than is possible through a monopolistic system.

Individualism. This word needs to be defined because it is used here in its simple reference to individual freedom. According to the *Random House Dictionary,* individualism is, "A social theory advocating the liberty, rights, or independent action of the individual." This definition is linked to the philosophical roots of capitalism and is consistent with the concept of freedom. It is related to competition, equality of opportunity, and especially to private property rights. The prospect of ownership provides the incentive for competition and hard work. It also provides protection from state encroachment. A limited state role, with the individual taking precedence over the state, is essential to individualism.

Consumer sovereignty. This is exercised through freedom of choice. It is assumed that large numbers of buyers and sellers, given a competitive market and freedom of choice, will make rational decisions. Since production is the means and consumption is the end, the producers must respond to the consumers' desires. Since the government role is limited, the consumer must apply the principle of "caveat emptor" to his decisions.

The work ethic. Hard work produces profits that lead to savings and investments. These produce interest and provide capital with which to multiply future products. Work brings rewards for those who are competent and ambitious, and is a desirable and essential aspect of life.

Limited government. In theory, the government should apply the doctrine of *laissez faire,* limiting its activity to a few general functions that individuals cannot do for themselves, such as national defense, law and order, diplomacy, and public construction and institutions. Each individual is more capable of determining his own interests than the government. A free-enterprise, market economy has its own built-in discipline. Intervention is not desirable or necessary. This concept has been applied in varying degrees, and in reality all governments have participated in economic activities to some extent.

These capitalistic institutional arrangements control the distribution of income and the process of savings and capital formation. Savings are translated into investments through the market mechanism. Interest rates and entrepreneurial judgments determine the allocation of available capital. Individuals and corporations have varied reasons for savings and investments. Banks serve as intermediaries between savers and borrowers. Schnitzer and Nordyke do an excellent job of summarizing these arrangements:

> Capitalism is an economic system which is characterized by a set of institutional arrangements. The centerpiece of capitalism is a freely competitive market where buyers satisfy their wants and sellers supply those wants in order to make

a profit. The price mechanism determines resource allocation, and freedom of enterprise and private property ownership provide incentives to save and produce. Individualism
is also at the core of the capitalist or free market ideology. It
was assumed by Adam Smith and others that people were
rational and would try at all times to promote their own
personal welfare. The individual, in promoting his or her
self-interest, works in the interest of society.

Competition is an indispensable part of a free enterprise system. In economic life, self-reliant individuals must
compete for economic rewards (good jobs, high pay, and
promotions) and business must compete for consumer
incomes. The Protestant work ethic stressed rewards in this
life, not in the hereafter. Hard work included thrift, which
could provide the savings necessary for investment. The
role of government is minimal in a capitalist economy.[8]

This is the most non-polemic and secular description of
capitalism I have been able to find. It should give you an adequate,
factual basis on which to compare the system's principles with
scriptural teaching. Because this book is theological in orientation,
permit me to point out some of the characteristics of capitalism
that relate more directly to scriptural concepts.

Freedom. A look at the elements of capitalism reveals that
capitalism requires freedom. It is impossible for the principles of
capitalism to exist and function under totalitarianism. They are
mutually exclusive by definition, because totalitarianism involves
total control. It is theoretically possible for capitalism to flourish
within a benevolent monarchy, oligarchy, or dictatorship. Given
the sinful nature of man with its bent toward self-aggrandizement,
however, such an arrangement is unlikely. If it were to exist, there
is little chance of its long-term survival. The temptations that
accompany absolute power are too great.

Proponents of capitalism are motivated by the fear of

tyranny. Freedom and liberty are their highest priorities. Regimented equality is the enemy. That is why it is necessary to use the word "democratic" to fully describe capitalism. Modern democracy developed with modern capitalism. They go hand-in-hand because, in their best manifestations, both are based on the same principles. Integrity, dignity, and value of the individual coupled with the necessity of community are basic to both concepts. Novak describes this relationship well.

> The two revolutions—political and economic—in practice, but also in theory, nourish each other. Both spring from the same logic, the same moral principles, the same nest of cultural values, institutions, and presuppositions. . . .
>
> The natural logic of capitalism leads to democracy. For economic liberties without political liberties are inherently unstable. . . .
>
> Not only do the logic of democracy and the logic of the market economy strengthen one another. Both also require a special moral cultural base. Without certain moral and cultural presuppositions about the nature of individuals and their communities, about liberty and sin, about the changeability of history, about work and savings, about self-restraint and mutual cooperation, neither democracy nor capitalism can be made to work. Under some moral-cultural conditions, they are simply unachievable. . . .
>
> What do I mean by "democratic capitalism"? I mean three systems in one: a predominately market economy: a policy respectful of the rights of the individual to life, liberty and the pursuit of happiness: and a system of cultural instructions moved by ideals of liberty and justice for all. In short, three dynamic and converging systems functioning as one: a democratic policy, an economy based on markets and incentives, and moral-cultural system which is pluralistic and, in the largest sense, liberal.[9]

Capitalism requires freedom. This is provided by democracy in the political realm, by the free market system in the economic realm, and by diverse, voluntary communities in the moral-cultural realm. In this arena of freedom, man's nature can be fully expressed.

Sin. There is room within capitalism for the recognition of sin. Since sin lies in man's heart, all man-made systems will be defective. These defects are rooted in man's sinful nature and will be expressed in any system. "Sin is rooted in the free personality beyond the reach of any system."[10]

Recognition of sin does not in itself guarantee anything, but makes it possible to construct a system based on reality. God chose to take the risk of giving man the freedom to sin. It is futile to attempt to create a system that eliminates sin. This would take away the freedom that is essential to man's nature. Since liberty is the highest priority within capitalism, economic virtue cannot be imposed.

Man's sin will manifest itself within capitalism, just as within any system. Sin will take a different form within each system, and can be based on the strengths of the system itself. God recognized the opportunities for evil present in Israel's system. He warned against some of them, such as the temptation to forget God and to rely on their self-sufficiency. He warned them against the selfish and unlimited acquisition of wealth. He gave instructions that would prevent many potential problems, such as the selfish disregard for the poor, the exploitation of the weak, and injustice for the helpless.

Community. The freedom of the individual includes the free choice of communities. This freedom is provided under capitalism, and makes possible an unlimited range of voluntary communities. Freedom also enhances the function of the natural community of the family. Communities form a powerful buffer against the extension of the state's power and against totalitarianism. Since government is to be limited under capitalism, communities play a vital role in capitalistic society.

Pluralism. The variety of institutions that are free to develop in capitalism stand in sharp contrast to a unitarian order. The economic, political, and cultural-moral systems serve as checks and balances to each other. In addition to this are the many communities. "Grave dangers to the human spirit lurk in the subordination of the political system and the economic system to a single moral-cultural vision. . . . Christianity has helped to shape the *ethos* of democratic capitalism, but this ethos forbids Christians (or any others) from attempting to *command* the system."[11]

Diversity. Since freedom and liberty are the highest priorities and the enemy is regimented equality, diversity is to be accepted. This diversity includes inequality of economic results. Equality of opportunity is desirable, but the economic inequality that results from individuality, freedom, and diversity is accepted as natural and inevitable. Each individual is equal in dignity and standing, but not in wisdom, diligence, or ambition. Great diversity results from freedom.

Socialism

Socialism "advocates the resting of the ownership and the control of the means of production, capital, land, etc., in the community as a whole."[12] Stated more elaborately, socialism is the "general term for any economic doctrine that challenges belief in the sanctity of private property and favors use of property for the public welfare. In this broad sense it embraces a great variety of economic theories, from those holding that only certain public utilities and natural resources should be owned by the community or the state with remaining property still private, to thoroughgoing Marxian socialism and, farther, to the edges of Anarchism."[13]

The historic development of modern socialism may be traced to the aftermath of the French Revolution. The conflict between purely utopian socialist dreamers and a practical socialism was largely resolved with the ascendance of Karl Marx who, with

Friedrich Engels, issued the *Communist Manifesto* in 1848. From this time on, Marxist thought dominated socialism, and the terms "communism" and "socialism" were used interchangeably. The socialistic doctrines that I will outline were developed during this time and the ensuing period. I will list the major characteristics and institutions of Marxist socialism.

The dialectic. Marx adopted from Hegel the idea of the dialectic, which was originally applied to explain progress in the realm of ideas. By applying this concept to the material world, Marx sought to explain how historic changes occur through the clash of opposites; a thesis conflicts with its antithesis, producing a synthesis, which in turn becomes a thesis for further progress. Thus history proceeds according to a series of violent conflicts.

Materialism. The character of a society depends entirely on its economic system. Thus matter becomes primary and ideas derivative. Ultimate reality is found in matter and material things. Nothing is transcendent. God does not exist.

Dialectical materialism. The concept of dialectical materialism results from the previous two considerations and is the dialectic applied to the economy. Progress is made through a continuing series of clashes of opposites. History is a progressive conflict. These clashes, based on class conflict, inevitably transform society into the socialist ideal.

Economic determinism. Economic matters determine all other aspects of society. All political, religious, and cultural systems depend on the economic system. When the economy becomes truly socialistic, government, conflict, classes, and scarcity will disappear.

Labor theory of value. All value is determined by the amount of "socially necessary labor" (average conditions, skill, and intensity), measured in time, required to produce it.

Theory of surplus value. The difference between the value created by the workers and what is paid to them as wages is surplus value. In a capitalistic system, surplus value is expropriated by the owners. Since all value in socialism is attributed to labor (capital is the result of previous labor), the workers are entitled to all of it. Expropriation by owners will eventually destroy the capitalistic system.

Class conflict. All history is the story of class struggles between the oppressor and the oppressed. This struggle is inevitable and will occur until a classless society emerges. Because they are expropriating the surplus value, the rich get richer and the poor get poorer. This process accelerates until, in advanced capitalistic societies, the situation will become intolerable and the proletariat will revolt. Violent revolution *must* occur. It is inevitable. Eventually, after the revolution, conditions causing class distinctions will disappear, conflict will cease, and the state will disappear.

Communities. The "bourgeois family" and other institutions, including religion, will vanish. They will be unnecessary in the perfected society. Children will be the responsibility of the state, which will provide their training and education.

Nature of man. Evil lies within the system, not in man himself, and has its foundation in the unequal distribution of wealth. When the system is perfected, all sources of evil will be eliminated. Cooperation will replace individualism. Social motivation will replace the private motivation of concern for the welfare of the individual and family. Man will be free to live in accordance with his altruistic nature.

State ownership of property. Private ownership of property is regarded as the cause of class conflict. So the community as a whole must own and control all means of production (capital). This requires state ownership until the very final stage of communism. Private ownership of property is severely limited. Eventually private property will not exist, and since the state came into being to protect private property, it, too, can disappear.

Centralized planning and control. A controlled economy is preferable to one directed by the marketplace. Equality, efficiency, and the direction of production to desirable ends are the objectives of control. Leaders will make these decisions, and will be altruistic in doing so.

Disintegration of capitalism. Economic cycles have historically developed into crisis and depression. This is an integral part of the capitalistic system. Workers are not paid enough to purchase the goods produced, surpluses develop, failures and unemployment result, owners turn to technology to increase profits, unemployment increases, and exploitation becomes more severe due to a desperate attempt to restore profits. Cycles will become increasingly severe until the capitalistic system collapses and is replaced by a new economic system. Since all other aspects of society are determined by economics, an entirely new society will result.

Socialism is directed against inequality. Inequality of economic results is the supreme evil, the essence of social injustice. This is extremely important because of materialistic determinism: the belief that economic factors determine everything else. Other values are not important when compared to this one.

Mixed Systems

The previous descriptions of capitalism and classic or Marxist socialism have seldom—perhaps never—been applied in their entirety. It is certainly not an exaggeration to say that every contemporary system is a mixed system. "The economy of the United States today by no means represents a pure laissez-faire capitalist system. It is rather a mixed economic system, since there are public enterprises, considerable government regulation and control and various other elements that hinder the unrestrained functioning of market forces."[14] This reality does not prove that pure capitalism would not work; it simply indicates that capitalistic societies accommodate aspects of opposing systems.

The advanced capitalist countries of today have modified the institutions of capitalism. In the operation of capitalist economies, problems have arisen that seemed impossible for private individuals to solve and whose impact upon their lives brought a demand for government intervention. As a result, government intervention and regulation is a very common feature of life under capitalism. Consumers are not left to depend solely on competition to furnish them with foods and drugs of acceptable quality and purity; there are laws that provide certain standards in these matters. Capitalistic societies have never been willing to extend complete freedom of enterprise to any individual. That is, it has always been recognized that an individual, in selecting the field of activity that would be most profitable to him or her, might well choose something that would be clearly antisocial. In such cases, government has not hesitated to step in with restrictions. But government has also altered the economic institutions of capitalism through, for example, subsidies to farmers and protection of inefficient business firms from competition.[15]

Similarly, socialist societies have deviated far from the socialistic ideal in practice. In fact, there has always been great diversity in socialistic doctrine, before and after Marx, and continuing into the present. Modern socialists are still redefining socialistic theory. The primary direction of change is to permit more private ownership of property. Some socialists insist on public ownership of only natural resources and public utilities. Others include land and all capital used in large-scale production. This allows private ownership of farms, small businesses, and sometimes even industries that the state does not feel the need to control completely. Still others deviate from ideal socialism only to the extent of permitting ownership of consumer goods.

Modern socialists who permit private ownership of portions of the means of production have not necessarily abandoned the objective of equality. Equality is attempted through control, taxation, and redistribution. More confidence to produce efficiently and direct the society's production toward profitable ends is placed in control than in the marketplace. In modern societies, this central planning takes place through bureaucracies that exercise the determined amount of control over the economic life of nations. In some societies, these controllers become a new elite with special status and privileges. Schnitzer and Nordyke summarize this process:

> By the early 1960's, many of the European social democratic parties severed completely whatever remaining ideological ties they had with Marx and communism. They abandoned their traditional opposition to private property and their goal of social ownership, and turned their attention to improving the public mix of total goods and services. Thus what have developed in Western Europe are mixed capitalist-socialist economies. When socialists come into power, the tilt is toward socialism; there is still reliance on a market economy, but also heavy government direction and planning in order to achieve desired social and economic objectives.[16]

I'm not sure the above statement is correct in saying that there are no more ideological ties to classical socialism. In spite of the many departures from socialistic doctrine, the objective of modern socialism remains unchanged. It is still aimed against inequality, with the inequality of economic results considered as the foundation of social injustice. Values that are primary in capitalism, such as the sanctity of private property ownership and the freedom of the individual, can be sacrificed to reach the socialistic objective of equality. Other aspects of classic socialism are present in modern socialism to varying degrees: the idealistic concept of man's nature, the suppression of communities other than the state, the necessity of class conflict and antagonism, and the primacy of the material.

Communism

Communism, as we have come to use the term, includes all the doctrines of socialism with several significant extensions and additions. The dictionary definition begins with the description of state ownership of property, but continues with, "a system of social organization in which all economic and social activity is controlled by a totalitarian state dominated by a single and self-perpetuating political party."[17]

Distinctions have been made between communism and Communism with a capital "C." The first is equivalent to socialism, "The system of society in which property (especially real property and the means of production) is held in common, i.e., by all members of the society and not by individuals."[18] Socialism became dominated by the theories of Karl Marx and developed into the forms we have already examined.

Modern Communism, however, began in the early twentieth century with a split in the Russian party between the Bolsheviks and the Mensheviks. The division was over "gradualism," the use of gradual, constitutional means to bring about capitalism's downfall, rather than through violent revolution. Violence was present in Marx's theory and its emphasis is significant to Communism. Under Lenin's leadership, the Bolsheviks prevailed within the party and in the 1917 Revolution. Lenin's program called for:

> The uniting of all the workers of the world for the coming revolution.
> The establishment of a dictatorship of the proletariat and state socialism.
> The emergence of a classless society that would allow the state to wither away.
> Universal communism with work and plenty for all.
> Perpetual peace.

The elevation of the state to supreme power, with this power concentrated and directed by the Communist Party, can be attributed to Lenin. In Communism, the state controls every aspect of life: political, economic, cultural, and moral. Individuals become the property of the state. Religion is eliminated if possible, and strictly regulated or proscribed when allowed to exist. All forms of voluntary community are prohibited. Even the family is perceived as a threat to state control and has suffered various degrees of intrusion. Children are wards of the state and their indoctrination is the state's responsibility. Schnitzer and Nordyke describe the Russian Communist Party as follows:

> The Communist Party is supposed to represent the interests of the working class. It is the sole repository of political power and is involved in all phases of economic activity. For example, the election of trade union officials is usually arranged by the Communist Party, and higher union positions are mostly occupied by party members. In all factories, collective farms, military units, or organizations, the Communist Party maintains local units or cells. Under the supervision of higher Party organizations, they attempt to improve the discipline and political education of the workers, and spur them on to the fulfillment of planned economic goals.
>
> In spite of the democratic facade which some communist countries maintain, the government is a complete dictatorship, with the leaders of the Communist Party in complete control. The Communist Party controls the armed forces and the electoral process. All candidates for office must have the approval of the Party if they hope to be successful. The Communist Party maintains Party officials and agencies to match the various officials and agencies of government. For all practical purposes Party and state are one and the same.[19]

Similar parties were established in other countries, with the following general, characteristic pattern:

> The parties were organized on a hierarchial basis with
> secret and active cells of believers as the broad base; there
> was established the rule of iron discipline, and not even the
> least of individual or group deviation from the established
> policy of the party was tolerated. The party is made up only
> of the elite, only those approved by the higher members of
> the party as being reliable, active, and subject completely to
> party rule. Thus . . . it constitutes only a relatively small
> number of people.[20]

The objective of these parties was to foment unrest leading to revolution and the downfall of capitalism. Often their prime targets were the labor movements, considered to be the vanguard of the proletariat.

In summary, Communism emphasizes philosophical materialism. The corollary, of course, is atheism. Religion is decadent, "the opiate of the people." Because of economic determinism, the organization of the economy becomes the predominant priority. Without God, there are no moral absolutes, so truth and morality can be defined as anything that advances Communism's cause. The mission of Communism is to extend its rule to the entire earth. No sacrifice or zeal is too great in realizing this purpose. Success is inevitable.

Pseudo-systems

We have talked about capitalism, socialism, mixed systems, and Communism. The economic systems of many countries cannot accurately be called any of these, for these countries have fallen into the hands of autocrats who may claim to represent an ideology, but in reality are manipulating the country for self-aggrandizement. These systems need to be recognized for what they are.

Our tendency is to use the word "capitalism" to include any system not avowedly socialistic or communistic. The fact that such greatly differing societies are lumped together in one category makes analysis difficult. Attributing past characteristics to the present increases the difficulty. To some people the word "capitalism" stimulates the image of the exploitation, gross inequity and unfairness, child labor, slavery, and injustice of the Industrial Revolution. Many individuals in the Third World remember their own experience with military or civilian dictatorships or oligarchies that systematically exploited their countries' resources and oppressed their citizens. Some people I have observed in the "flavellas" of Brazil or the "Tondo" of Manila see capitalism as an image of grinding poverty due to oppression. Others think of "rugged individualism" and vast private wealth gained ruthlessly at the expense of others. Many fear large, multinational corporations with excessive power.

Mercantilism and feudalism limited the benefits of capital ownership to the elite, a situation that is similar to the economic systems in many countries today. A Latin American nation may have a tradition of private ownership of property, but the ownership of land, factories, banks—the entire economic structure—may be owned by a few families. So the opportunities of capitalism are not available to the majority of people. In this situation, another essential element of capitalism, the element of competition, is also eliminated.

A military dictatorship may claim to be capitalistic, meaning, that it is not socialistic or communistic. But if the people are deliberately and systematically kept in poverty while the country's assets are drained off and deposited in foreign bank accounts, the system cannot be described as truly capitalistic. An African despot may talk about capitalism, but murder tens of thousands of his countrymen and confiscate their property. At best, these societies are pseudo-capitalistic.

In a similar way, exploitation occurs under the guise of socialism. Corrupt leaders pretend to accept ideologies in order to gain the benefits of money and munitions from socialistic and communistic powers. We must be careful not to blame the ideologies for the results.

Making an Appropriate Evaluation

The predominance of mixed systems and pseudo-systems, together with the fact that all systems are flawed due to man's sin, necessitate the need for careful evaluation on the basis of biblical criteria. We need to go back to our basic question, "Do the underlying principles of the system conform to those taught in the Scriptures?" The potential success of any system will be directly related to the answer to that question.

A Christian needs to evaluate the system in which he or she lives for several reasons. The first is to determine the available opportunities for stewardship. The second is to determine how to direct whatever influence we have as individuals and communities within the system. The third is to determine the specifics of our prayers for our leaders. "I urge, then, first of all, that requests, prayers, intercession and thanksgiving be made for everyone—for kings and all those in authority, that we may live peaceful and quiet lives in all godliness and holiness" (1 Timothy 2:1-2).

The criteria I listed as the ideal characteristics of a system can serve as the basis for our evaluation. None of these characteristics are unimportant, but several key questions seem to be the most crucial requirements of a system that can serve the needs of man as God created him.

> Does the system permit me to serve God according to my conscience?
> Does the system permit the freedom that God Himself has given in regard to my individuality, freedom of choice, personal responsibility, and diversity?
> Does the system give me freedom to associate in voluntary communities?
> Do I have the right to own property and be a steward of

capital, assuming the responsibilities of stewardship
and generosity?

Is the system realistic about man's willingness to accept the
fact of sin?

Does the system make possible the development of virtue
and righteousness?

Conclusion

Man's sinfulness will manifest itself within any system. Weaknesses inherent in the system's structure will provide opportunities for the expression of this sinfulness. This will take different forms within different systems. Many readers of this book, like myself, live in a mixed system that is predominantly capitalistic. Perhaps the greatest weakness within capitalism is the tendency toward excessive individualism. If this is true, Christians need to apply the biblical teaching on community to counteract this tendency. Individualism, coupled with economic freedom, provides the opportunities for exploitation and injustice. The biblical insistance on justice, Jesus' exhortation to treat others as we desire to be treated, and Paul's instruction to place our brothers' interests on a level equal with our own, should prevent us from taking unfair advantage of others. Biblical teaching also includes the positive aspects of constructive participation in the lives of others. We need to make a concerted effort to avoid participating in errors that are inherent in the system in which we live.

As Christians, our responsibility goes beyond the world's systems and extends to the Kingdom of God. I have emphasized the fact that all systems are made by man and are therefore unrighteous. I have encouraged you to compare the principles underlying today's systems with biblical teaching. The greater the system's conformity to biblical teaching, the greater the potential for man in general and for Christians in particular. For men in general, the potential is that they might find God: "From one man he made every nation of men, that they should inhabit the whole earth; and he determined the times set for them and the exact places where they should live. God did this so that men would seek him and perhaps reach out for him and find him" (Acts 17:26-27). For Christians, the potential is that they might be free to follow and proclaim God. Whatever the system, Christians will not fully conform to it. "Do not conform any longer to the pattern of this world." (Romans 12:2).

As Christians, we are instructed to do certain things in relationship to the system in which we live. In general, these correspond to our responsibilities as good citizens:

We will submit to the governing authorities and pay taxes (Romans 13:1-7).

We will pray for those in authority that we might live "peaceful and quiet lives in all godliness and holiness" (1 Timothy 2:2).

We will refuse to disobey God when authority is in conflict with His commandments. "Judge for yourselves whether it is right in God's sight to obey [the authority] rather than God" (Acts 4:19).

We will exert our influence on the side of God by actively participating in our society.

We will identify with what is right within the system and speak out and effect change in respect to what is wrong.

We will recognize that all systems are imperfect because man is sinful.

We will respect man's freedom and will not attempt to command the system to enforce conformity.

Our responsibility is proportionate to our opportunity. "From everyone who has been given much, much will be demanded; and from the one who has been entrusted with much, much more will be asked" (Luke 12:48). Jesus made this statement in relationship to stewardship. Those of us who enjoy greater opportunity will also have to account for stewardship of this opportunity.

Because all of man's economic systems are imperfect, there will never be an ideal situation for living out God's truth. Christians have always had to struggle to apply biblical principles within a hostile system to the greatest possible extent. History reveals that Christians can thrive in adversity and can become lethargic in situations that appear more advantageous.

Some who will read this may live within a system that seemingly provides very little opportunity or freedom. If so, please keep in mind that the New Testament instruction is given to help Christians live within whatever system we find ourselves. Those of us who enjoy the freedom to do so, should speak out against what is wrong in the system. However, that would be futile in many historic and contemporary situations.

Jesus and Paul, for example, did not attempt to command the system, or make an effort to reform it. In fact, they did not even speak to society at large on some of the most crucial issues of the day, such as slavery, subjugation of women, infanticide, and many other gross injustices. When they did speak, their instruction was to Christians; Christians were to be different. The Roman Empire was a ruthless, oppressive system. Living within it did not free Christians from their responsibilities to live by biblical principles.

Christians are expected to live according to scriptural principles to whatever extent possible. In any given society, some opportunities may be limited, but others may be enhanced. My friends who have worked within totalitarian societies have found that community assumes a new vitality in these difficult situations. The security found in brotherhood can surpass that found in financial reserves.

The implementation of biblical principles will be quite different within different social, political, and economic structures. No situation frees us from our responsibility to apply biblical principles to the greatest extent possible.

One consideration is more basic than the tenets of the system in which people live; it is the character of the people. In fact, too much emphasis on the philosophy of the system can cause us to misdirect our efforts to influence society. The character of the people is fundamental to any system. Systems may be temporarily imposed, but over the long term they reflect the nature, integrity, and wishes of the people within them. This fact is widely recognized, as evidenced by the old proverb, "Like people, like priest." In general, people get the kind of leadership they desire and deserve. Any system's success is due in greater degree to the people's character than the system's doctrines. Man's basic problem—even in the field of economics—is not philosophical, but moral.

Christians are not to conform to the world's systems (Romans 12:1), but are to be "salt" and "light" within those systems (Matthew 5:13-14). We must demonstrate truth through the integrity of our lives. This is the process Jim Petersen refers to as "affirmation evangelism in practice."[21] In the economic realm, the first step in this process is to become communitarian individuals. We must also make every effort to influence our society in the right direction by communicating truth within our sphere of influence. The second effort is absolutely impossible without the first.

We affect our society by introducing truth in a way that initiates change. If the fundamental aspect of a society is the character of the people, then the change must begin there. That is why Jesus and Paul did not attempt to change the system of their day, but focused on the transformation of individuals. Jesus' final instruction to His followers was to communicate the good news about Himself with the objective of making disciples. Changing society at large would be accomplished through their presence and influence in society.

I do not believe that Jesus and the New Testament writers were mistaken, or that God's strategy has changed significantly since that time. Jesus made it clear that the majority of people of all times would reject Him. "Small is the gate and narrow the road that leads to life, and only a few find it" (Matthew 7:14). Jesus asks, "When the Son of Man comes, will he find faith on the earth?" (Luke 18:8). In 2 Thessalonians 2, Paul says that Jesus will return only after a great, final rebellion that will be led by a lawless leader who deceives the majority of mankind. Man's systems are doomed to deterioration, not destined to progress.

> But you are a chosen people, a royal priesthood, a holy
> nation, a people belonging to God . . . aliens and strangers
> in the world. (1 Peter 2:9,11)

NOTES:
1. Pennington Haile, *The Eagle and the Bear* (New York: David McKay Company, Inc., 1965 [1950]), page 2.
2. Haile, page 5.
3. Joseph A. Schumpeter, *Capitalism, Socialism, and Democracy* (New York: Harper & Brothers, 1947 [1942]), page 200.
4. *The Random House Dictionary* (New York: Random House, 1973 [1966]), page 219.
5. *The Columbia Encyclopedia* (Morningside Heights, New York: Columbia University Press, 1950 [1935]), page 317.
6. Martin C. Schnitzer and James W. Nordyke, *Comparative Economic Systems* (Cincinnati: South-Western Publishing Co., 1983), page 3.
7. Schnitzer & Nordyke, pages 3-9.
8. Schnitzer & Nordyke, pages 18-19.
9. Michael Novak, *The Spirit of Democratic Capitalism* (New York: Simon & Schuster, 1982), pages 14-16.
10. Novak, page 82.
11. Novak, page 68.
12. *The Random House Dictionary,* page 1351.
13. *The Columbia Encyclopedia,* page 1844.
14. Schnitzer & Nordyke, page 3.
15. Schnitzer & Nordyke, pages 18-19.
16. Schnitzer & Nordyke, page 26.
17. *The Random House Dictionary,* page 298.
18. *The Columbia Encyclopedia,* page 1844.
19. Schnitzer & Nordyke, page 41.
20. *The Columbia Encyclopedia,* page 433.
21. Jim Petersen, *Evangelism as a Lifestyle* (Colorado Springs, Colorado: NavPress, 1980), page 64ff.

Conclusion

Whether or not you agree with the position I have presented in this book, I'm sure you agree that the Scriptures speak extensively on the subject of man's utilization of God's material creation. Scripture provides an adequate basis for a comprehensive, biblically based philosophy of material possessions. There is every reason to expect this, since we are physical-spiritual beings living in a material universe that God created for our benefit and over which He gave us dominion. God's material provision is a cause for thanksgiving and celebration.

God could have given detailed blueprints for our economic systems and our personal, economic affairs. He could have imposed a perfect system that required no thinking on our part. But He chose not to give us a "cake recipe" (as one of the men in Brazil put it) for living the Christian life and making financial decisions. Instead, He gave us principles that we must learn to apply, which makes our relationship to material things an aspect of spiritual growth. This is consistent with God's purpose in bringing His children to maturity. He has created us as individuals in His image and His likeness, and has endowed us with freedom of choice, personal responsibility, and great diversity. Discovering and applying God's truth in the process of growth is always exciting and rewarding. Scriptural truth is profitable for "teaching, rebuking, correcting and training in righteousness" (2 Timothy 3:16). Perseverance in its application will cause us to be "mature and complete, not lacking anything" (James 1:4).

In the course of this study, every concept that we discovered in Scripture and have developed is intended to help us build and clarify our convictions—to establish a set of values as the basis for our economic lives. We need to build our lives around these biblical principles, not simply subscribe to an ideology. Christians who do this could be characterized as communitarian individuals.

The application of biblical principles in our economic lives has several important effects. The first is what takes place within us as we "become mature, attaining to the whole measure of the fullness of Christ" (Ephesians 4:13). The second is the enhancement of community when we, as individuals, "look not only to our own interests, but also to the interests of others" (Philippians 2:4). The third is our effect on those around us when we season as salt and when we "shine like stars in the universe as you [we] hold out the word of life" (Philippians 2:15-16).

In closing, I want to emphasize this last result, which I mentioned in the introduction. If our economic lives are patterned on scriptural principles, we will stand in sharp contrast to the world around us. Our financial life and philosophy will demonstrate God's grace. There will be a "radical difference" in the way we handle our financial affairs. Our economic conduct, even without any verbal witness on our part, will cause us to be "redemptive in our relationships."

If we are to be "redemptive in our relationships," we must be *involved* in relationships. We must have "radical indentification" with the world around us. We dare not isolate ourselves from the world only to seek a comfortable refuge in the Christian community. Yet some Christians today seem to want to do just that!

Jesus talked of the need to keep light in a position to illuminate darkness. "You are the light of the world. . . . let your light shine before men, that they may see your good deeds and praise your Father in heaven" (Matthew 5:14,16). As His followers, we are likened unto a city on a hill or a lamp on a lampstand! Jesus emphasized our presence in the world in His special prayer for the disciples: "My prayer is not that you take them out of the world. . . . As you sent me into the world, I have sent them into the world" (John 17:15,18). Jesus' own conduct is our example. He enjoyed the company of sinners, and they were more comfortable around Him than the religious leaders were. The latter accused Jesus of being the friend of tax collectors and sinners.

I have heard one lecturer say, "There will come a time when the maturing Christian has no real friendships among nonChristians." Another advised, "As we become more mature, we become less and less effective with the world." By their standards, Jesus was very immature. The tragedy is, such withdrawal from the world often takes place, and these leaders encourage it.

Responsible Christian leaders like Dr. Joseph Aldrich deplore this situation. Speaking to pastors, he said, "The average Christian has no nonChristian friends after he has been a Christians for two years. . . . You need to open up your relationships to the nonChristians. . . . They are not the enemy; they are victims of the enemy; and that's a very important difference."[1]

Separation from the world is not isolation. Sanctification is not a matter of limiting our contact with the world, but a condition of the heart. In the passage from John quoted above, Jesus sent His disciples into the world, but defined the source of their sanctification as the truth of God's Word and the power of Jesus Himself. Light is meant for dark places. Our economic affairs can provide real opportunities for the beginning of relationships.

A friend moved to another state a year ago, purchased a home, and cultivated a relationship with one of the professionals who assisted him in that purchase. In our most recent telephone conversation, he rejoiced that his new friend had become a Christian. Opportunities such as this are lost when Christians limit their business dealings to other Christians. Except in cases where a brother is in difficulty and needs help, it may be wise to deliberately choose involvement with nonChristians.

Productive relationships with the victims of the Enemy require more freedom than Christians are often willing to give each other. To be in the world, we have to participate in the lives of those around us. This thought leads directly to the subject of liberty, which is too extensive to discuss here. Paul summarizes Christian liberty in the statement, "I have become all things to all men so that by all possible means I might save some" (1 Corinthians 9:22). We need to give each other all the liberty that God has given us if we are to build relationships with those outside of Christ.

One of my Brazilian friends had been confused by one of the syndromes of false assumptions and misinterpretation of Scripture that we talked about in chapter 2. When he began to understand the freedom God has given us to enjoy and to use material things in His Kingdom, my friend said, "The liberty this brings is too good to be true!" When I heard his remark, I could not help but think of Jesus' statement, "Then you will know the truth, and the truth will set you free" (John 8:32). And I could have added to my friend's statement, "The opportunity this freedom presents to relate to those who need the light is too good to be true."

God created the material universe to meet our needs and "for our enjoyment." He uses it as an instrument to bring us to spiritual maturity. We can use it for eternal purposes. God's material provision is a *cause for continuing celebration*!

NOTE:
1. Tape entitled "Developing Vision for Disciplemaking," Glen Eyrie, Colorado Springs, Colorado, 1980.

Subject Index

Scripture Index